IMPORTANT NOTICE

The Forest Service is in the process of renumbering all of the forest roads in western Washington. They expect to make the change in 1982, at which time the forest maps and road signs will show the new numbers.

The present numbering system was derived thirty years ago before road planners had any indication of the maze of roads that would eventually be developed. The new numbering system should make road directions easier to follow.

A NOTE ABOUT NUMBERING OF HIKES:

When Mt. St. Helens exploded May 18, 1980, five trails in this book were wiped off the map. Five other trips, in different geographical locations, have been substituted. Thus you will find peculiarities of numbering in the table of contents, so that the *listings* of these "new" trips may be presented in their true geographical areas, while the *descriptions* of the trips are located in the section of the book formerly covering the Mt. St. Helens region.

D1468904

102 hikes

IN THE ALPINE LAKES, SOUTH CASCADES AND OLYMPICS

Text: Ira Spring and Harvey Manning
Photos: Bob and Ira Spring

THE MOUNTAINEERS • SEATTLE
Second edition

The Mountaineers: Organized 1906 ". . . to explore, study, preserve and enjoy the natural beauty of the Northwest."

Copyright © 1971, 1974, 1978 by The Mountaineers

Published by The Mountaineers, 719 Pike Street
Seattle, Washington 98101

Published simultaneously in Canada by
Douglas & McIntyre Ltd., 1615 Venables Street
Vancouver, British Columbia V5L 2H1

Manufactured in the United States of America
First edition, June 1971; revised September 1974
Second edition, June 1978; second printing, August 1979;
third printing, May 1980; fourth printing (revised), June 1981

*Designed by Marge Mueller; maps by Helen Sherman, Gary Rands
  and Judith Siegel*
Cover: Lake Viviane and McClellan Peak, Enchantment Lakes region–Hike 8
Frontispiece: Toleak Point–Hike 102

Library of Congress Cataloging in Publication Data

Spring, Ira.
  102 hikes in the Alpine Lakes, South Cascades and Olympics.

  Includes index.
  1. Hiking—Washington (State)—Guide-books. 2. Trails—Washington (State)
—Guide-books. 3. Washington (State)—Description and travel—1951-
—Guide-books. I. Manning, Harvey, joint author. II. Spring, Robert, 1918-
III. Mountaineers, Seattle. IV. Title.
GV199.42.W2S67   1978   917.97   80-12388
ISBN 0-916890-24-4

PRESERVATION AGENDA

In a variety of ways over the years The Mountaineers have worked "to preserve the natural beauty of Northwest America." One means, adopted in the early 1960s, is the publication of hiking guides, the aim being to put more boots on certain trails, into certain wildlands. The organization doesn't suffer from any delusion that large numbers of boots improve trails, enhance wildness. However, it is ruefully certain that only by making new friends for threatened areas will they be preserved.

Those who benefit from the guidance of this book have the obvious obligation to become defenders of trails and wilderness. Nowadays, when the large numbers of wilderness lovers are in themselves a threat of sorts, more attention is required to rules of "walking light," as discussed later herein. Yet the ultimate threat to natural beauty is not hikers, no matter how destructive their great, vicious boots may be, but doomsday, as represented by motorcycles, bulldozers, and forces for change in the name of "progress."

Some things have been won since The Mountaineers began guidebook publishing — a North Cascades National Park, to cite the grandest victory of the 1960s. In 1976 came this decade's triumph, the Alpine Lakes Wilderness — too small, of course, the preserves always are, but a splendid foundation for future expansion.

Folks who arrived late need have no fear there's nothing left for them to do. The situation cries out for heroes and heroines. Following is a capsule summary of the current preservation agenda for the many provinces of the Cascades and Olympics to which the 102 hikes offer an introduction. Those who find this book a useful guide to hours and days of wandering forests and meadows owe it to themselves, and to their children and grandchildren, to make the agenda their own.

De Facto Wilderness

A quarter-century ago the mountain areas of Washington were mostly pretty much as they always had been — wild. Then, after World War II, the loggers and road-builders began pushing deeper into the backcountry, farther up valleys, higher on ridges. The action caused an equal and opposite reaction in the form of a great reinforcement of the preservation movement. By the 1970s all observers realized that exploiters and preservers were both so busy there soon would be no overlooked lands. Everything was either going to be "locked up" or logged.

The U.S. Forest Service, manager of most of the "de facto" (just sitting there) wilderness, is trying to satisfy all concerned with another roadless area inventory (RARE II). The odds are that in the future, as in the recent past, there'll be a dogfight over each wild valley and hill. Therefore, every hiker should participate, striving to preserve as much wilderness as should and can be preserved in the Olympics and Cascades.

Cougar Lakes

Hikes 45-52 and 54 are in the 150,000 acres of the proposed two-section Cougar Lakes Wilderness; a bill to establish this area was introduced in Congress in 1970 and hearings held in 1977-78. The north section is bounded on the south by the Chinook Pass Highway, on the west by the Crystal Mountain Ski Area, and on the north by the lowering of the crest into wooded terrain. The larger south section includes the entire Cascade Crest between Chinook Pass and the White Pass Highway, bounded on the

Beargrass on Huckleberry Mountain, Page 232
(John Spring photo)

west much of the way by Mount Rainier National Park, and extends eastward over valleys of virgin forests and ridges of flowers punctuated by such rugged peaks as Mt. Aix.

The Cougar Lakes Wilderness is needed as wild living room to complement increasingly-crowded Mount Rainier National Park and to prevent high-use road-oriented recreation (and logging) the fragile beauty cannot tolerate.

Mount Rainier National Park

Ultimately the National Park boundaries must be pushed outward on the south, west, and north to take in the entirety of Mt. Rainier and all its flanking ridges and the intervening valleys; though many of these have been savagely clearcut, the Park is for the centuries and in time wounds will heal. Certain as yet unspoiled lands, notably in the Tatoosh Range, should be placed in the Park immediately.

On the north, where the Forest Service is thrusting logging roads almost to the boundary, logging should be halted, or at the very least, the roads "put to bed" when the cutting is complete in order to preserve the remoteness of Park meadows. Hunting should be controlled in all areas adjacent to the Park to maintain a complete summer-and-winter range for the animal population.

Pacific Crest Trail

The route of the Pacific Crest National Scenic Trail southward from Snoqualmie Pass should be designated as a no-logging strip, and protected from any further road intrusions.

The historic Naches Wagon Trail (Hike 42) deserves particularly urgent attention. The little that remains of the old emigrant route should be saved by placing it entirely off-limits to jeepers and trailbikers and logging.

South Cascades

The area sampled by Hikes 53-76 is large, varied, and badly abused. The Goat Rocks and Mt. Adams Wildernesses consist mainly of snow and rocks and meadows; boundaries should be adjusted outward to include more of the approach ridges and valleys.

The Mt. St. Helens area (Hikes 72-74) is one of the worst examples of mismanagement in the Northwest. Faced by an impossible checkerboard of private and public ownership, the U.S. Forest Service has capitulated to the exploiters. On three sides the graceful volcano rises above a sea of stumps, only the Spirit Lake side so far spared — and here the Service is planning to log the beautiful forest described in Hike 74. Further, the Service has opened many popular trails to motorized travel, so that children, old people, horses, and hundreds of hikers must compete with trailbikes. Because the Forest Service seems totally unwilling to radically alter its management philosophy, conservationists are now seeking a Mt. St. Helens National Monument.

The broad expanse of forested valleys and ridges between Adams and St. Helens has been criss-crossed with a spider web of roads in the years since World War II, obliterating hundreds of miles of trails. But small pockets of splendor remain relatively pristine and to preserve these a number of small Wildernesses are proposed.

Olympics

Hikes 78-102 are on the Olympic Peninsula, for the most part in Olympic National Park, most of which soon will be permanently classified as wilderness. The Park Service must be strenuously urged to acquire private lands within the Park, particularly in the Quinault Valley, and under no circumstances to eliminate from the Park portions of the Valley now included.

Eventually the Park must be enlarged along the eastern side, where, for example, the summits of such peaks as Cruiser, The Brothers, and Constance lie exactly on the boundary, their east slopes and drainage valleys excluded. Looking west from Seattle to the Olympic horizon, the only portions of the Park that can be seen are the summits of several peaks. All the rest of the visible range is in Olympic National Forest, subject to logging, as can be vividly realized in winter, when snows demark the clearcuts, which grow larger year by year. To prevent further damage, Wildernesses must be established bordering the National Park on the northeast, southeast, and southwest.

Park Lake and Chikamin Ridge, Hike 28

The Mountaineers: An Invitation

The Mountaineers, with groups based in Seattle, Everett, Tacoma, and Olympia, warmly invite the membership of all lovers of outdoor life who sympathize with the purposes of the organization and wish to share its activities.

The Mountaineers sponsor a year-around program of climbing, hiking, camping, ski-touring, snowshoeing, canoeing and kayaking, and bicycling. Many hundreds of outings are scheduled each year, ranging from afternoon walks to trips lasting 2 weeks or more. On a typical weekend as many as 50 excursions may be offered, from ocean beaches to the summit of Mt. Rainier. In addition, members engage in countless privately-organized trips of all kinds; the opportunity is boundless to make new friends with similar interests.

Enjoying wildlands is one side of the coin; the other is working to preserve the natural beauty of Northwest America. Here, The Mountaineers continue their role of leadership as they have for 72 years, and seek new members to share the effort.

For membership application, and further information on club activities, write The Mountaineers, 719 Pike Street, Seattle, Washington 98101.

March 1978   HARVEY MANNING

HIKER/MOTORCYCLE SCOREBOARD

A dozen-odd years ago hiking trails were seldom if ever molested by motorcycles. It wasn't until Yankee ingenuity and Japanese mass production combined that the trouble began; since then the situation has gotten completely out of hand.

When Congress enacted the "Multiple Use Concept," it certainly never intended the Forest Service to adhere to the literal interpretation and mix together every use everywhere no matter how incompatible. However, forest supervisors do just that, saying, "Let the hikers and motorcyclists learn to live together." But they can't. A major reason hikers go hiking is to get away from machines, and until the middle 1960s, once on the trail they were free of noise and pollution. But where, now, can they escape? In dedicated wilderness areas — that are so full of people escaping machines one needs a permit to enter. In the European Alps all trails are closed to motorcycles. Even service roads used by farmers and foresters are closed to recreational use of motors. In Japan where most of the machines come from, things are not as bad as here. Only in America . . .

Unlike the trees, wildlife, water, and minerals of national forests, whose benefits are measurable in dollars, the benefits of hiking trails are hard to determine. Who can put a cash value on the mental stimulation of meeting a challenge? The spiritual and physical therapy of getting away from the contraptions of civilization? As any doctor will testify, hiking is one of the best exercises known for lungs, heart, and muscles. And many a case of hypertension, many a case of crumbling nerves, has been successfully treated by a walk in the wildlands. While the Forest Service hasn't yet put a dollar value on good health, some health insurance companies are beginning to.

The Forest Service has been conditioned to think in terms of the value of logs; rangers are trained to manage timber, not to provide mental and physical therapy, much less esthetic pleasure. As a consequence, unless an area is specifically set aside by Congress as a wilderness, some forest supervisors adhere to a literal interpretation of "multiple-use," meaning every use everywhere, no matter how incompatible. Even the best supervisors, placed in the position of compromising between user-group pressures, make terrible blunders of judgment. Congress is going to have to set strict controls. Until it does, though, we hikers have to keep after the supervisors, letting them know where we stand (and where we walk).

Recreational use of off-road vehicles had become so serious a problem by 1976 that the President ordered all federal land-managers to inventory off-road vehicle use, listing where environmental damage had been done, where user conflict existed, and where off-road vehicle use should be permitted. It was a golden opportunity to give hiking trails back to the hiker. It failed. After months of study, public reviews costing millions of dollars nationwide, virtually nothing happened. Except the roar went on.

We made a few gains and for them are thankful. But the scoreboard as of now is grim reading. Surely it will improve in the future. How could it get worse?

In the Gifford Pinchot National Forest, trails around Spirit Lake (Hikes 72 and 73) were closed to wheels in 1977 after a barrage of written and verbal complaints; the Lewis River trail (Hike 76), Goat Mountain trail (Hike 68), and Packwood Lake trail (Hike 58) were closed for various reasons. However, not all the news is good. The Gifford Pinchot Forest has relatively few trails left after the road-building surge of the last 20 years, and an incomplete list of trails open to motorcycles runs to 26 entries, plus the entire proposed Shark Rock Wilderness (Hikes 65, 66, and 67).

In Wenatchee National Forest, no trails were closed to motorized travel in Naches and Tieton Districts except in wilderness-study areas where Congress forbids them, and Crow Creek Way (Hike 46), too steep for wheels. In Ellensburg and Cle Elum

Districts hikers fared better; Kachess Ridge trail and all trails leading into or near the Alpine Lakes Wilderness were closed. However, those still open to motorcycles are too numerous to list.

In Mt. Baker-Snoqualmie National Forest motorcycles were eliminated from Summit Lake trail (Hike 41), Pratt River trail (the bridge has been gone for years so there are no hikers either), and Pratt Lake (Hike 19). But they are still allowed on such heavily hiked trails as Echo Lake (Hike 43), Huckleberry, Dalles, Fawn Ridge and some 18 others; jeeps, as well, are allowed on the historic Naches Wagon Trail (Hike 42).

In Olympic National Forest trails have been closed only in the two wilderness-study areas, Mt. Colonel Bob (Hike 97) and Lena Lake (Hike 82), the latter after overwhelming public demand. This hardly begins to balance the partial list of 23 trails still open.

The future could bring a number of things. The hikers could unite and throw the machines out. Unlikely. The machines could become so ubiquitous and commonplace that a whole generation of walkers would grow up accepting them as a matter of course. Unthinkable. The answer lies in designating low grade logging roads for motorcycles and jeeps and keeping the little roadless area left for wilderness use. For unthinkable as is the prospect of future generations accepting motorcycles as normal use for trails, it could happen, just as our generation accepts the use of automobiles for doing errands our parents would have done on foot. When this happens, our dedicated wilderness areas and national parks will be lost too. We, as organizations and individuals, must press all those in any position of influence—by letter, by verbal remonstrance, by sheer presence at hearings, by visibility on the trails—to save every scrap of wildland left.

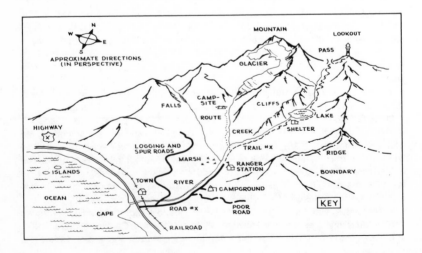

INTRODUCTION

The country sampled by the 102 hikes has many characteristics in common throughout, but also significant differences from place to place caused by variations in climate and geology and elevation and people-pressure. Three "provinces" may be distinguished.

First, the Alpine Lakes Cascades (Hikes 1-40), extending some 50 or so miles west to east from maritime greenery of Puget Sound lowlands to golden hills above the semi-arid Columbia River valley, and roughly 25-35 miles south to north from the Snoqualmie Pass Highway to the Stevens Pass Highway—beyond which lies the domain of a companion book, **101 Hikes in the North Cascades.**

On the windward slopes of the Cascades the precipitation is heavy enough to nourish near-rain forests. The leeward slopes, in the rainshadow, often are sunny when the crest is lost in mists and drizzles, and the forests are generally more open. However, the range is much narrower here than it is to the north and the contrasts in climate from one edge to the other less marked. The hiking season is everywhere about the same because though snows pile deeper on the west, elevations average higher on the east. Past glaciation has left in all parts a legacy of sharp-sculptured peaks, plus cirque basins and scoured valleys now filled by lakes high and low—some 600 in all.

The second province, the Washington South Cascades (Hikes 41-77), is really an assemblage of quite diverse sub-provinces: the 25 miles south from Snoqualmie Pass, in which the Cascade Crest follows relatively low and heavily wooded ridges; the next 25-odd miles from north of Chinook Pass to White Pass, with the Crest rising to meadows and small crags of the proposed Cougar Lakes Wilderness; the 30 miles south from White Pass, where the Crest climbs more, from flowers to glaciers of the Goat Rocks and finally to the nearly 2½-mile-high summit of Mt. Adams; and a last 30 miles in which the Crest drops to the Columbia River. But the Cascade Crest is not the whole story: though the alpine realm of the Crest proper is rather narrow, westward 35 miles from Adams over forested ridges is the graceful volcano of Mt. St. Helens; and of course, adjoining the Cougar Lakes area is the grandest volcano of them all, and the trail country described in a companion book, **50 Hikes in Mount Rainier National Park.**

The South Cascades offer isolated eruptions of spectacular violence—the volcanoes, the ice-plucked Goat Rocks and a few other peaks—but also the friendliest parklands of the entire range, and because of the distance from major cities, and the overshadowing fame of mountains farther north, some of the lonesomest.

The third province, the Olympic Peninsula (Hikes 78-102), extends some 55-85 miles from the Pacific Ocean east to Hood Canal and roughly 70 miles from the Strait of Juan de Fuca south to foothills, encompassing wilderness ocean beaches, westside rain forests, a wilderness interior of glaciers and rock needles and flower gardens, and rainshadow ridges standing high above lowlands of Hood Canal and Puget Sound

Within these three provinces many varieties of trail experience are available. There are short and easy hikes that can be done by small children and old folks with no training or equipment for mountain travel. And also there are long hikes, and difficult hikes, and long-and-difficult hikes, which should be attempted only by experienced wilderness roamers.

There are hikes that can be done by any person capable of putting one foot in front of another for a morning or afternoon. And there are adventures that can take a party back through time to the frontier, into wildlands where the walker is utterly on his own, with no help from anyone if things go wrong.

Administration

The three provinces are administered by the National Park Service, by the U.S. Forest Service in the Mt. Baker-Snoqualmie, Wenatchee, Gifford Pinchot, and Olympic National Forests, and in small but important part by the Washington State Department of Natural Resources. Because regulations on use vary, hikers should be aware of which administrative units they are traveling.

Mount Rainier and Olympic National Parks have been set aside, to use the words of the National Park Act of 1916, "to conserve the scenery and the natural and historic objects and wildlife . . . " Each visitor must therefore enjoy the Parks "in such manner and by such means as will leave them unimpaired for the enjoyment of future generations." A good motto for Park users is: "Take only a picture, leave only a footprint."

Much of both Parks soon will be dedicated as wilderness, so that not only the National Park Act of 1916 but the Wilderness Act of 1964 will apply, giving a still higher degree of protection. Motorized travel on Park trails is forbidden and horse travel closely regulated. Hunting is banned—but not fishing. Pets are not allowed on trails, since their presence disturbs wildlife.

Backcountry permits are required for all overnight hikers in National Parks, and may be obtained at ranger stations on the entry roads.

Under U.S. Forest Service jurisdiction are the Goat Rocks, Mt. Adams, and Alpine Lakes Wildernesses (and hopefully, in the near future, the proposed Cougar Lakes Wilderness), where "the earth and its community of life are untrammeled by man, where man himself is a visitor who does not remain." Motorized travel is forbidden absolutely and horse travel is beginning to be regulated or even eliminated at some points; foot travel and camping are currently less restricted, though the backcountry population explosion will require increasing controls to protect the fragile ecosystems. Wilderness permits, available at ranger stations and National Forest headquarters, are required for all travelers in most dedicated Wildernesses.

Other portions of the National Forests are designated now, or may be in future, as recreation areas, scenic areas, roadless areas, or primitive areas, each of which has certain limitations on commodity exploitation and recreation. Multiple-use areas are devoted mainly to logging, though with some consideration of other uses; here things often change violently from one year to the next and the hiker may find roads and trails radically different from descriptions in this book.

Large areas of the Alpine Lakes and South Cascades are in a checkerboard ownership dating from the Northern Pacific Land Grant. The presence of private land intermixed with public land so far has interfered with trail use only here and there, but poses a future threat. The Forest Service is seeking to "block up" the public land by exchanges, but some private owners are uncooperative and the program is not moving as rapidly as could be wished.

Maps

Each hike description in this book lists the appropriate topographic maps (if such are available) published by the U.S. Geological Survey. These can be purchased at mountain equipment shops or map stores or by writing the U.S. Geological Survey, Federal Center, Denver, Colorado 80225. The USGS maps are the hiker's best friend.

The National Forests publish recreation maps which are quite accurate and up-to-date. These maps may be obtained for a small fee at ranger stations or by writing the Forest Supervisors at:

Bogachiel rain forest, Hike 95 (John Spring photo)

Mt. Baker-Snoqualmie National Forest
1601 2nd Avenue
Seattle, WA 98101

Gifford Pinchot National Forest
500 W. 12th Street
Vancouver, WA 98660

Wenatchee National Forest
P.O. Box 811
Wenatchee, WA 98801

Olympic National Forest
Federal Building
Olympia, WA 98501

Clothing and Equipment

Many trails described in this book can be walked easily and safely, at least along the lower portions, by any person capable of getting out of a car and onto his feet, and without any special equipment whatever.

To such people we can only say, "welcome to walking—but beware!" Northwest mountain weather, especially on the ocean side of the ranges, is notoriously undependable. Cloudless morning skies can be followed by afternoon deluges of rain or fierce squalls of snow. Even without a storm a person can get mighty chilly on high ridges when—as often happens—a cold wind blows under a bright sun and pure blue sky.

No one should set out on a Cascade or Olympic trail, unless for a brief stroll, lacking warm long pants, wool shirt or sweater, and a windproof and rain-repellent parka, coat, or poncho. (All these in the rucksack, if not on the body during the hot hours.) And on the feet—sturdy shoes or boots with rugged lug soles and a 5-9-inch top to keep out mud and dirt plus two pair of wool socks and an extra pair in the rucksack.

As for that rucksack, it should also contain the Ten Essentials, found to be so by generations of members of The Mountaineers, often from sad experience:

1. Extra clothing—more than needed in good weather.

2. Extra food—enough so something is left over at the end of the trip.

3. Sunglasses—necessary for most alpine travel and indispensable on snow.

4. Knife—for first aid and emergency firebuilding (making kindling).

5. Firestarter—a candle or chemical fuel for starting a fire with wet wood.

6. First aid kit.

7. Matches—in a waterproof container.

8. Flashlight—with extra bulb and batteries.

9. Map—be sure it's the right one for the trip.

10. Compass—be sure to know the declination, east or west.

Camping and Fires

Indiscriminate camping blights alpine meadows. A single small party may trample grass, flowers, and heather so badly they don't recover from the shock for several years. If the same spot is used several or more times a summer, year after year, the greenery vanishes, replaced by the dusty, muddy barrens of "slum camps." The respectful traveler always aims to camp in the woods, or in rocky morainal areas. These alternatives lacking, it is better to use a meadow site already ruined—a slum—rather than extend the destruction into pleasanter virginal places nearby. (If the site is messy, clean it up and feel the warm glow of virtue.) As time goes on and people pressure grows, more and more meadows necessarily will be posted against camping.

Particularly to be avoided are camps on meadows (rocky or bare-dirt sites may be quite all right) immediately beside streams or lakes. Delightful and scenic as such sites are, their use may endanger the water purity, as well as the health of delicate plants. Better to camp at a distance and leave the riverbanks and lakeshores undisturbed for all visitors to enjoy. In many jurisdictions camping is now expressly forbidden within 100 or 200 feet of lakes and streams.

Shelter cabins are on a first-come first-served basis, so always carry a tent or tarp. (But never ditch the sleeping area unless and until essential to avoid being flooded out—and afterwards be sure to fill the ditches, carefully replacing any sod that may have been dug up.) Most shelters are crummy and foul from years of abuse and are best avoided; in fact, many shelters are expected to be removed by land administrators in the next few years on the grounds that they are "attractive nuisances."

The bough bed, beloved of the frontier past, is so damaging to vegetation it is obsolete in areas worthy of preservation in a natural condition, including all the country covered by this book. Instead, carry an air mattress or a foam-plastic pad.

The wood fire, another age-old tradition, also should be considered obsolete in the high country. At best, dry firewood is hard to find at popular camps; the easy wood was burnt years ago. What remains now is from picturesque silver snags and down logs, and in burning these one erodes the very beauty that makes the hike worth taking. Needless to say, green, living wood must never be cut; it doesn't burn anyway.

Both for reasons of convenience and conservation, The Mountaineers strongly urge the highland hiker to carry a lightweight stove for cooking and to depend on clothing and shelter (and sunset strolls) for evening warmth. The pleasures of a roaring blaze on a cold mountain night are indisputable, but for the sake of these pleasures a single party on a single night may use up ingredients of the scenery that were long decades in growing, dying, and silvering.

At remote backcountry camps, and in forests, fires may still be built (for a while) with a clear conscience. Again, one should minimize impact by using only established fire pits and using only dead and down wood. When finished, be certain the fire is absolutely out—drown the coals and stir them with a stick and then drown the ashes until the smoking and steaming have stopped completely and a finger stuck in the slurry feels no heat. Embers can smoulder underground in dry duff for days, spreading gradually and burning out a wide pit—or kindling trees and starting a forest fire.

Litter and Garbage and Sanitation

Ours is a wasteful, throwaway civilization—and something is going to have to be done about that soon. Meanwhile, it is bad wildland manners to leave litter for others to worry about. The rule among considerate hikers is: **If you can carry it in full, you can carry it out empty.**

On a day hike, take back to the road (and garbage can) every last orange peel and gum wrapper.

On an overnight or longer hike, burn all paper (if a fire is built) but carry back all unburnables, including cans, metal foil, plastic, glass, and papers that won't burn.

Don't bury garbage. If fresh, animals will dig it up and scatter the remnants. Burning before burying is no answer either. Tin cans take as long as 40 years to disintegrate completely; aluminum and glass last for centuries. Further, digging pits to bury junk disturbs the ground cover, and iron eventually leaches from buried cans and "rusts" springs and creeks.

Don't leave leftover food for the next travelers; they will have their own supplies and won't be tempted by "gifts" spoiled by time or chewed by animals.

Especially don't cache plastic tarps. Weathering quickly ruins the fabric, little creatures nibble, and the result is a useless, miserable mess.

Keep the water pure. Don't wash dishes in streams or lakes, loosing food particles and detergent. Haul buckets of water off to the woods or rocks, and wash and rinse there. Eliminate body wastes in places well removed from watercourses, and cover the evidence with loose dirt, humus, dead bark, or rocks. Increasingly, popular camps are provided with privies of sorts; use them.

Pets

It is time to leave pets at home. Dogs have become so numerous on trails they sometimes outnumber hikers and, like humans, are having an impact on the fragile environment. Pets have always been forbidden on national park trails, and park rangers issue hundreds of citations every year to hikers who choose to violate the regulation. Outside of the parks, dogs have had free rein, but their impact on meadows and wildlife has been so great the Forest Service has been forced to prohibit dogs in the Enchantment Lakes (Hike 8), and as the problem is better documented, there will be more closures in the future.

Where pets are permitted, even a well-behaved dog can ruin someone else's trip. Some dogs noisily defend an ill-defined territory for their master, snitch someone else's food, and are quite likely to defecate on the flat bit of ground the next hiker will want to use for a campsite.

Dogs belong to the same family as coyotes, and even if no wildlife is visible, a dog's presence is sensed by the small wild things into whose home they are intruding.

Theft

Twenty years ago theft from a car left at the trailhead was rare. Not now. Equipment has become so fancy and expensive, so much worth stealing, and hikers so numerous, their throngs creating large assemblages of valuables, that theft is a growing problem. Not even wilderness camps are entirely safe; a single raider hitting an unguarded camp may easily carry off several sleeping bags, a couple tents, and assorted stoves, down booties, and freeze-dried strawberries — maybe $1000 worth of gear in one load! However, the professionals who do most of the stealing mainly concentrate on cars. Authorities are concerned but can't post guards at every trailhead.

Rangers in Olympic National Park have the following recommendations.

First and foremost, don't make crime profitable for the pros. If they break into a hundred cars and get nothing but moldy boots and tattered T shirts they'll give up. The best bet is to arrive in a beat-up 1960 car with doors and windows that don't close and leave in it nothing of value. If you insist on driving a nice new car, at least don't have mag wheels, tape deck, and radio, and keep it empty of gear. Don't think locks help — pros can open your car door and trunk as fast with a picklock as you can with your key. Don't imagine you can hide anything from them—they know all the hiding spots. If the hike is part of an extended car trip, arrange to store your extra equipment at a nearby motel.

Be suspicious of anyone waiting at a trailhead. One of the tricks of the trade is to sit there with a pack as if waiting for a ride, watching new arrivals unpack—and hide their valuables—and maybe even striking up a conversation to determine how long the marks will be away.

The ultimate solution, of course, is for hikers to become as poor as they were in the olden days. No criminal would consider trailheads profitable if the loot consisted solely of shabby khaki war surplus.

Water

Hikers traditionally have drunk the water in wilderness in confidence, doing their utmost to avoid contaminating it so the next person also can safely drink. But there is no assurance your predecessor has been so careful.

No open water ever, nowadays, can be considered safe for human consumption. Any reference in this book to "drinking water" is not a guarantee. It is entirely up to the individual whether he wants to take a chance—or to treat the water with chemicals or boil it for 20 minutes.

Protect This Land, Your Land

The Cascade and Olympic country is large and rugged and wild—but it is also, and particularly in the scenic climaxes favored by hikers, a fragile country. If man is to blend into the ecosystem, rather than dominate and destroy, he must walk lightly, respectfully, always striving to make his passage through the wilderness invisible.

The public servants entrusted with administration of the region have a complex and difficult job and they desperately need the cooperation of every wildland traveler. Here, the authors would like to express appreciation to these dedicated men for their advice on what trips to include in this book and for their detailed review of the text and maps. Thanks are due the Superintendent of Olympic National Park, the Supervisors of the Mt. Baker-Snoqualmie, Wenatchee, Gifford Pinchot, and Olympic National Forests, the director of the Washington State Department of Natural Resources, and their district rangers and other staff members.

On behalf of the U.S. Forest Service and National Park Service and the Washington State Department of Natural Resources and The Mountaineers, we invite Americans—and all citizens of Earth—to come and see and live in their Washington Cascades and Olympics, and while enjoying some of the world's finest wildlands, to vow henceforth to share in the task of preserving the trails and ridges, lakes and rivers, forests and flower gardens for future generations, our children and grandchildren, who will need the wilderness experience at least as much as we do, and probably more.

TABLE OF CONTENTS

Page

SKYKOMISH RIVER
1 Lake Serene 22
2 Snoqualmie Lake 24
3 Tonga Ridge-Mount Sawyer 26
4 Necklace Valley 28
5 Foss Lakes 30
*67 Deception Creek 154
6 Surprise Lake and Mountain 32
*68 Lake Josephine 156

NASON CREEK
7 Larch Lake 34

ICICLE CREEK
8 Enchantment Lakes 36
9 Lake Caroline 38
10 Lake Stuart-Colchuck Lake 40
11 Lake Mary 42

PESHASTIN CREEK
12 Ingalls Creek 44

NORTH FORK SNOQUALMIE RIVER
13 Lennox Creek 47

MIDDLE FORK SNOQUALMIE RIVER
14 Mount Si 48
15 Hester Lake-Myrtle Lake .. 50
16 Dutch Miller Gap-La Bohn Gap 52

SOUTH FORK SNOQUALMIE RIVER
17 McClellan Butte 54
18 Bandera Mountain 56
19 Pratt Lake 58
20 Granite Mountain 60
21 Melakwa Lake 62
22 Annette Lake 65
23 Silver Peak 66
24 Snow Lake 69
25 Ridge and Gravel Lakes 70
*72 Commonwealth Basin 166

Page

LAKE KEECHELUS
26 Mount Margaret-Lake Lillian 72

LAKE KACHESS
27 Rampart Ridge 74
28 Mineral Creek Park 76

CLE ELUM RIVER
29 Kachess Ridge 78
30 Polallie Ridge 80
31 Spectacle Lake 82
32 Jolly Mountain 84
33 Spade and Waptus Lakes .. 86
34 Fish Eagle Pass 88
*73 Paddy Go Easy Pass 168
35 Deep Lake 90
36 Marmot Lake 92

NORTH FORK TEANAWAY
37 County Line Trail 94
38 Beverly Turnpike 97
39 Esmerelda Basin 98
40 Ingalls Lake 100

CARBON RIVER
41 Summit Lake 102
42 Naches Wagon Trail 104
43 Echo Lake 107
44 Crystal Ridge 108
45 Big Crow Basin- Norse Peak 110

AMERICAN RIVER
46 Crow Lake Way 113
47 Sourdough Gap 114

BUMPING RIVER
48 American Ridge 116
49 Nelson Ridge-Mount Aix .. 118
50 Cougar Lakes 120
51 Tumac Mountain 122

TIETON RIVER
52 Dumbbell Lake 124
53 Shoe Lake 127
54 Blankenship Lakes 128

*see note, page 1

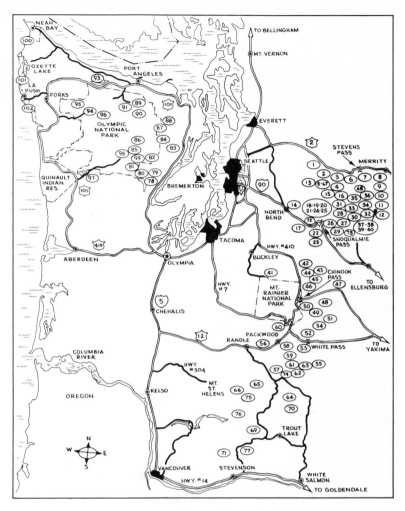

	Page
55 Devils Horns	130
*74 McCall Basin	170

COWLITZ RIVER

56 Trails End (Purcell Mountain)	132
57 Klickitat Trail	134
58 Packwood Lake	136
59 Lily Basin-Heart Lake	138
60 Tatoosh Ridge	140

CISPUS RIVER

61 Snowgrass Flat	142
62 Nannie Ridge	144

	Page
63 Goat Rocks Crest	146
64 Adams Glacier Meadows	148
65 Juniper Mountain	150
66 Boundary Trail	152

TROUT LAKE

69 Indian Heaven	158
70 Mount Adams Highline Trail	160

WIND RIVER

71 Observation (Trapper) Peak	163

see note, page 1

TOUTLE RIVER
Mt. St. Helens 165

LEWIS RIVER
75 Shark Rock and Craggy
    Peak.....................172
76 Lewis River Trail 174
77 Pacific Crest Trail 176

HOOD CANAL
78 Mount Ellinor 180
79 Mildred Lakes 183
80 Flapjack Lakes 184
81 Home Sweet Home 186
82 Upper Lena Lake 188
83 Mount Jupiter 191
84 Lake Constance 192
85 Anderson Glacier 194
86 Hayden Pass 196
87 Marmot Pass.............198
88 Mount Townsend 200

STRAIT OF JUAN DE FUCA
89 Mount Angeles...........202
90 Grand Valley 204
91 Whiskey Bend to Low
    Divide....................206
92 Appleton Pass 208
93 Pyramid Mountain 210
94 High Divide 212

PACIFIC OCEAN
95 Bogachiel River 214
96 Hoh River................216
97 Colonel Bob Mountain ...218
98 Enchanted Valley 220
99 Lake LaCrosse-
    O'Neil Pass 222
100 Point of the Arches 224
101 Rialto Beach to
    Cape Alava..............226
102 Third Beach to Hoh River 228

Mountain goats on Mt. Angeles, Hike 89

1 Lake Serene

Round trip 2 miles
Hiking time 4 hours
High point 2509 feet
Elevation gain 1300 feet
Best June through November
One day or backpack
USGS Index

Like Jack climbing the beanstalk, scramble up a ladder of roots from a busy valley of rumbling trains and speeding autos into the quiet haven of a lake held in a tiny scoop in the side of the giant, Mt. Index, whose rough walls leap a dizzying 3000 feet above the serene waters.

Drive US 2 east from Gold Bar 8 miles and just before a bridge over the Skykomish River, turn right on Index River road. In ¼ mile is a Y, 650 feet. Take the right fork, on wheels or afoot — frequently the steep, clay-slippery road becomes undrivable at some point short of the end. By whatever means, proceed 1½ miles to the end, on the way passing a side-road dropping left to Bridal Veil Creek, coming at last to an interesting mess of mine junk and diggings from the 1950s. Park here (if not before), elevation 1200 feet.

The obvious trail ascends past a mine tunnel and across a rockslide, bearing toward Bridal Veil Falls. The way climbs moderately at first, with views over the Skykomish valley, and then bumps against the foot of the forested cliff and the beginning of the ladderway. The trail was never "constructed," but was beaten out by boots of miners and fishermen and climbers, and scarcely can be recommended as an easy stroll for beginners. However, the tree roots provide convenient steps—plus handholds on the steepest sections—and there is no real danger. But here and the whole way to the lake, keep glancing back to see how the trail will look on the descent; it's easy to go astray and get in bad trouble. The ascent is strenuous but not long.

The trail soon passes remnants of a cabin. Walk around the ruins for a close-up look at Bridal Veil Falls. A bit past the cabin is the tunnel of the old Honeymoon Mine. The mine area has the last flat ground and the last drinking water before the lake. From here the way is straight up through forest on roots and rocks and mud, finally easing in grade at the lip of the basin.

Though the lake elevation is only 2509 feet, the Index-shadowed cirque is cold and snowy and alpine. For the most impressive inspections of the great precipice, wander westward and southward along the shores to large boulders fallen from above and to talus thrusting into the waters. (Watch out for falling rocks!) For views of the Skykomish valley, walk a short bit to the outlet, but don't bother going beyond—cliffs make a circuit of the east shore tough and tricky.

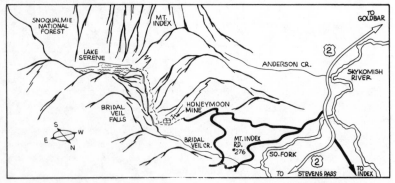

Lake Serene and towering cliffs of Mt. Index

Campsites at the lake are heavily used, badly mauled, and thoroughly unappealing. If camping is planned anyway, be sure to carry a stove; the easy firewood is long gone.

The trail is usually free of snow in May, when the lake still remains frozen and partly covered by enormous avalanche fans. However, spring avalanches sometimes send rocks bounding into the woods and even down the trail. Forest Service rangers therefore recommend staying away until June.

SKYKOMISH RIVER

2 Snoqualmie Lake

Round trip to Snoqualmie Lake 13 miles
Hiking time 6 hours
High point 3800 feet
Elevation gain 1600 feet in, 650 feet out
Best July through October
One day or backpack
USGS Snoqualmie Lake

A string of four large subalpine lakes, some of the most popular in the Alpine Lakes Wilderness. For many decades, even when the hike was very long, they were thronged by fishermen and Scouts. Now that logging roads have pushed far up the Miller River, the first couple are mobbed on summer weekends.

Drive US 2 east 17½ miles from Gold Bar and just before the highway tunnel turn right, at a sign for Money Creek Campground, on Old Cascade Highway. At a Y in 1¼ miles turn right onto gravel Miller River road and drive 9.3 miles to the end and the trailhead, elevation 2200 feet.

The trail climbs through forest to Dorothy Lake at 1½ miles, 3058 feet. Passing over-used camps, it follows the east side of the 2-mile-long lake, crosses the marshy inlet, begins climbing, and at 4½ miles from the road tops the 3800-foot ridge dividing the Miller and Taylor Rivers. Views are down to island-dotted Dorothy amid forest and gray-white cliffs and southeast to the dominant peak of the area, 6670-foot Big Snow Mountain.

From the pass the way is downhill to Bear Lake, 3610 feet, and, at 6 miles, Deer Lake, 3583 feet. At 6½ miles is Snoqualmie Lake, 3147 feet, second-largest of the group and the least-visited. The trail continues 2¼ miles down the Taylor River and then, on long-abandoned logging road, and passing lovely Otter Slide Falls, 6¼ miles more to the Middle Fork Snoqualmie River road.

To protect the vegetation, campers are asked to use sites 100 feet from lakeshores.

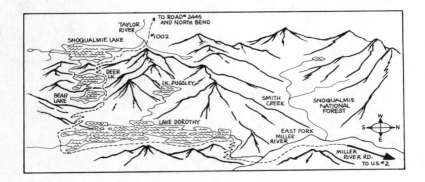

Snoqualmie Lake

3 Tonga Ridge- Mount Sawyer

Round trip to pass 6½ miles
Hiking time 3 hours
High point 4800 feet
Elevation gain 400 feet
Best July through October
One day or backpack
USGS Scenic

The easiest ridge walk on the west side of the Cascades, with grand views, beautiful meadows, and flowers throughout the summer.

Drive US 2 east from Skykomish 1.8 miles and turn right on the Foss River road. At 1.2 miles keep right on the main road. At 2.5 miles go straight ahead at the intersection just after passing under a railroad bridge. At 3.6 miles turn left on Tonga Ridge road No. 2605 for 7 miles. Turn right at a junction marked "Tonga Ridge," No. 2605A, and continue 1.5 miles to the road-end, elevation 4400 feet.

The hike begins on an old fire trail climbing to the ridge crest. In a couple hundred feet the foot trail turns off the fire trail into forest, winds through woods a while, and then follows the ridge top in meadows. At about 1½ miles the trail leaves the crest to contour around Mt. Sawyer, finally dropping a bit to Sawyer Pass, 3 miles, 4800 feet, dividing the drainages of Burn Creek and Fisher Creek. Good campsites, and also the first water of the trip, in the gentle swale of the pass, a large green meadow (commonly called N. P. Camp) that turns a brilliant red in fall.

For a wide-view side-trip, scramble up 5501-foot Mt. Sawyer, the second large hill seen from the Tonga Ridge approach. Leave the trail wherever the slopes look appealing and plow upward in huckleberry brush, gaining 700 feet. Try it in late August and eat your way through delicious berries. The summit panorama includes Mt. Rainier, Mt. Baker, and Glacier Peak, plus Hinman, Daniel, Sloan, and more. Immediately below are two lakes of the Jewel Lake string, easily reached from Sawyer Pass by consulting a contour map.

The most obvious tread at Sawyer Pass is on the west side, but this is a fishermen's path toward Fisher Lake and soon fades out. The main trail stays to the east side of the pass, then descends 1600 feet into valley forest, crossing several small creeks. At 5½ miles skirt a clearcut, cross another clearcut and road, and at 6 miles reach Deception Creek trail.

If pick-up transportation can be arranged, interesting one-way hikes can be made from here, exiting via Deception Creek, or Deception Lakes and Surprise Creek (Hike 6), or Deception Pass, a side-trip to Marmot Lake, and Hyas Lake (Hike 36).

Note: Road No. 2605 is open to public travel to the end; to get there, instead of turning right at the junction 7 miles from Foss River road No. 2622, one would

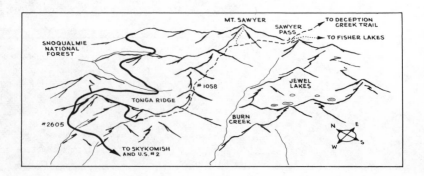

Tonga Ridge trail

continue on road No. 2605 for 11 miles to the trailhead below Sawyer Pass. Obviously this shortcut would give much quicker access to goals in and beyond upper Deception Creek. However, hikers seek challenges, not shortcuts, and it is therefore fervently urged (and demanded) that the Forest Service live up to its "multiple use" theory by closing off the last 3-4 miles of road No. 2605 once the logging is finished, thus preserving as trail country an area that is very heavily used as such, and that certainly doesn't need "improved" access by automobile.

Necklace Valley, LaBohn Gap in distance

SKYKOMISH RIVER

4 Necklace Valley

Round trip to Jade Lake 16 miles
Allow 2-3 days
High point 4600 feet
Elevation gain 3000 feet
Best late July through October
USGS Skykomish, Big Snow Mountain, Mt.
  Daniel

A narrow alpine valley carved from the side of Mt. Hinman and appropriately named for its string of small gems—Jade, Emerald, and Opal Lakes. Nearby are Locket and Jewel Lakes. And others. Thanks to the long trail, this is much more lonesome country than the Foss Lakes area described in Hike 5.

Drive US 2 east from Skykomish 1.8 miles. Turn right on the Foss River road 3.6 miles to the Tonga Ridge junction, as described in Hike 3, and continue to the East Fork Foss River trail at 4.2 miles. On the left side of the road find a small parking area and the trailhead, elevation 1600 feet.

The trail sign reads 9 miles to Necklace Valley, but the Forest Service log says 8, the figure used here. Be prepared for 8 miles that feel like 9.

The first 5 miles gain only 600 feet and are very pleasant going through forest, following the valley bottom, passing the marshes of Alturas "Lake."

The trail this far is very worthwhile in its own right, and can be hiked on a day walk or a weekend backpack in May and June when the high country is buried in snow.

The trail crosses a log over the river which flows from the Hinman Glacier on Mt. Hinman and from the Lynch Glacier on Mt. Daniel. On the far bank the trail leaves the river and climbs into the hanging glacial trough, gaining 2400 feet in the 3 miles to the first gem of the necklace, Jade Lake, 4600 feet.

Necklace Valley is a delightful mixture of forest, heather, ice-polished granite—and of course, the lakes. Possibilities for roaming are endless. Campsites are available along the river and at most of the lakes.

From Emerald Lake, about ¼ mile up-valley from Jade Lake, cross a low saddle west to Jewel and Locket Lakes or cross the ridge east to Lake Ilswoot.

From the east side of Opal Lake, another ¼ mile up-valley from Emerald Lake, climb a short step up a tributary creek to Cloudy Lake.

Tougher to attain are La Bohn Lakes, set in granite bowls near the summit of 5600-foot La Bohn Gap. The off-trail route from the head of Necklace Valley goes abruptly up through cliffs, and though an easy way can be found, at least one hiker has been killed here, and the route cannot be recommended for any but experienced mountain travelers.

To preserve vegetation, campers are asked to use sites 100 feet from lakeshores. Until the Alpine Lakes Management Plan is complete, they also are asked to carry stoves and abstain from building wood fires.

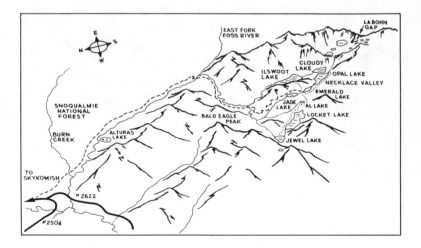

SKYKOMISH RIVER

5 Foss Lakes

Round trip to Copper Lake 8 miles
Hiking time 6-8 hours
High point 3961 feet
Elevation gain 2300 feet
Best July through October
One day or backpack
USGS Big Snow Mountain

Lovers of alpine lakes look at the Big Snow Mountain topog map and drool. Crowded onto this single sheet are 10 large lakes and numerous small ones, the rich legacy of ancient glaciers. The West Fork Foss River trail passes four of the lakes and fishermen's paths lead to others. Don't expect privacy—the area has long been famous and extremely popular for its numerous, unusually big, and readily accessible lakes.

Drive US 2 east from Skykomish 1.8 miles. Turn right on the Foss River road 4.2 miles to the East Fork Foss River trail, as described in Hike 4, and continue to West Fork Foss River road No. 2622 at 4.8 miles. Turn left 2 miles to the road-end and trailhead, elevation 1600 feet.

Hike an easy 1½ miles in cool forest to the first of the chain, Trout Lake, 2000 feet. Trees line the shore; through branches are glimpses of rugged cliffs above. This far makes a leisurely afternoon, and the trail is free of snow in May. Many campsites.

The steep, hot, 2-mile climb to Copper Lake, gaining 2000 feet, is something else in late summer. Water is plentiful but always out of reach—splashing in falls on the far

Copper Lake

hillside, rushing along a deep gully below the trail. The way at last opens into the cliff-walled basin of 3961-foot Copper Lake, surrounded by alpine trees and meadows and talus slopes. The campsites here are heavily used and crowded; others are available at the other lakes, but for any of them be sure to carry a stove.

Though much can be seen in a day or weekend, 3 days or more are needed for a satisfying exploration. Copper Lake is the beginning of highland terrain, with miles of heather and blueberries amid groves of alpine trees, and glacier-smoothed rock knolls and granite buttresses. The crowds steadily diminish beyond Copper.

The lovely cirque of Malachite Lake, 4089 feet, is reached by a steep ¼-mile path branching from the main trail ½ mile before Copper Lake.

Beyond Copper Lake the main trail climbs gently along a stream, passing the best and maybe the only flower display of the trip, to 4204-foot Little Heart Lake, 1 mile from Copper, then crosses a 4700-foot ridge and drops to 4545-foot Big Heart Lake, 2½ miles from Copper.

The formal trail continues beyond the outlet of Big Heart Lake 1 mile over the end of the ridge to the outlet of 4609-foot Lake Angeline. Chetwoot Lake, 4905 feet, coldest and rockiest of the group, may be reached by leaving the formal trail at about its high point on the ridge and traveling south over the very summit of the high and narrow ridge between Big Heart and Angeline Lakes, down into a saddle, and up once more over the next ridge. The route is a bit rugged but quite feasible, with a beaten footpath much of the way. There is a campsite at Chetwoot from which the upper end of Lake Angeline is readily accessible.

There are also Delta, Azurite, and Otter Lakes, and a dozen or more smaller ones, many visible from the trail and each a jewel in its own right. Routes known to hardy fishermen exist to all of them, and even semblances of boot-beaten track, but essentially these lakes are for the experienced cross-country hiker.

To preserve the vegetation, campers are asked to use sites 100 feet from lakeshores.

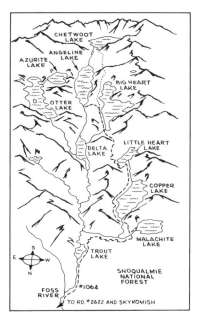

SKYKOMISH RIVER

6 Surprise Lake and Mountain

Round trip to Surprise Lake 8 miles
Hiking time 5 hours
High point 4500 feet
Elevation gain 2300 feet
Best late June through October
One day or backpack
USGS Scenic

Round trip to Surprise Mountain 15 miles
Hiking time 9-12 hours
High point 6330 feet
Elevation gain 4100 feet
Best late July through October
One day or backpack
USGS Scenic

Two alpine lakes surrounded by forest with mountain tops looming over the trees and reflected in the quiet water.

Drive US 2 east from Skykomish 10 miles to Scenic, the west portal of Burlington-Northern Railroad's Cascade Tunnel. Drive into the hamlet of Scenic, cross the railroad track, and in several yards turn right to a small parking lot at the trailhead, elevation 2200 feet.

Hike west along the old road beside the railroad tracks for approximately ½ mile to a powerline. The trail begins from the powerline service road, climbs through the hot-and-brushy clearcut area along the powerline, then enters cool forest. The tread is well-constructed and maintained but the nature of the soil makes for much mud in the first mile. In fact, a few horses can render the path unusable.

In 1 mile the trail fords Surprise Creek; if the water is high, look for a footlog a bit downstream. The steadily-ascending route is mostly in deep woods, but at around 3 miles climbs a rocky knoll with views back toward the Skykomish valley and up to Surprise Mountain. In 4 miles the way passes the old route of the Pacific Crest Trail from Stevens Pass; here too a path drops 100 feet to Surprise Lake, 4508 feet. Campsites at the lake, which also is a good destination for a day trip.

The valley trail continues uphill, in ¾ mile joining the new Pacific Crest Trail from Stevens Pass. At 1 mile from Surprise Lake is 4806-foot Glacier Lake and at 1½ miles is a lovely little meadow; camps here and at the lake.

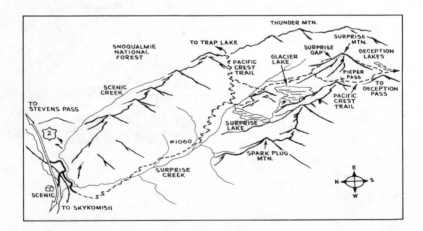

Mt. Daniel from Surprise Gap

Now the way opens from greenery into a granite basin under the cliffs of Surprise Mountain and ascends to a junction 2¼ miles from Surprise Lake. The new Crest Trail turns right, climbs to 5900-foot Pieper Pass, and swings around the south slopes of Surprise Mountain. The old trail switchbacks ¼ mile to 5780-foot Surprise Gap. North-slope snow patches linger until mid-July; proceed with caution.

Views from the gap are fine, but for really magnificent vistas find the lookout trail on the west side of the gap and climb 1 steep mile through meadows to the 6330-foot summit of Surprise Mountain. Look south across valley forests of Deception Creek to glacier-gleaming Mt. Daniel and other peaks of the Alpine Lakes Wilderness.

Deception Lakes lie 1 mile and 700 feet below Surprise Gap. They can also be reached by the 10 percent-grade Crest Trail over Pieper Pass. From the junction, the distance to the lakes via the gap is 1¼ miles, via the pass (Crest Trail) 2¾ miles.

To preserve the vegetation, campers are asked to use sites 100 feet from lakeshores.

NASON CREEK

7 Larch Lake

Round trip via Chiwaukum Creek 20 miles
Allow 2-3 days
High point 6078 feet
Elevation gain 3700 feet
Best mid-July through October
USGS Chiwaukum Mountains

A high mountain lake, rimmed by rocks and groves of larch, in the shadow of the tall and rugged Chiwaukum Mountains on the northeast edge of the Alpine Lakes Wilderness.

Tragically, much of the surrounding region is privately owned as a consequence of the infamous Northern Pacific Land Grant of 1864, and in 1973, despite strenuous efforts by conservationists, Wenatchee National Forest and Pack River Lumber Company began building a system of new roads to allow logging of both private and public timber. Take the hike—and return mourning the destruction.

There are two approaches to Larch Lake: a well-graded trail over McCue Ridge; or a valley walk along Chiwaukum Creek, easy except for 2 very steep, hot miles. Despite the mean stretch, the creek route is recommended. The forest is lovely, there are frequent charming views of the stream, and the way crosses three nice bridges, one of them just below a waterfall. Both approaches are the same length but the ridge trail climbs 300 feet higher going in and makes a 500-foot ascent coming out.

For the McCue Ridge route, which has been messed up by Pack River's logging operations, drive US 2 east from Stevens Pass 17 miles. Just opposite a highway rest area turn south around a pasture. There are numerous logging spurs but the correct way is well-marked. At 1.5 miles find Lake Julius trail No. 1584, elevation 2500 feet.

The trail follows a ridge above Roaring Creek, crossing a private (gated) logging road four times, climbing to a junction with McCue Ridge trail No. 1574 at 5½ miles, 5600 feet. Keep left, ascending to the ridge top at 5750 feet. At this point the ridge is timbered; for views, walk a path a few hundred feet east on the crest and look over a big patch of buckbrush, or snowbrush (ceanothus). Below is the vast Chiwaukum valley, west are the Chiwaukum Mountains, and south are Snowgrass Mountain and the Stuart Range. From the ridge the trail drops 550 feet to Chiwaukum Lake at 7½ miles; campsites near the shores and in a large, horsey area at the head of the lake in

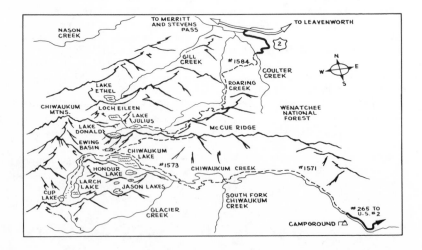

Larch Lake and Chiwaukum Mountains

Ewing Basin. A way trail traverses the long basin and climbs steeply into meadow-lands, at 10 miles reaching 6078-foot Larch Lake and many good camps.

For the Chiwaukum Creek route, drive US 2 east from Stevens Pass 25 miles and about ½ mile before reaching Tumwater Campground turn south on a rough road leading in 2 miles to the trailhead, elevation 2200 feet.

Trail No. 1571 follows close by the creek in deep forest, gradually ascending. At 4 miles turn right on trail No. 1573 and at 5 miles begin climbing steeply, with many switchbacks, on a badly-eroded tread consisting mainly of loose schist, gaining 1200 feet in a little more than a mile. At 7 miles the unpleasantness ends as 5210-foot Chiwaukum Lake is attained. Follow the shore ½ mile to a junction with the McCue Ridge trail described above and continue to Larch Lake at 10 miles.

Among the possible explorations from Larch Lake are a scramble up among the 8000-foot Chiwaukum Mountains and a walk to tiny Cup Lake, set in a little north-facing cirque that doesn't melt free of snow until September, if then.

To preserve the vegetation, campers are asked to use sites 100 feet from lakeshores.

Gnome Tarn and Little Annapurna

ICICLE CREEK

8 Enchantment Lakes

Round trip to Snow Lakes 13½ miles
Allow 2 days
High point 5415 feet
Elevation gain 3800 feet
Best July through mid-November
USGS Mt. Stuart and Liberty

Round trip to Lower Enchantment Lakes 20 miles
Allow 3-4 days
High point 7000 feet
Elevation gain 5400 feet
Best late July through mid-October

A legendary group of lakes in rock basins over 7000 feet high amid the splintered Cashmere Crags of the Stuart Range; one of the most famous places in the entire Cascade Mountains. Large lakes, small ponds, gigantic slabs of ice-polished granite, flower gardens, heather meadows, groves of larch, lone trees gnarled and twisted by the elements, waterfalls, snowfields, and glaciers. Visit in summer for flowers, in late September to see the autumn gold of larch.

This is not a trip for beginners. The way is long, steep, and grueling. A strong hiker needs at least 12 hours to reach the high lakes. The average hiker takes 2 days. The rest never make it.

Drive US 2 east from Stevens Pass to Leavenworth. On the west outskirts of town turn south on Icicle road. At 4 miles turn left into the Snow Lakes trail parking area, elevation 1600 feet.

Snow Lakes trail No. 1553 crosses the river and immediately starts up—and up. Motorbikes long have been prohibited, and now horses are not allowed prior to early September. The way switchbacks upward in forest, with views in the early part to the granite cliffs of Snow Creek Wall. Small camps at approximately 2 miles, 2800 feet, offer a break in the journey for parties with heavy packs or not too much energy and wishing to make the approach in easy stages. At 5½ miles is Nada Lake, 5000 feet, and good camps. At 6¾ miles the trail passes between the two Snow Lakes at 5415 feet. For camping here, find sites to the left at the lower lake. To the north rises 8292-foot Mt. Temple and to the south 8364-foot Mt. McClellan. All beginners and most average hikers find this far enough, and these lakes magnificent enough—as indeed they are, but it just happens their beauty can't hold a candle to what lies above.

To continue to the Enchantments, cross the low dam between the two lakes. Pause to note this rather weird interference with nature: like a bathtub, water is drained through a hole in the bottom of the upper lake (which thus has a fluctuating shoreline) and is used to guarantee a pure intake for the Leavenworth Fish Hatchery; probably few people imagined, when the project was perpetrated back in the 1930s, that Snow Lakes would become as popular as they now are.

Follow the trail winding along the left shore. At the south end cross the inlet stream and proceed up Snow Creek, climbing into granite country.

The nomenclature of the lakes, which until recently had only a group name, is disputed. The Starks, who know the area over many years, and in every season, proposed individual names appropriate to the theme of "enchantment," drawing on various mythologies. A lake and its sword-like rock peninsula became Lake Viviane and Excalibur Rock. Other lakes and tarns they called Rune, Talisman, Valkyrie, Leprechaun, Naiad, Lorelei, Dryad, Pixie, Gnome, Brisingamen, Brynhild, Reginleif, Sprite, and Titania. And there is Troll Sink (a pond), Valhalla Cirque, Tanglewood, and many more. The Forest Service, however, chose to decorate the map with trite, conventional names that immediately became "official"—except that nobody who knows and loves the area uses them.

Lower Enchantment Basin, at 7000 feet, is friendliest. Upper Enchantment Basin, at 7500 feet, has a wild, desolate splendor. Some of its lakes are clear and some are jade-colored by rock milk and some are frozen solid all summer. There are small glaciers, great slabs of ice-sculptured granite, and grand views of a cold high wilderness.

Despite the arduous approach the Enchantments are mobbed, with over 60,000 visitor-days a year. Great care is thus required to protect the vegetation: no wood fires, whenever possible, walk on rock or snow rather than plants, camp on bare ground at established sites, limit party size to six, bring no dogs.

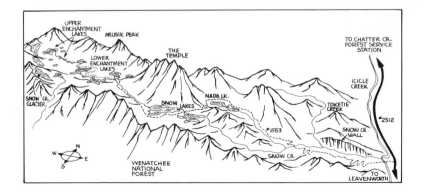

ICICLE CREEK

9 Lake Caroline

Round trip 11 miles
Hiking time 8 hours
High point 6190 feet
Elevation gain 2400 feet
Best mid-July through October
One day or backpack
USGS Chiwaukum Mountains

Another famous beauty spot of the Alpine Lakes Wilderness. Meadows, a wealth of rugged granite crags, spectacular views—and lovely lakes, of course. A special treat is the great north face of 9415-foot Mt. Stuart, seen from close enough to make out crevasses in the hanging glaciers.

Drive US 2 east from Stevens Pass to Leavenworth. On the west outskirts of town turn south on Icicle Creek road. At 8.5 miles turn left across a new bridge on road No. 2412 up Eight Mile Creek, climbing steeply 3 miles to the trailhead, elevation 3800 feet. Eight Mile Lake trail No. 1552, on the uphill side of the road, is clearly signed.

The trail ascends moderately through splendid old forest, following along Eight Mile Creek 2½ miles to Little Eight Mile Lake, 4400 feet, and a junction. The left fork goes ½ mile up the valley to 4641-foot Eight Mile Lake and good camps. The lake is ringed by woods but awesome rock walls rise far above the trees.

The right fork climbs an endless series of switchbacks (hot and thirsty on sunny days) up from the valley, first in timber, then emerging into meadows. The labor is rewarded by steadily improving views to the jagged spires of the Stuart Range and finally the tall thrust of Mt. Stuart itself. At 5½ miles the way reaches the alpine basin of Lake Caroline, 6190 feet. The most attractive campsites are ½ mile farther and 200 feet higher at Little Lake Caroline, surrounded by meadows.

The best is yet to come. The 2-mile hike to 7200-foot Windy Pass, on good trail amid flowers and larches, is an absolute must. For broader views walk the ridge towards 8501-foot Mt. Cashmere—but don't try for the summit; the last pitches are strictly for climbers.

An alternate return route to civilization—though not to the starting point—can be made by going 8 miles from Windy Pass down the Trout Creek trail to Chatter Creek Guard Station.

To preserve the vegetation, campers are asked to use sites 100 feet from lakeshores.

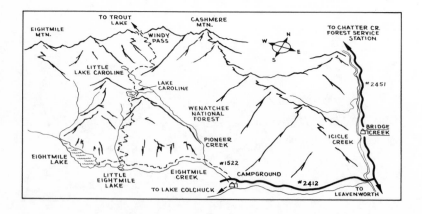

Mt. Stuart from near Windy Pass

ICICLE CREEK

10 Lake Stuart-Colchuck Lake

Round trip to Colchuck Lake 7 miles
Hiking time 8 hours
High point 5570 feet
Elevation gain 2000 feet
Best mid-July through October
One day or backpack
USGS Chiwaukum and Mt. Stuart

Round trip to Lake Stuart 9 miles
Hiking time 7 hours
High point 5064 feet
Elevation gain 1500 feet
Best mid-July through October
One day or backpack

Two beautiful lakes amid alpine forests and granite cliffs of the Stuart Range. Hike to the emerald waters of Colchuck Lake and contemplate the towering crags above, decorated with two small glaciers. Or, to cure itchy feet, visit nearby Lake Stuart and explore onward to higher and lonesomer country and grand views of Mt. Stuart.

From Icicle Creek road (Hike 9) drive 4 miles on road No. 2412 to the trailhead, elevation 3600 feet. Find Lake Stuart-Colchuck Lake trail No. 1599 at a sharp turn of the road on the creek side.

The trail parallels Mountaineer Creek on a constant upward grade for 1 mile, then switchbacks up the steepening valley to a junction at 1½ miles, 4600 feet.

The left trail (a rough path) crosses Mountaineer Creek and ascends with many switchbacks, in open forest among numerous granite knolls, along the cascading waters of the East Fork Mountaineer Creek. During the final ¼ mile the way bypasses a waterfall, leaves the creek, and comes to a tiny, almost landlocked lagoon of Colchuck Lake, 5570 feet, 3½ miles. Incredibly, this lovely blue-green lake, like others in the area, is drained for use by the Icicle Irrigation District. Camping at the lagoon or near the outlet.

The right trail proceeds gently up the main fork of Mountaineer Creek to the wooded shores, clear blue water, and tall cliffs of Lake Stuart, 5064 feet, 4½ miles. Campsites near the point where the trail first reaches the lake and around the south shore. Follow the trail ¾ mile beyond the lake to a marshy meadow under the towering cliffs of Mt. Stuart. Experienced and determined wilderness travelers may then bust brush and

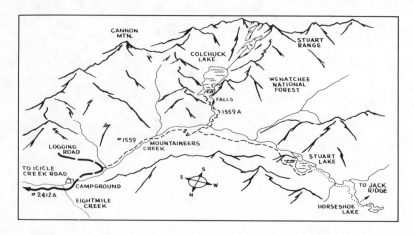

Mt. Stuart from Lake Stuart

scramble rocks dotted with isolated larches to Horseshoe Lake, well above timberline at 6200 feet. Continue to the crest of Jack Ridge for better views of the north wall of 9415-foot Mt. Stuart.

To preserve the vegetation, campers are asked to use sites 100 feet from lakeshores.

Icicle Ridge trail. Mt. Stuart in distance

ICICLE CREEK

11 Lake Mary

Round trip to Lake Mary 16 miles
Allow 2-3 days
High point 6200 feet
Elevation gain 3300 feet
Best mid-July through October
USGS Chiwaukum Mountains

Some hikers claim this is the lovliest part of the entire Alpine Lakes Wilderness. None denies the extraordinary beauties of the miles of flowers, grass, heather, and huckleberries, lakes and ponds and snowfields, and a succession of dream-like views—a highland designed for endless roaming.

Drive US 2 east from Stevens Pass to Leavenworth. On the west outskirts of town turn south on Icicle road. At 8.5 miles pass Eight Mile junction and at 16.7 miles cross Icicle Creek on a concrete bridge (road No. 2512). At 18.5 miles are the road-end and trailhead, elevation 2900 feet.

Icicle Creek trail No. 1551 goes upstream in forest, over several little creeks with campsites, to a junction at 2½ miles, 3000 feet. Turn right on Wildhorse trail No. 1592, cross Icicle Creek, and start up. Within a mile cross Frosty Creek (fill canteens—the next steep miles are long and waterless and can be scorching). Now comes a punishing series of switchbacks and hot traverses as the trail ascends the valley of Frosty Creek, gaining 3000 feet in less than 4 miles and leaving woods for parkland. At 6¾ miles pass a side-trail descending to tree-ringed Lake Margaret, and at 7½ miles attain the open crest of 5800-foot Frosty Pass and a junction with Icicle Ridge trail No. 1570.

Ascend the ridge trail east ½ mile along the alpine slopes of Snowgrass Mountain and find a short way trail dropping to Lake Mary, 6100 feet, a grand place for a basecamp. If the basin is crowded, go another long mile over a little pass to Upper Florence Lake, 6500 feet. Many other fine camps can be found elsewhere in the area.

Plan to spend a full, rich day wandering the Icicle Ridge trail to 6800-foot Ladies Pass, overlooking Lake Brigham and Lake Flora. The distance from Lake Mary is only 2 miles but the constant views of meadows and peaks and valleys slow the pace to the speed of a worm.

Other explorations abound: from Ladies Pass, ascend a path up a shoulder of Cape Horn and then scramble to the 7300-foot summit; also from Ladies Pass, take the trail traversing slopes of Cape Horn to the cold and rocky tarn of Lake Edna; from Lake Mary, follow the easy ridge crest to the very top of 7993-foot Snowgrass Mountain and a panorama of the Chiwaukum Mountains, the Wenatchee Mountains, the Stuart Range, and much more; from Frosty Pass, walk the Wildhorse trail north a bit more than a mile and then climb to 6242-foot Lake Grace. A week of rambling is scarcely enough.

If transportation can be arranged, a one-way trip can be made down the South Fork Chiwaukum Creek trail 12 miles from Ladies Pass to the road. Maps show a trail down Chatter Creek; the way is rough, steep, and in spots hard to find.

To preserve vegetation, campers are asked to use sites 100 feet from lakeshores.

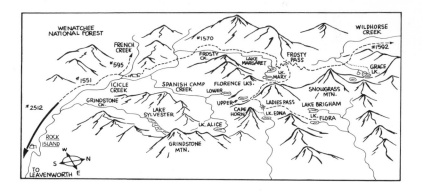

PESHASTIN CREEK

12 Ingalls Creek

Round trip to Falls Creek Camp 12 miles
Hiking time 6 hours
High point 3200 feet
Elevation gain 1200 feet
Best late May through November
One day or backpack
USGS Liberty and Mt. Stuart

Round trip to Stuart Pass 32 miles
Allow 3-5 days
High point 6400 feet
Elevation gain 4400 feet
Best July through October

The longest wilderness valley remaining in the Cascades outside the far north, 16 miles of trail climbing from low forest to high meadows, passing constantly changing views of the spectacular Stuart Range.

Hike this trail the first week of June when the first 5 miles are lined with trillium, gold-colored paintbrush, and a few calypso orchids thrown in. If you're too early for trillium, there will be glacier lilies. If you're too late for trillium, there will be queen's cup.

Drive US 97 north from Swauk (Blewett) Pass 12.5 miles and turn left on the Ingalls Creek road about 1 mile to the road-end and trailhead, elevation 1953 feet.

The trail ascends steadily but gently, alternating between groves of trees and patches of avalanche brush, mostly in sight and always in sound of roaring Ingalls Creek, with tantalizing glimpses of the rocky summits of the Stuart Range, and later, looks to fantastic spires.

In early June hikers usually will encounter snow patches from 4 miles or so, and difficult going beyond the vicinity of Falls Creek, 6 miles, 3200 feet. The lovely Falls Creek Camp is reached by a side-trail across Ingalls Creek, which is much too deep and swift to ford while melt-water is rushing. In any season this point makes a good turnaround for day-trippers.

The way continues upward along the almost-straight fault-line valley (granite on one side, sediments and metamorphics on the other), the forest becoming subalpine and open, the views growing and shifting. Tributary creeks are crossed often enough to satisfy thirst; pleasant camps are frequent.

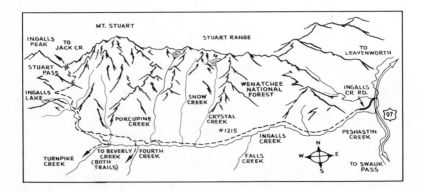

Ingalls Creek near Falls Creek

From Porcupine Creek, about 10 miles, 4100 feet, the path steepens a bit and sidehills above Ingalls Creek, the timber increasingly broken by meadows. Now the dramatic cliffs and buttresses of 9415-foot Mt. Stuart, second-highest nonvolcanic peak in the state, dominate the scene.

At about 13½ miles, 4800 feet, the trail nears Ingalls Creek and commences a comparatively earnest ascent, climbing parkland and flowers and talus to Stuart Pass, 16 miles, 6400 feet. On the far side the tread descends Jack Creek to Chatter Creek Forest Station on Icicle Creek.

All along the upper valley the open country invites easy off-trail wanderings, such as to Longs Pass (Hike 39). From a camp in the delightful basin under Stuart Pass one can spend days exploring—begin by contouring meadows from the pass to 6463-foot Ingalls Lake (Hike 40).

Anderson Lake, snow-covered in late June. Treen Peak, left, and Garfield Mountain, center

**NORTH FORK
SNOQUALMIE RIVER**

13 Lennox Creek

Round trip to Anderson Lake 7½ miles
Hiking time 5 hours
High point 4600 feet
Elevation gain 1900 feet in, 400 feet out
Best July to early November
One day or backpack
USGS Mt. Si and Snoqualmie Lake

Waterfalls, broad slopes of heather meadows, views of peaks and valleys, and a quiet lake—all in a little-traveled portion of the Cascades. After lying in limbo for many years, this particular trail was reopened in 1970, and hikers gradually are coming to discover the beauties of the North Fork Snoqualmie country.

Drive Interstate 90 to North Bend, take the first exit into the town and onto the main street, the former highway. Turn north on North Ballart Street (second street east from the stoplight), and proceed through town to the outskirts, where the street changes in name to North Fork Road (county), sometimes called the Lake Hancock road. In 7.5 miles pass the Lake Hancock junction and at about 21 miles (mostly and increasingly rough) enter Snoqualmie National Forest; note a marked improvement in the road, now designated No. 250. At the boundary the road forks; keep right, cross Lennox Creek, and drive 4 miles to two small bridges over island-divided channels of Lennox Creek. About ¼ mile farther is a fork; keep right on road No. 250B, heading up Cougar Creek drainage a short, switchbacking mile to the road-end at a hogback in a clearcut, elevation 2700 feet.

The trail starts steeply up the hogback on a bulldozer track, in less than ¼ mile going from logged barrens into forest and passing a miner's cabin. Now the way contours the east side of Dog Mountain, traversing shoulders of a large avalanche chute. At about 2 miles the route enters a land of heather laced by numerous creeklets. Directly below the meadows and a bit hard to see is the spectacular waterfall of one of the tributaries of Lennox Creek.

At about 3¼ miles, 4600 feet, the trail gains a wooded saddle in the ridge. Enjoy the views down to Taylor River and across the valley to Treen Peak and a most unfamiliar aspect of Garfield Mountain.

From the saddle the trail switchbacks down 400 feet in a rough ½ mile to little Anderson Lake, surrounded by patches of heather and lots of trees. Camping is nice and quite private.

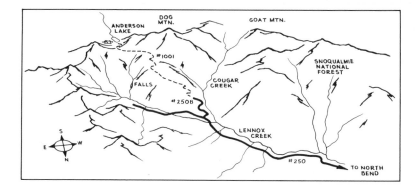

MIDDLE FORK
SNOQUALMIE RIVER

14 Mount Si

Round trip 8 miles
Hiking time 8 hours
High point 4167 feet
Elevation gain 3500 feet
Best April through November
One day
USGS on the corner of Mt. Si, Snoqualmie,
North Bend, and Bandera

Climb steeply to the top of a fault scarp rising high above lowlands at the west edge of the Cascades. Look down to the Snoqualmie River meandering by the towns of North Bend and Snoqualmie and through green farms. If the smog isn't too thick, look west to Seattle and Puget Sound and the Olympic Mountains.

Si is a striking landmark at the gateway to the Cascades and is close to the city and therefore is perhaps the most heavily-traveled peak in the state. Mountaineers use the trail for conditioning, Scouts come in troops, and families with little children, and elderly folk and young lovers and lone roamers—a cross-section of humanity (in fact, about 10,000 hikers a year) may be encountered on a typical Sunday.

By May of normal years the way is entirely clear of snow. Sometimes the mountain is briefly bare even in midwinter, and the trail usually can be hiked to high viewpoints in any month.

Drive Interstate 90 to North Bend, take the first exit into town, and continue east on North Bend Way, the old route of I-90. Exactly 1 mile from the east edge of town turn left on 432nd S.E. (Stilson Road) and cross the Middle Fork Snoqualmie River. Turn right at the first intersection. Drive 2.5 miles to a parking lot for 175 cars, a picnic area, and the trailhead, elevation 650 feet. The trail is signed for hikers only.

The first ½ mile is in alders, then second-growth firs 60-70 years old—except for a 1976 clearcut. At 1 mile is a vista point on a big rock alongside the trail. At 1¾ miles enter Snag Flat, covered by a mixture of old snags and huge fir trees, some 8 feet in diameter, that survived the fires. Water here about 200 feet off the main trail on a spur going ½ mile to a viewpoint.

The trees get smaller but views are scarce until the old trail is intersected at 3 miles, just below the ridge, a mile from the top. The way follows a rocky shoulder with broad panoramas to Haystack Basin, at the foot of the cliffs of the final peak. The Department of Natural Resources, which relocated the trailhead and built the new path after the old one was partially obliterated by logging operations, has installed pit toilets and

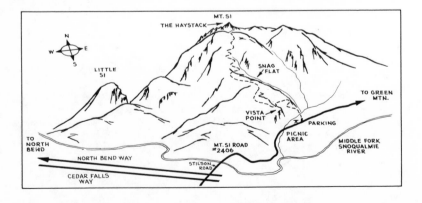

North Bend from edge of Haystack Basin

primitive campsites. However, there is no water after the last snow melts, usually in May, so carry enough for cooking or else hike up after dinner, enjoy the night on top—thousands of lights below and millions of stars above—and return to the car for breakfast. There are no other camps on the route.

The Haystack can be climbed by crossing the basin to the northeast side and scrambling a steep, loose-rock gully, but the ascent is a bit difficult and quite hazardous, and the summit view is only slightly better than that from the basin.

**MIDDLE FORK
SNOQUALMIE RIVER**

15 Hester Lake- Myrtle Lake

Round trip to Myrtle Lake 10 miles
Hiking time 7 hours
High point 3777 feet
Elevation gain 2400 feet
Best July through October
One day or backpack
USGS Snoqualmie Lake

Round trip to Hester Lake 9 miles
Hiking time 7 hours
High point 3886 feet
Elevation gain 2500 feet

Two high lakes, one offering some scenery and lots of solitude, the other lots of scenery—and people. However, the fishermen crowds don't climb the ridge where the views and meadow-wandering are.

Drive Interstate 90 east past North Bend and take the Edgewick exit. Go left past Ken's Truck Town and follow signs for Middle Fork Snoqualmie River road No. 2445, which in 15 miles crosses the Taylor River bridge. Once across the bridge, go another 6 miles to the road end and Dingford Creek trailhead, elevation 1400 feet.

The trail switchbacks steeply and hotly upward 1 mile through second-growth trees seeded after logging operations in the late 1940s, then gradually gentles out in cool virgin forest of tall, old Douglas fir and hemlock, going along constantly close to the tumble and roar of Dingford Creek. At about 2 miles, 2600 feet, is a ford of Goat Creek and an unmaintained fishermen's side-trail climbing a rough 1 mile to Horseshoe Lake and Goat Lake. At 3 miles, 2900 feet, the trail forks; a nice campsite here beside the creek.

The right fork, to Hester Lake, is in poor shape and will be allowed to stay that way for people wanting to get away from people. The trail crosses Dingford Creek, ascends moderately at first in subalpine meadow-marshes and patches of trees, then goes straight uphill to Hester Lake, 3888 feet, 2 miles from Dingford Creek. The deep blue lake is set in a cirque gouged in the side of 5600-foot Mt. Price; impressive cliffs rise from the shores, around which are good camps.

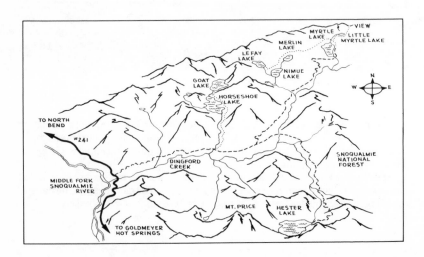

Oyster mushrooms along the trail to Hester Lake

The left fork, to Myrtle Lake, is being improved for hikers and horses. The trail ascends easily in open forest, passing several meadows; the biggest difficulty (in season) is making any progress at all through the delicious blueberries. At 3 miles from the forks is Myrtle Lake, 3777 feet, amid clumps of alpine trees interspersed with huckleberry-covered meadows. Campsites at the lake and on higher benches; to protect the vegetation, campers are asked to use sites 100 feet from the shore.

For explorations, go around the east shore and find (if possible—it's not easy) a faint trail to Little Myrtle Lake. Continue another ¼ mile to the 4400-foot top of the ridge and views north to Lake Dorothy and south to Big Snow Mountain, 6670 feet. Alternatively, climb the slopes west from Myrtle Lake and roam the ridges and fields of blueberries to Merlin, Niume, and LeFay Lakes.

Williams Lake and Little Big Chief Mountain

**MIDDLE FORK
SNOQUALMIE RIVER**

16 Dutch Miller Gap-La Bohn Gap

Round trip to Dutch Miller Gap 27 miles
Allow 2 days
High point 5000 feet
Elevation gain 2200 feet
Best mid-July through October
USGS Big Snow Mountain and Mt. Daniel

Round trip to La Bohn Gap approximately
    28 miles
Allow 2 days
High point 5600 feet
Elevation gain 2800 feet
Best late July through October

Hike a glorious valley of forests and meadows and waterfalls, rockslides and cliffs and jagged peaks, to wilderness headwaters of the Middle Fork Snoqualmie River. Then follow either the main trail to Dutch Miller Gap, named for an early prospector, or a way-trail to La Bohn Gap, where he dug his holes in the ground.

Drive the Middle Fork Snoqualmie River Road (Hike 15), cross the Taylor River bridge and continue to the present road end at Dingford Creek. Hike the now abandoned road 6 miles to the trailhead, elevation 3000 feet.

The trail enters forest and ascends gently with ups and downs, passing a riverbank camp at 1½ miles.

The transition from low country to high is abrupt: at about 4 miles the trail switchbacks up a step in the valley, going by a splendid cataract of the river, and at the top emerges into heather, grass, flowers, large talus slopes, and views of craggy peaks. The way is flat and frequently marshy and muddy to 6 miles, where the river is so wide and slow and meandering as almost to be a lake, surrounded by a broad meadow. Here, at superbly scenic Pedro Camp, 4100 feet, the trail crosses a branch of the river on a bridge; shortly beyond prowl around to find remnants of an old miner's cabin (Dutch Miller's?).

The way goes moderately upward in heather and alpine trees another ½ mile to a junction with the Williams Lake—La Bohn Gap trail, an easy ¾ mile to the heather-fringed lake.

For the main event, follow tread a long mile or so and then climb rockslides and/or snowfields to a magnificent basin of cold little tarns set in granite bowls, of flower patches and waterfalls, and of the mineral outcroppings and diggings and garbage of Dutch Miller's old mine—and his contemporary successors. Climb a bit more to the 5600-foot crest of La Bohn Gap (2 miles from the junction) and more tarns and views of Bears Breast Mountain and down into Necklace Valley (Hike 4). Experienced roamers can walk to panoramas from 6585-foot La Bohn Peak west of the gap or make a more difficult scramble to the summit of 7492-foot Mt. Hinman. Many delightful camps in the basin and in the gap.

One-half mile from the Williams Lake junction the main valley trail fords the river and ascends between the walls of Bears Breast and Little Big Chief, with grand views of Little Big Chief, Summit Chief, Middle Chief, and Overcoat, to the gardens of Dutch Miller Gap, 7½ miles, 5000 feet. Look immediately below to Lake Ivanhoe and out the valley east to Waptus Lake. Look westerly back down the long Snoqualmie valley. The trail drops ½ mile to rock-shored Ivanhoe, 4652 feet, at the foot of the cliffs of Bears Breast. Good camps at the shelter by the lake. The trail continues down to Waptus Lake and the Cle Elum River (Hike 33).

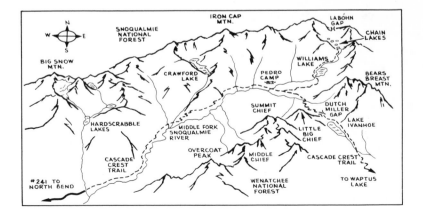

SOUTH FORK
SNOQUALMIE RIVER

17 McClellan Butte

Round trip 8 miles
Hiking time 8 hours
High point 5162 feet
Elevation gain 3700 feet
Best July through October
One day
USGS Bandera

The sharp little peak looks formidable from I-90, and because of avalanche snows in a gully it is dangerous until early July. However, a steep and rugged trail climbs to a viewpoint only 50 feet below the rocky summit for panoramas west over lowlands to Seattle, Puget Sound, and the Olympics, south over uncountable clearcuts to Mt. Rainier, and east to Snoqualmie Pass peaks. The lower part of the route contains numerous scars and artifacts of man's present and past activities; the recorded history of the area dates to 1853, when Captain George B. McClellan journeyed approximately this far up the valley during his search for a cross-Cascades pass suitable for Indian-fighters and immigrants. The trail is very popular even though rough in spots.

Drive Interstate 90 east from the center of North Bend 12 miles and at the great huge sign announcing the McClellan Butte Trail take Exit 42 to road No. 222. Immediately beyond the Snoqualmie River bridge, turn right to the trailhead and parking lot, elevation 1500 feet.

The trail follows remnants of a wire-wrapped wooden waterline to a bridge (built by Scouts) over Alice Creek, climbs a bit, crosses a powerline swath, enters woods again, reaches a long-abandoned, overgrown railroad grade, and at ½ mile crosses the Milwaukee Railroad tracks and enters a vast clearcut. In the woods again, the trail passes mouldering mining relics and at 1 mile, 2200 feet, crosses a private (gated) logging road, Find a little spring left along the road—the last sure water after July.

The way steepens, going by a sometime spring in a cool grove of large trees, then switchbacks up the wooded north face of the butte. At about 2½ miles the trail rounds

Yellow violets

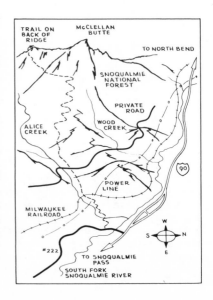

*Interstate 90, logging roads, powerline, and railroad
from summit ridge of McClellan Butte*

the east side of the butte and crosses an avalanche gully with a treacherous snow-bank that usually lasts into July. From here, with numerous switchbacks, the way sidehills below cliffs and occasional views, attaining the south ridge of the peak at 3¼ miles, 4500 feet. The trail follows the crest a short bit, with looks down into Seattle's Cedar River watershed, rounds the east side of the mountain, drops 100 feet to a small pond (possible campsites) and climbs again, passing recent mining garbage to a magnificent viewpoint on the ridge crest about 100 vertical feet from the summit.

Ancient cables of doubtful security give treacherous handholds for an exposed scramble to the actual summit. As in the case of nearby Mt. Si, the majority of hikers are content with the ridgetop view and leave the summit for experienced moun-taineers.

SOUTH FORK
SNOQUALMIE RIVER

18 Bandera Mountain

Round trip 7 miles
Hiking time 6 hours
High point 5240 feet
Elevation gain 2800 feet
Best mid-May through November
One day
USGS Bandera

Even though there is no real trail, just a boot-beaten track and follow-your-nose scramble, Bandera offers the easiest-to-reach summit panoramas in the Snoqualmie area, with superb views to the valley and lowlands, into the Alpine Lakes Wilderness, and up and down the length of the Cascades. Because of the southwesterly exposure, snow melts off early; the ascent can be made when trails to nearby peaks are still buried in winter white.

In the summer of 1958 a fire started by loggers swept Bandera to timberline. Long before that, in the past century, the upper slopes were burned (probably by nature's lightning, not by man's carelessness) and forest has not yet begun to come back. Thus the entire ascent is in the open, and can be hot. To compensate, scenery is continuous every step of the way.

Drive Interstate 90 east from North Bend 15 miles and go off on Exit 45, signed "Bandera Airport, Talapus Lake Trail." Go under the highway and turn left onto Forest Service road No. 2218, heading westward parallel to the highway. At a junction in a short mile, go straight on road No. 2218A, signed "Mason Lake Way 4." Continue upward to where the road is closed at 4½ miles from the highway. Park here, elevation 2400 feet.

Walk the abandoned road, passing the Mason Lake trail, 1½ miles to the end. Fill canteens at the creek here; there is no water above.

Begin by scrambling uphill near the creek, on boot-built tread, a short bit to a bulldozer track. Go rightward up the road a few hundred feet to a point where green timber at the margin of the burn is very close above. Climb the bank (where others obviously have done so) and a few yards of sparse brush to the edge of timber and there intersect the rough path hacked out by the fire-fighters of 1958.

Ascend the rude, steep tread with hands and feet to the upper limit of the burn, then follow any of the paths directly upward, first over and around down logs, then in low greenery of small shrubs and bear grass. Admire picturesque bleached snags from

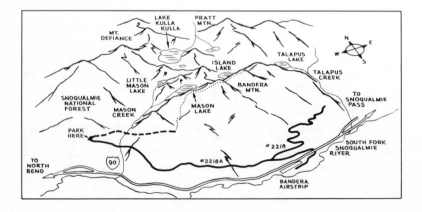

Island Lake from Bandera Mountain

the 19th century blaze. Off to the left, see a lichen-gray granite talus; listen for marmots whistling there.

The ridge crest is attained at around 4700 feet; immediately below on the far side is Mason Lake. The ridge is a good turnaround point for those who've had enough; the views are nearly as broad as those from the summit. The route to here often melts free of snow in early May.

Climb east on the crest through subalpine trees, then scramble granite boulders up a step in the ridge to the first summit, 5150 feet, and down-and-up a bit farther to the highest summit, 5240 feet. Look north to lakes in forest bowls below and far away to Glacier Peak and Mt. Baker, northeasterly to Snoqualmie peaks, south down to the highway, and beyond to omnipresent Rainier, and west past the portal peaks of Washington and Defiance to lowlands. Civilization is near, but also wilderness.

SOUTH FORK SNOQUALMIE RIVER

19 Pratt Lake

Round trip to Pratt Lake 11 miles
Hiking time 8 hours
High point 4100 feet
Elevation gain 2300 feet in, 700 out
Best July through October
One day or backpack
USGS Snoqualmie Pass and Bandera

Miles of deep forest and a lovely lake amid subalpine trees. A network of trails leads to other lakes and to meadow ridges and high views. From a basecamp hikers and fishermen can spend days exploring.

Drive Interstate 90 east from North Bend 17 miles to a U-turn signed "Denny Creek." Turn left onto the westbound lanes and go ½ mile to the trailhead parking lot, elevation 1800 feet. (Upon completion of I-90 construction, access will be slightly changed.)

The first steep mile gains 800 feet in cool forest to a junction with the Granite Mountain trail; just beyond is a nice creek for drinking and resting. Turn left and sidehill upward on a gentler grade in young forest, through patches of twinflower, Canadian dogwood, salal, and bracken, by many good examples of nurse logs, to Lookout Point, 3 miles, 3400 feet, site of a demolished shelter and still a much-used camp. A rough fishermen's track drops ½ mile to Talapus Lake in the narrow valley below.

At 3½ miles is a short side-path down to Olallie Lake, around whose basin the main trail swings in open subalpine forest to a 4100-foot saddle, 4 miles, a logical turn-around point for day hikers. Lots of huckleberries here in season, plus a view south to Mt. Rainier, and a junction with the Mt. Defiance trail (see below). The Pratt Lake trail switchbacks down a steep hillside of much mud, some of it covered with new puncheon, flattens out and contours above the lake, then drops to the outlet, 5½ miles, 3400 feet, and popular camps.

Now, for explorations. (These are only a few; connoisseurs of the country have many other private favorites.)

In a short ½ mile from Pratt Lake is Lower Tuscohatchie Lake, 3400 feet, and a choice of three directions for wandering: A fishermen's path beats brush 1½ miles to 4023-foot Tuscohatchie Lake. From the outlet of Lower Tuscohatchie a trail ascends

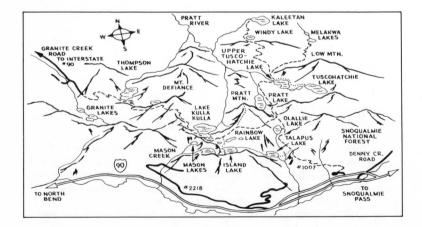

Pratt Lake from Pratt Mountain

gently then steeply 3 miles, in trees with glimpses outward of alpine scenery, to 4500-foot Melakwa Lake (Hike 21). Also from the outlet of Lower Tuscohatchie, a less-used trail climbs northward to 4800 feet and drops past little Windy Lake to 3900-foot Kaleetan Lake, 3½ miles. The way is entirely in forest, with only occasional views over the Pratt River valley, logged in the 1930s, but the lonesome lake has a splendid backdrop in the cliffs of Kaleetan Peak.

From the Olallie-Pratt saddle (see above), the Mt. Defiance trail ascends westward through beargrass and heather and huckleberry meadows (fine views 1100 feet down to Lake Talapus) on the side of Pratt Mountain, whose 5099-foot summit is an easy scramble via huge boulder fields on the southwest side, passes Rainbow Lake (Island Lake lies ½ mile away on a side-path and actually is a more rewarding objective for hikers than Pratt Lake), comes near Mason Lake, traverses high above Lake Kulla Kulla, and climbs in flower gardens almost to the summit of 5584-foot Defiance, about 3 miles, and broad views. The trail continues westward on the ridge a mile, drops to Thompson Lake, 3400 feet, 5½ miles, and descends to the Granite Creek road, 7 miles.

At some of the lakes campers are asked to keep 100 feet from the shores.

Snoqualmie Pass from Granite Mountain

**SOUTH FORK
SNOQUALMIE RIVER**

20 Granite Mountain

Round trip 9 miles
Hiking time 8 hours
High point 5629 feet
Elevation gain 3800 feet
Best June through November
One day
USGS Snoqualmie Pass

The most popular summit trail in the Snoqualmie region, and for good reason. Though the ascent is long and in midsummer can be blistering hot, the upper slopes are a delightful garden of granite and flowers and the panorama includes Mt. Rainier south, Mt. Baker and Glacier Peak north, Chimney Rock and Mt. Stuart east, and infinitely more peaks, valleys, and lakes.

Drive Interstate 90 east from North Bend 17 miles to a U-turn signed "Denny Creek." Turn left onto the westbound lanes and go ½ mile to the trailhead parking lot, elevation 1800 feet. (Upon completion of I-90 access will be slightly changed.)

The first steep mile on the Pratt Lake trail gains 800 feet in cool forest to the Granite Mountain junction and a creek for drinking and resting. Be sure to fill canteens; this may be the last water.

Go right from the 2600-foot junction, traversing in trees ½ mile, then heading straight up and up in countless short switchbacks on an open south slope where fires and avalanches have inhibited the growth of forest. (On sunny days, start early to beat the heat.)

At 4000 feet the trail abruptly gentles and swings east across an avalanche gully—an area of potentially extreme danger perhaps through May. Hikers seeking the summit before Memorial Day of cold springs should be very wary of crossing this gully; a better alternative in avalanche season is to leave the trail and climb directly to the peak on the rough but safe granite felsenmeer ("rock sea") of the southwest ridge, which melts free of snow while the trail route has another month of winter whiteness left.

Beyond the gully the trail sidehills through rock gardens, passing a waterfall (early summer only) from snows above, and then switchbacks steeply to grass and flowers, reaching the summit ridge at 5200 feet. In early summer the route beyond here may be too snowy for some tastes; if so, wander easterly on the crest for splendid views over the Snoqualmie Pass peaks, down to alpine lakes, and through the pass to Lake Keechelus.

The trail ascends westward in meadows, above cosy cirque-scoop benches, and switchbacks to the fire lookout, 5629 feet, 4½ miles, and full compensation for the struggle.

Experienced highland rovers depart from the trail on secret routes to solitudes of hidden lakes and alpine nooks. It is possible to camp near the summit, either for the sunset and dawn views or to allow time for exploration.

The hike has special appeal in early summer when flowers are blooming and in fall when blueberries are ripe and the slopes are flaming.

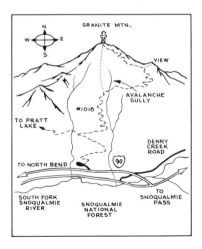

SOUTH FORK
SNOQUALMIE RIVER

21 Melakwa Lake

Round trip to Melakwa outlet 8 miles
Hiking time 6 hours
High point 4600 feet
Elevation gain 2300 feet
Best mid-July through October
One day or backpack
USGS Snoqualmie Pass

The most spectacular alpine scenery of the Snoqualmie Pass vicinity, with snow-fields and walls of Kaleetan, Chair, and Bryant Peaks rising above the little lake, one shore in forest, the other in rocks and flowers.

Drive Interstate 90 east from North Bend 17 miles to a U-turn signed "Denny Creek." (Upon completion of I-90 construction, go off the freeway on the Denny Creek exit.) Turn left over the westbound highway lanes onto the Denny Creek road and continue 3 miles to Denny Creek Campground. Just beyond, turn left on a road over the river and follow it ¼ mile, passing private homes, to the road-end parking area and trailhead, elevation 2300 feet. (On busy summer weekends it may be necessary to park before crossing the Snoqualmie River bridge.)

The trail ascends moderately along Denny Creek in forest, passing under the freeway, crossing the stream on a bridge at ½ mile and recrossing at 1 mile, 2800 feet, below water-smoothed slabs of a lovely cataract. The way leaves forest and strikes upward in avalanche greenery to Keekwulee Falls, 1½ miles.

The next ½ mile of tight switchbacks ascends around cliffs past Snowshoe Falls.

At 2 miles, 3500 feet, the path flattens out into the upper basin, shortly crosses the creek, goes from trees to low brush to trees again, and switchbacks to wooded Hemlock Pass, 3½ miles, 4600 feet. From here the trail drops a bit in forest to the outlet of Melakwa Lake, 4 miles, 4550 feet.

Enjoy views of talus, snowfields, and cliffs falling abruptly from the 6200-foot summits of Kaleetan and Chair. Good camps are numerous—those on a peninsula across the lake are sunniest.

For explorations, roam meadows and boulders to tiny Upper Melakwa Lake and 5300-foot Melakwa Pass. Experienced cross-country travelers can descend past Iceberg (Chair Peak) Lake to intersect the Snow Lake trail (Hike 24) for an alternate return to the highway.

For another way back to the highway, and for lonesome walking, take the 3-mile trail from Melakwa Lake to Pratt Lake (Hike 19).

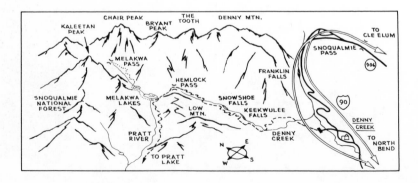

Keekwulee Falls

Annette Lake and cliffs of Abiel Peak

SOUTH FORK SNOQUALMIE RIVER

22 Annette Lake

Round trip 6 miles
Hiking time 4 hours
High point 3600 feet
Elevation gain 1400 feet
Best June through November
One day or backpack
USGS Snoqualmie Pass

A very popular and often crowded little subalpine lake, with cliffs and talus of Abiel Peak above the shores of open forest, pleasant for camping. Scouts of the Chief Seattle Council are helping the Forest Service maintain and improve the trail. For lonesome walking here, try early summer or late fall.

Drive Interstate 90 east from North Bend. Until I-90 construction is complete, the best approach is from the Tinkham exit, driving 7 miles on Tinkham Road to the Annette Lake parking lot at Humpback Creek. When I-90 is complete, take the Denny Creek exit and drive upstream on Humpback Creek ½ mile to the parking lot, elevation 2200 feet.

The way starts in an old clearcut, crosses Humpback Creek, and in 1 mile passes under a powerline and enters forest. At 1¼ miles, 2400 feet, cross the Milwaukee Railroad tracks.

Now comes the hard part, switchbacking steeply upward in nice, old forest on the slopes of Silver Peak, occasional talus openings giving looks over the valley to Humpback Mountain. After gaining 1200 feet in 1½ miles, at the 3600-foot level the way flattens out and goes along a final mile of minor ups and downs to the lake outlet, 3 miles, 3600 feet.

Wander along the east shore for picnic spots or camps with views of small cliffs and waterfalls.

Some cross-country hikers continue to the summit of Silver Peak via the draw between Silver and Abiel Peaks, a good but quite brushy route.

To preserve the vegetation, campers are asked to use sites 100 feet from the lakeshore.

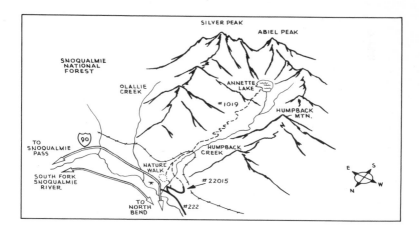

**SOUTH FORK
SNOQUALMIE RIVER**

23 Silver Peak

Round trip via powerline 7 miles
Hiking time 4 hours
High point 5603 feet
Elevation gain 1200 feet
Best early July through October
One day or backpack
USGS Snoqualmie Pass

Round trip from Lost Lake road 8 miles
Hiking time 5 hours
Elevation gain 2000 feet

Hike the Pacific Crest Trail through subalpine forest, then wander easily up heather and flowers to a rocky summit with views north to Snoqualmie Pass peaks, east to Lake Keechelus, south over rolling green ridges to Mt. Rainier, and west down to Annette Lake and out to the Olympics.

However, though some beauty remains, long gone is the sense of remoteness and solitude that 50 years ago, and even 20 years ago, made this one of the most popular hikes in the Snoqualmie Pass vicinity. Much of the way is within the roar of Interstate 90 and the route is cut by powerlines, a radio relay, a road, and several logging spurs—including one up Cold Creek to Olallie Meadow, from around whose lovely greensward loggers recently have removed the enclosing forest. Silver Peak can be approached by three routes: from the Crest Trail starting at Snoqualmie Summit Ski Area, 7½ miles of trail leading to the summit scramble; from a powerline road, 3 miles of trail; and from Lost and Mirror Lakes, also 3 miles of trail.

To start the hike from the powerline road, drive Interstate 90 east 2 miles from Snoqualmie Pass and take the Hyak exit. A short bit before the entrance to the Hyak ski area turn right several hundred feet, then left onto a logging road that climbs through the ski area, past Hyak Lake (the logging road becomes the powerline road) to the road-end and Pacific Crest Trail 3 miles from the highway, elevation 3400 feet.

The Pacific Crest Trail enters woods and climbs gradually to Olallie Meadow, 3800 feet, and swings upward around the east side of Silver Peak. At about 2½ miles, 4400 feet, below the saddle between Silver and Tinkham Peak, find unmarked Gardner Mountain trail No. 1018 heading west and uphill. (Here is the junction with the approach via Lost Lake.)

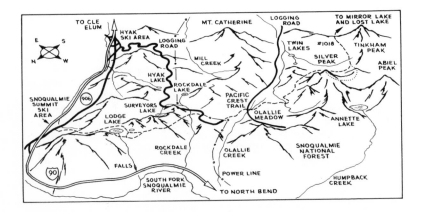

Mt. Rainier from Silver Peak, Abiel Peak on right

Ascend the Gardner Mountain trail about 500 feet in ½ mile to heather meadows on the south ridge of Silver Peak. Leave tread and pick an obvious route to the top, first on a wide slope of flowers, then on a narrow crest of heather and trees; when the trees are too thick, keep to the east side. The final 200 feet climb steeply up shattered rock to the 5603-foot summit.

To reach Lost Lake, drive Interstate 90 east from Snoqualmie Pass 10.5 miles and take the Stampede Pass-Lake Kachess exit. Turn right toward Stampede Pass 1 mile, then right 4 miles to a five-way intersection at Lost Lake. Take the road on the north side of the lake for a very rough 2 miles (best to walk the last ½ mile) to the end, elevation 3600 feet. Hike 1½ miles to the Crest Trail at Mirror Lake, then 1½ miles north on the Crest Trail to the Gardner Mountain junction.

SOUTH FORK
SNOQUALMIE RIVER

Round trip 8 miles
Hiking time 6 hours
High point 4400 feet
Elevation gain 1300 feet in, 400 feet out
Best July through October
One day or backpack
USGS Snoqualmie Pass and Bandera

24 Snow Lake

The largest alpine lake (more than a mile long) in the Snoqualmie Pass area. On one side cliffs rise steeply to Chair Peak, and on the other forest slopes fall into the broad gulf of the Middle Fork Snoqualmie River. The trail and lake are extremely popular (some 10,000 visitors a year) but there is plenty of room to escape crowds.

Drive Interstate 90 east from North Bend 21.7 miles and turn right on the Snoqualmie Pass exit, then left 2 miles on the Alpental road through the ski area and subdivision to the parking lot and trailhead, elevation 3100 feet.

The trail climbs a bit in forest to intersect the generations-old hiking route from the pass, obliterated by the Alpental subdividers, and ascends gradually, sometimes in cool trees, sometimes on open slopes with looks over Source Creek to Denny Mountain, now civilized, and to The Tooth and Chair Peak, still wild.

The way swings around the valley head above the 3800-foot droplet of Source Lake and switchbacks a steep ½ mile in heather and flowers and parkland to the saddle, 3½ miles, 4400 feet, between Source Creek and Snow Lake. Day hikers may well be content with the picnic spots in blossoms and blueberries and splendid views.

The trail drops sharply ½ mile from the saddle to meadow shores of Snow Lake, 4 miles, 4016 feet. Many good—but usually mobbed—camps along the lake, which often is partly frozen through July. More secluded sites in the saddle and at various secret places.

The trail rounds the north side of the lake and descends the Rock Creek valley to the Middle Fork Snoqualmie.

To get away from overpopulation, follow a faint fishermen's path west from the trail, over the Snow Lake outlet, and up to 4800-foot Gem Lake. This is alpine roaming country at its best. With map and compass and a sharp eye, experienced wanderers can find easy routes to Upper and Lower Wildcat Lakes, to the summits of Wright Mountain and Preacher Mountain. And more.

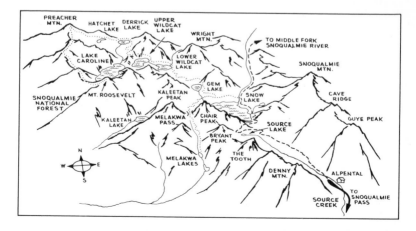

A church hike at Snow Lake

SOUTH FORK SNOQUALMIE RIVER

25 Ridge and Gravel Lakes

Round trip to Ridge Lake 12½ miles
Hiking time 6 hours
High point 5600 feet
Elevation gain 2900 feet in, 300 feet out
Best July to mid-October
One day or backpack
USGS Snoqualmie Pass

Walk a new stretch of the Pacific Crest Trail along a knife-edge ridge to the most beautiful views in the Snoqualmie Pass vicinity, including looks down on Alaska and Joe Lakes, two of the most beautiful in the Alpine Lakes Wilderness.

Beyond any question this section of the Crest Trail should have been placed down in the Gold Creek valley, a safer route, snowfree more of the year, and able to withstand heavy use. The high ridge and lakes already were getting as many visitors as they could absorb and met a need for close-in off-trail exploring. Now, with the miniature freeway brutally thrust into the heart of the wilderness, the crowds will be misdirected to an inappropriate area. The only excuse that can be made for this blunder is that at the time the Forest Service planned the route it was inexperienced at building trails, not having done any such work to speak of since the 1920s-30s, and even less experienced at conversing with any other of its clients than the loggers. The project was managed by logging-road engineers and they built a narrow-gauge road and called it a "scenic trail." The Forest Service belatedly revealed its plans to hiking-conservation organizations and they screamed bloody murder, but the engineers declared it was then too late to reconsider. However, after enough hikers are slaughtered the trail will be moved where it belongs, down in Gold Creek.

Drive Interstate 90 to Snoqualmie Pass and go off on the Alpental exit. Within 200 feet of the highway, on the north side, find the Pacific Crest Trail parking lot, elevation 3004 feet.

The trail climbs in forest at an easy 10 percent grade 2 miles, loses 300 feet entering Commonwealth Basin, and at 2¾ miles passes the Commonwealth Basin trail. Flattening briefly, the way then switchbacks up to alpine meadows high on west slopes of Kendall Peak, with views out to Rainier and down to bugs whizzing along I-90. At 4 miles the trail is blasted around a rock spur of Kendall and soon after, rounding the north side of the peak, at 5 miles it tops the ridge crest, 5500 feet (only 200 feet from Kendall's summit), between Commonwealth and Gold Creeks.

Mainly contouring, the way proceeds north along the west side of the ridge, then switches to the east side to cross a 100-foot-tall, near-vertical, granite slab. The 5-foot-wide path blasted in solid rock is safe enough when snowfree and stormfree

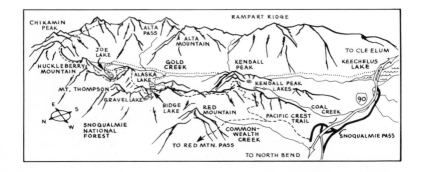

Pacific Crest Trail and Kendall Peak

but before this story is finished a few intrepid souls who insist on trying to make the passage in dangerous conditions are surely going to fall off.

Beyond the slab the mountainside moderates to heather meadows. At 6¼ miles is the 5600-foot saddle between tiny Ridge Lake and larger Gravel Lake. To preserve the vegetation, campers are asked to use sites 100 feet from the shores.

For more views continue northward on the Crest Trail. Experienced cross-country travelers can drop in (1000 feet down in each case) on Alaska and Joe Lakes.

At the same time it was building the Pacific Crest Freeway, the Forest Service was letting the ancient and honorable Gold Creek trail, which led to these two lakes, go to pieces, maintained solely by boots. The Service now is debating whether to rebuild the trail, relocating to bypass a housing development, or abandon it altogether. The debate will end when the high freeway has killed enough hikers attempting to force their ways through (from Canada to Mexico, or Mexico to Canada) in the snows of early summer or the storms of any season.

LAKE KEECHELUS

26 Mount Margaret-Lake Lillian

Round trip to Mt. Margaret 6 miles
Hiking time 5 hours
High point 5520 feet
Elevation gain 1500 feet
Best late June through October
One day
USGS Snoqualmie Pass

Round trip to Lake Lillian 9 miles
Hiking time 6 hours
High point 5200 feet
Elevation gain 1300 feet in, 500 feet out
Best July through October
One day or backpack

A short climb to a little mountain with big views, then onward in meadows to a secluded alpine lake, a fine basecamp for highland roaming on Rampart Ridge.

Drive Interstate 90 east from Snoqualmie Pass 2 miles to the Hyak exit and find the Forest Service road on the north side of the highway. This road parallels I-90 for 2½ miles to Rocky Run and then climbs another 1½ miles, passing several well marked intersections to a large parking lot, elevation 3800 feet. Walk the road a few hundred feet farther and take a steep abandoned logging track which eventually turns into a trail and enters forest. The trail climbs, with numerous switchbacks, to the ridge top at 5000 feet, a few hundred feet below the summit of Mt. Margaret. From here the Margaret Lake trail drops over the far side of the ridge and descends to the lake 300 feet below. For a view of forest and three or four small lakes, step a few feet over the crest of the ridge and look down. Besides Margaret, there are Stonesthrow, Swan, and Rock Rabbit Lakes.

From the ridge the trail climbs a bit then contours around the west side of Mt. Margaret. (For more views, scramble to the summit. One place is as good as the next as there is no trail.) On the north side of the mountain the trail descends in meadows to shallow Twin Lakes and campsites at 3 miles, 4700 feet (boil your water before drinking). Now the trail becomes more difficult. The tread is rough and at times steep as it loses another 200 feet and then climbs back up 300 feet. At 4½ miles, 4800 feet, is lovely Lake Lillian amid glacier-polished rocks and heather and flowers and alpine

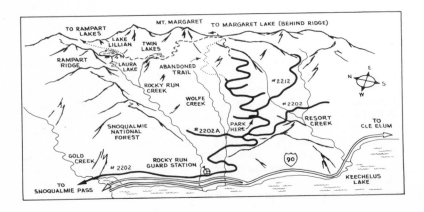

Lake Lillian and Rampart Ridge

trees. The mountains around the lake are so steep there are only three or four level places with room for a small tent.

For wandering, climb the steep slopes at the head of the lake to lonesome little basins or climb Rampart Ridge for broad views.

LAKE KACHESS

27 Rampart Ridge

Round trip to Rachel Lake 8 miles
Hiking time 6 hours
High point 4700 feet
Elevation gain 1900 feet
Best mid-July through October
One day or backpack
USGS Snoqualmie Pass

Round trip to Rampart Lakes 11 miles
Hiking time 8 hours
High point 5200 feet
Elevation gain 2400 feet

A cool and green valley forest, a large alpine lake walled by glacier-carved cliffs which drop straight into the water, and a heaven of rock-bowl lakelets and ponds, gardens of heather and blossoms, and ridges and nooks for prowling. On summer weekends hundreds of hikers throng the shores of Rachel Lake—which is magnificently beautiful even amid a crowd. And dozens of people are in every pocket, on every knob, of the high ridge, where hikers have stomped out a spiderweb of paths.

The trail, posted "hikers only," was never built, but simply beaten into existence by thousands of feet. The way goes around, up, or down to avoid obstacles, and hardly knows how to switchback. But bad is good—if the route were built to freeway standards the highland would be visited not by regiments but swarming hordes.

Drive Interstate 90 east from Snoqualmie Pass 12½ miles, take the Lake Kachess exit, and follow signs 5 miles to Kachess Lake Campground. Turn left 4 miles on Box Canyon road No. 2214 to a junction. Turn left ¼ mile to the bridge over North Fork Box Canyon Creek and hope to find space for your car in the enormous parking lot. Just before the bridge is the Rachel Lake trailhead, elevation 2800 feet.

The hike begins with a mile of moderate ascent to a mandatory cold drink and rest stop by water-carved and pot-holed and moss-carpeted slabs. The trail levels out along the creek for 1½ miles. In an open swath of avalanche greenery, look above to 6032-foot Hibox Mountain. At 2½ miles the valley ends in an abrupt headwall and rough tread proceeds straight up, rarely bothering to switchback, gaining 1300 feet in a cruel mile, suffering alleviated by a glory of a cool-breeze rest-stop waterfall. Suddenly the angle eases and forest yields to meadows and at 4 miles, 4700 feet, is Rachel Lake.

Follow fishermen's tracks around the lake, admiring blue waters ringed by trees and cliffs—and numerous campsites. Go left past the narrows to the secluded south bay.

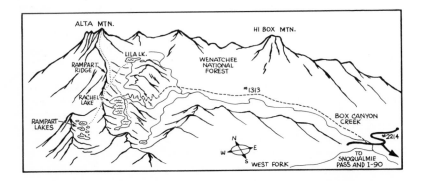

Lila Lake and Hibox Mountain

To visit the higher country, turn right at the shore on a boot-built path climbing above the cirque, with views down to the lake and out Box Canyon Creek. After a steep ½ mile the trail flattens in a wide parkland saddle, 5200 feet, and reaches an unmarked junction offering a choice.

Go right 1 mile to 5200-foot Lila Lake, or ramble the easy ridge to the summit of 6240-foot Alta Mountain.

Go left an up-and-down mile to 5100-foot Rampart Lakes. Examine in detail each of the little lakes and tiny ponds, the surrounding buttresses, waterfalls, and peaceful mountain homes. Note the mixture of basalts, conglomerates, and rusty mineralized lobes. Snoop into a flowery corner, climb a heather knoll, think about roaming the short but rough way south to Lake Lillian (Hike 26), and before you know it, arrive on the crest of 5800-foot Rampart Ridge and enjoy views down to Gold Creek, west to Snoqualmie Pass, south to Rainier, east to Stuart, and north to Three Queens and Chimney Rock.

When the Alpine Lakes Wilderness management plan is complete, camping will be greatly restricted at the lakes. Best not to count on staying overnight on summer weekends.

Chikamin Ridge from slopes above Park Lakes

LAKE KACHESS

28 Mineral Creek Park

Round trip from Cooper Pass road 10 miles
Hiking time 8 hours
High point 4700 feet
Elevation gain 2300 feet
Best July through October
One day or backpack
USGS Snoqualmie Pass and Kachess Lake

Round trip from Kachess Lake
  Campground 20 miles
Allow 2 days
Elevation gain 3300 feet

Heather and huckleberry meadows surrounding alpine lakes, mountains to climb, and views. The trail is tough and not many fish are in the lakes, so the area currently offers more solitude than nearby Spectacle and Rachel Lakes.

Once upon a time—until 1968, in fact—the trip began with a lovely walk along Kachess Lake. Now, in the name of progress, a logging road has intersected the route right in the middle, cutting the hike in half. Since the challenge and satisfaction of traveling the entire distance in unmarred wilderness have been lost, the most practical plan probably is to use the new road as an approach to the upper half and maybe some other day walk the lower half.

To reach the halfway point, drive to Cooper Lake (Hike 31) and keep left on road No. 229 climbing over Cooper Pass and dropping into the Kachess valley. At 11 miles from the Cle Elum River road, at the road-end, find the trailhead, elevation 2400 feet. The path goes through a broad valley-bottom clearcut to a crossing (difficult in early summer) of the Kachess River and on the far side ascends to join the trail from Kachess Lake.

Just in case there are die-hard hikers willing to ignore the new road to recapture a semblance of the old wilderness experience, the trip will be described here from Kachess Lake.

Drive Interstate 90 east from Snoqualmie Pass 12½ miles, take the Kachess Lake exit, and follow signs 5 miles to Kachess Lake Campground. Proceed .7 mile to the northernmost (uplake) point one can drive and find the trailhead in the tent-only camping area, elevation 2254 feet.

Little Kachess trail No. 1312 follows the lake more than 3 miles to its head, never over 200-400 feet above the water, but seldom level and with so many ups and downs that about 1000 feet of elevation are gained and lost. At the end of the lake the footpath merges into a mining road built in the days of the Model T and now abandoned. At about 4½ miles the route turns up Mineral Creek trail No. 1331, climbing steeply; here is the junction with the old Cooper Pass trail which joins the logging road in about ¼ mile; this latter trail is the beginning of the short version of the trip.

The mining road continues 1¼ mile to an end at a group of dilapidated buildings. From here on the tread mainly just grew, going up and down and around, never flat, often very steep. Most of the way is brushed out—thankfully so, for much of the route is on slopes of slick alder and vine maple. Beyond the mine buildings ¼ mile the trail crosses Mineral Creek, and at about 3¾ miles from the Cooper Pass logging road, crosses the outlet stream from lower Park Lake. At about 5 miles the path reaches upper Park Lake, 4700 feet, and the edge of meadow country. Excellent camps here; more are ½ mile to the west up a small stream.

For wide views join the Pacific Crest Trail in parkland up the steep 5600-foot ridge to the west. Look down into Gold Creek and across to Joe Lake, Huckleberry Mountain, Mt. Thompson, and Snoqualmie Pass peaks. Look north along the ridge to Chikamin Peak.

The Pacific Crest Trail allows an easy hike from Park Lakes to Spectacle Lake (Hike 31).

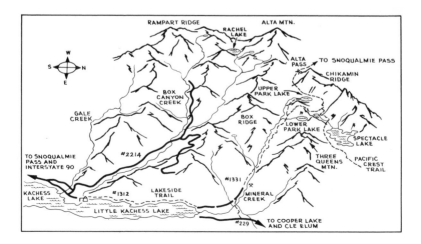

CLE ELUM RIVER

29 Kachess Ridge

Round trip 9 miles
Hiking time 7½ hours
High point 5850 feet
Elevation gain 2750 feet in, 600 out
Best July to November
One day
USGS Kachess Lake

Magnificent trail country of forest ridges and green meadows climaxing at Thorp Mountain Lookout. Views—Rainier, Stuart, Daniel, and the Dutch Miller Gap peaks. Other views, less esthetic—Kachess Lake (reservoir), powerlines, logging roads (which have shrunk the wildland and brought the ridge in easy reach of a day hike).

The Kachess Ridge trail extends 15 miles from road No. 2105 near Easton to Cooper Pass. The shortest route to Thorp Mountain is Knox Creek trail No. 1315A, starting at 4000 feet and meeting the Kachess Ridge trail in 1½ miles; the total distance to the lookout is 2½ miles, gaining 1800 feet. The way is fairly straightforward, climbing almost entirely in meadows of blueberries and flowers.

Described here is the French Cabin Creek trail, longer and with more ups and downs but giving views of the French Cabin Mountains, a panorama of the Knox Creek trail country, and eventually winding up in the same place.

Drive the Salmon la Sac road 12 miles from the City Hall, First and Dakota, in Roslyn. Just past the end of Cle Elum Lake (reservoir) turn left on French Cabin Creek road No. 2211 and drive 7 miles to the trailhead. On the way pass Knox Creek road No. 2211B at 5 miles (Knox Creek trail starts 2 miles up this road) and at an unmarked junction at 6 miles keep to the right side of the stream. The actual trailhead is up a short, rough spur; it may be best to park on the road, elevation 3700 feet.

French Cabin Creek trail No. 1305 starts in a clearcut and continues in an old burn. At spots very steep, at 1 mile it reaches a campsite with a good spring, then enters forest and at 1½ miles joins the Kachess Ridge trail (at 6½ miles from road No. 2105 near Easton). The ridge trail now grows extremely steep as it ascends a 5700-foot hump at 2 miles. The south side of this high point has great views back over the French Cabin peaks, Kachess Lake, and Rainier. At the start of the descent of the north side is a view down on Knox Creek trail.

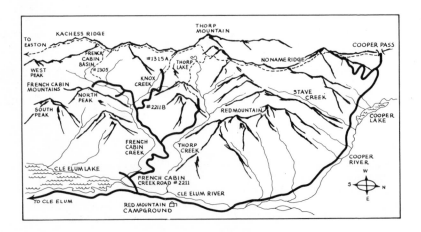

French Cabin Creek trail

From the high point the trail drops steeply 400 feet, contours a peak, passes Knox Creek trail at 3¾ miles, climbs, drops 200 feet, climbs another high point, and comes out atop a ridge bump 500 feet directly above Thorp Lake. At 4½ miles is a junction with the Thorp Mountain trail. The ridge trail proceeds 6½ more miles to Cooper Pass. The Thorp Mountain trail switchbacks 400 feet to the lookout at 4½ miles.

CLE ELUM RIVER

30 Polallie Ridge

Round trip to ridge top 6 miles
Hiking time 4 hours
High point 5300 feet
Elevation gain 2000 feet
Best late June through November
One day
USGS Lake Kachess

One-way trip from Tired Creek to Salmon la
 Sac 12 miles
Hiking time 5 hours
High point 5547 feet
Elevation gain 2200 feet, not counting
 side-trip to ridge crest
Best July through November
One day or backpack

A splendid hike to a high ridge overlooking Cooper Lake, with spectacular views of Dutch Miller Gap peaks, Mt. Hinman, and Mt. Daniel. A 6-mile round trip to the ridge top can be made, or if transportation can be arranged, a one-way trip for miles along the open crest, then more miles down through forest. The trail can be very hot and dry in sunny weather; be sure to carry water and start early.

Drive 7.3 miles on the Cooper road, then the Cooper River road (Hike 31) to the bridge over Tired Creek. A few feet beyond are the parking area and trailhead, elevation about 3300 feet. (To do the one-way trip, a party must first leave a car in the Salmon la Sac Campground.)

Tired Creek trail No. 1317 starts on a bulldozed fire trail climbing steeply around a clearcut and at the top joining the old trail, a rough but adequate path ascending steadily with many switchbacks. Views begin at the road and get better as elevation is gained. At about 1¾ miles two switchbacks on the edge of a ridge offer a look west to Pete Lake. At 2 miles forest yields to meadowlands as the trail traverses under the ridge and aims for a wooded pass at the head of Tired Creek.

The best views are from the top of this ridge, a logical turnaround for day hikers and an absolutely mandatory side-trip for those continuing on. Leave the trail at any convenient spot, scramble to the crest, and walk to the highest point, 5300 feet, a great place to soak up scenery and spend the day watching shadows move along distant mountains.   Many goodies remain in store for hikers choosing the one-way

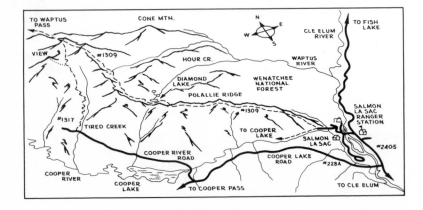

Peter Lake, Chikamin Peak, left; Lemah Mountain, right, from Polallie Ridge

trip. Regain the trail from the view crest and contour to the wooded pass, 3 miles, 5400 feet, and a junction. The left fork drops 2 miles to Waptus Pass; for a 10-mile loop trip, one can return to the car via this pass and Pete Lake (Hike 31). Turn right on the Polallie Ridge trail, traversing the ridge crest a mile, then going onward in high forest, meadows, and marshes to a possible campsite at tiny Diamond Lake, 5½ miles, 5200 feet. The lake is mostly surrounded by trees but there is a good view of the rounded top of 5295-foot Cone Mountain. At about 6 miles the ridge starts dropping rapidly. The trail more or less keeps on the crest, joining the Cooper River trail at 8½ miles and at 9 miles reaching recreation homes and the road near Salmon la Sac Campground.

The Forest Service plans eventually to close the road at Cooper Lake, adding about 2 miles of hiking each way.

Three Queens Mountain and Spectacle Lake

LAKE KACHESS

31 Spectacle Lake

Round trip 12½ miles
Allow 2 days
High point 4200 feet
Elevation gain 1300 feet in, 500 feet out
Best August through October
USGS Snoqualmie Pass and Kachess Lake

Only a scattering of miniature glaciers remain of the huge frozen streams that gouged out the Alpine Lakes region of the Cascades. However, the handiwork of ancient ice lies everywhere, and is beautifully exhibited by this delightful lake in a basin of glacier-polished rock.

Drive Interstate 90 east from Snoqualmie Pass about 27 miles and take the Salmon la Sac-Roslyn exit, following Highway 903 through Roslyn and Ronald and along Lake Cle Elum. At 15 miles from Roslyn and 1 mile short of Salmon la Sac turn left on Cooper road No. 229. At 4.7 miles from the junction turn right on Cooper River road No. 235, go by the recreation area, cross the river on a wooden bridge, pass the campground, and follow the main road, climbing steadily. At 8.3 miles is the road-end and Pete Lake trailhead, elevation 3400 feet.

The trail begins by following abandoned road, then descending in woods 500 feet in ½ mile, to intersect the Pete Lake trail—an easy enough way to start the hike but a murderous finish. With the usual valley ups and downs the route proceeds in deep forest 2½ miles to Pete Lake, 2980 feet, and much-used and often-crowded campsites. Unravel a confusion of paths at the shelter cabin and find the main trail, which climbs slightly over a rocky rib and drops to a double crossing of two swift creeks at about 4 miles. Both must be crossed. Footlogs may be available; if not, the boulder-hopping can be difficult in high water of early summer. When the water is impossibly high, follow Lemah Meadow trail No. 1323B some ¾ mile to the Pacific Crest Trail, which crosses the creeks on bridges; the detour adds 1 mile each way.

Shortly beyond the two creeks join the new Pacific Crest Trail that bypasses marshy Spectacle Meadows and switchbacks up toward Chikamin Ridge. The way is mostly in forest and views are scarce but occasionally Three Queens can be seen through the trees. At 5¾ miles the new trail proceeds onward toward the pass between Spectacle and Park Lakes and the Spectacle Lake trail branches right and climbs straight up the hillside with trees and roots for footholds. This is, and will remain, a hikers-only path; the Forest Service promises that horses never will be allowed at the lake.

The steep ascent is difficult but only ½ mile long, soon passing a lovely waterfall spilling from the lake, 4200 feet. For the best camps cross the outlet just above the falls and walk the south shore. The lake is like an octopus with a half-dozen arms, which makes the shoreline difficult to traverse but provides many glorious camps. To the south rises Three Queens, about 6800 feet. To the northwest is Chikamin Peak and to the north the spectacular spires of 7512-foot Lemah Mountain.

The Forest Service plans eventually to close the road at Cooper Lake, adding about 3 miles each way to the hike, and some lovely walking in virgin forest beside a rippling river.

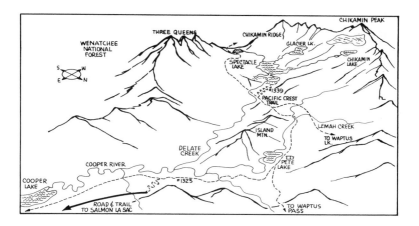

Mt. Stuart from Jolly Mountain

CLE ELUM RIVER

32 Jolly Mountain

Round trip from Salmon la Sac 12 miles
Hiking time 7-8 hours
High point 6443 feet
Elevation gain 4043 feet
Best July through September
One day
USGS Kachess Lake

An eastern outpost of the Alpine Lakes Cascades with 360-degree views east to Mt. Stuart and the freeway leading into Ellensburg, north to Mt. Daniel, west to Pete Lake and the Dutch Miller Gap peaks, south to Mt. Rainier, and directly down to Cle Elum Lake.

Drive Interstate 90 east from Snoqualmie Pass about 27 miles and take the Salmon la Sac-Roslyn exit, following Highway 903 through Roslyn and Ronald, beside Lake Cle Elum, and at 16 miles from Roslyn reaching the community of Salmon la Sac. Shortly before an historic old log building turn right on a road to the trailhead parking area by the Forest Service horse barn, elevation 2400 feet.

Go to the left side of the barn and find the trail in the woods. In ¼ mile briefly touch a service road and then return to trail, which climbs steeply with many switchbacks to a difficult crossing (easier by late July) of Salmon la Sac Creek. Fill canteens, since this is the only certain water on the entire route. At 3½ miles is a junction with the Paris Creek trail; keep right. The way ascends the valley a bit farther and then starts a series of switchbacks up the hillside. At 4½ miles is a junction with the Sasse Mountain sheep driveway (to use this as an alternate approach, see below). Keep left ¼ mile to a junction with the unmarked Jolly Creek trail. Go right, climbing steeply amid growing views for the final 1¼ miles to the 6443-foot summit, site of a fire lookout removed in 1968.

A jolly place to sop up panoramas. Carry a state road map to identify landmarks far out in Eastern Washington and a Forest Service map to name the innumerable peaks.

Though there may be snowfields to traverse then and the creek is difficult to cross, a magnificent time for the trip is June, when the way lies through fields of glacier lilies, spreading phlox, and lanceleaf spring beauty. Unfortunately, a band of sheep summers in the area and some of the meadows have been close-cropped.

An alternate approach saves about 1500 feet of climbing—at the cost of ½ mile or more of off-trail travel. Just .6 mile south of Salmon la Sac find two logging roads close together on the east side of the highway. Take the one nearest the resort (Little Salmon la Sac road No. 2216, sometimes gated) and drive 4½ miles to an elevation of about 4000 feet. Park at a sharp switchback. The road goes on another ¾ mile but gets very rough; it is best to walk the road to the end and then climb straight up the hill to intersect the Sasse Mountain sheep driveway on the crest of Sasse Ridge. The forested slopes are steep but mostly brushfree. Be sure to mark the spot where the ridge is reached in order to retrace steps on the return. Follow the sheep trail north a little over a mile to the junction with the Salmon la Sac trail and proceed to the top of Jolly Mountain.

If transportation can be arranged, a good loop trip can be made by going up the Little Salmon la Sac road and down the Jolly Mountain trail.

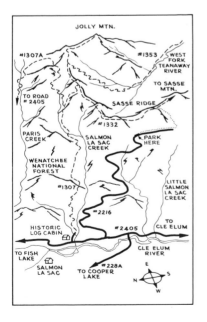

Yellow bell

CLE ELUM RIVER

33 Spade and Waptus Lakes

Round trip to Spade Lake 28 miles
Allow 3 days
High point 5400 feet
Elevation gain 3400 feet
Best mid-July through October
USGS Mt. Daniel

Round trip to Waptus Lake 18 miles
Allow 2 days
Best mid-June through October

Hike to Waptus Lake, largest in the Alpine Lakes Wilderness, lying in a broad glacial trough, its waters reflecting the spectacular spire of 7197-foot Bears Breast Mountain and snowfields on Summit Chief Mountain. Then climb to a cirque of glacier-scoured rocks holding lovely Spade Lake.

Though the trail makes a net gain of only 400 feet from road to Waptus Lake, there are many ups and downs, and as is typical of routes heavily used by horses, the tread alternates between powdery dust and cobblestones and seldom is as soft and smooth as a hikers-only path.

Drive to Salmon la Sac (Hike 32) and cross the Cle Elum River bridge. Just beyond, at the edge of the campground, find the head of Waptus River trail No. 1310, elevation 2400 feet.

The route starts on a private road past a group of summer homes, then begins a gradual ascent, first on remnants of a road used years ago for selective logging, soon becoming genuine trail. At 2 miles, 3000 feet, top the low divide and drop to the Waptus valley floor at the ford (a footlog upstream when needed) of Hour Creek, about 3 miles. The camp here is rather horsey; hikers will be happier in any of the numerous small riverside sites up the valley.

The trail now climbs 300 feet, again drops a little, and at about 4 miles touches the bank of the Waptus River. Views here of 5295-foot Cone Mountain rising above the route ahead. The way henceforth remains close to the river, whose clear waters sometimes dance over boulders, other times flow so quiet and smooth they seem not to move at all.

At about 6 miles the trail rounds the base of Cone Mountain, opening views toward the head of the valley, and at 8½ miles reaches a junction. The left fork leads along the west shore of Waptus Lake and climbs Polallie Ridge (Hike 30) to Waptus Pass and Pete Lake (Hike 31).

The Waptus trail goes right, turning downvalley ¼ mile to a steel-and-wood bridge

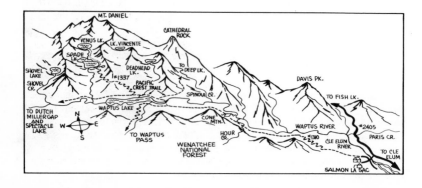

Glacier-carved rock at the outlet of Spade Lake

over the river, then heading upvalley again to cross Spinola Creek and join the Pacific Crest Trail coming from Deep Lake (Hike 35). At 9 miles the path arrives at Waptus Lake, 2963 feet, and a wonderful campsite with the best views of mountains reflected in water. However, this is also the most crowded camp; for other lakeside sites follow the Crest Trail 1½ miles along the shore.

The Crest Trail continues up the Waptus valley, ascending moderately for 3½ miles, then switchbacking 1400 feet in 2½ miles to Lake Ivanhoe at 4652 feet, 15 miles from the road. At 16 miles the trail reaches the 5000-foot summit of Dutch Miller Gap (Hike 16).

The best and worst is yet to come. From the Waptus outlet follow the lakeshore a short mile and find Spade Lake trail No. 1337, one of the lousiest trails in the Cascades because until a few years ago sheep and horses were allowed, making it just one steep rut. The way is mostly dry and hot but is forgiven for the pain when after 4 strenuous miles it reaches Spade Lake, 5210 feet. Campsites are located all around in meadows ribbed by outcrops of ice-polished rock. Don't camp on the heather— once broken down it takes many years to regrow.

Jack Creek Valley from Fish Eagle Pass

CLE ELUM RIVER

34 Fish Eagle Pass

Round trip 9 miles
Hiking time 7½ hours
High point 6200 feet
Elevation gain 2900 feet
Best July to November
One day or backpack
USGS The Cradle, Mt. Stuart, and
　　Chiwaukum Mountain

Located beneath rugged crags of Scatter Peak in the Wenatchee Mountains, Fish Eagle Pass boasts grand meadows and views. But the trail sure is nothing to brag about. Any resemblance to the trail shown on USGS and Forest Service maps (usually very accurate, but not here) is purely imaginary. The route is mostly straight up a sheep driveway and any tread that may once have existed has been obliterated by thousands of hooves. And the sheep are still regularly stomping and chomping through. Nevertheless, the trail, part of the County Line Trail system running from Blewett Pass to Deception Pass, has many beauties and provides a direct (if not easy) access to the vast trail system of Jack, Meadow, and French Creeks. Because of the difficulty there is a degree of solitude — when the sheep aren't around.

From the City Hall in Roslyn (First and Dakota Streets) drive 15½ miles to Salmon la Sac. Just before the main road crosses the river, turn right on road N. 2405 and drive 9 miles to Scatter Creek (underground much of the summer) and find Scatter Creek trail No. 1328, signed "County Line Trail 2 miles." Elevation, 3320 feet.

The trail start across a gravel flat is obscure, though marked by rock cairns, but becomes obvious at the hillside. With virtually no gesture toward switchbacks, it shoots up the slope, paralleling Scatter Creek, gaining 1500 feet in 2 miles (feels like 3). Cross a tributary of Scatter Creek to a junction signed "Sheep Drive." The right fork is signed "Fortune Creek." The left fork, "Fish Eagle Pass 1½ miles." The true distance is probably 2½ miles.

Take the left fork on a contour to a crossing of Scatter Creek. The seldom-maintained trail now grows hard to follow, and is easily lost in sheep-trampled meadows; hikers will want it for the passages through woods and thus upon losing the way should cast about to get back on track. Keep looking over your shoulder to spot landmarks for the return trip; especially do so in the first meadow after crossing Scatter Creek—the crossing must be made at this spot on the way out in order to not get lost.

The route passes a number of delightful campsites in the gently-sloping meadows that alternate with very steep stretches. At last there is the lovely small meadow at the summit of Fish Eagle Pass. Beyond, Mt. Stuart is a sharp pyramid. Behind, Mt. Daniel and Mt. Hinman are a great white sprawl of glacier. Below, the trail can be seen dropping steeply down Solomon Creek to join the Jack Creek trail.

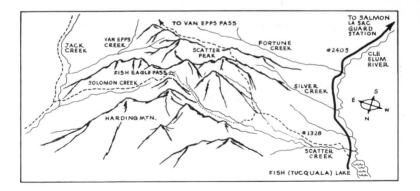

CLE ELUM RIVER

35 Deep Lake

Round trip 14½ miles
Hiking time 9 hours
High point 5500 feet
Elevation gain 2150 feet in, 1200 feet out
Best July through October
One day or backpack
USGS Mt. Daniel and The Cradle

Climb in forest to beautiful meadow country at the base of Cathedral Rock. Look in one direction down to the Cle Elum River and beyond to Mt. Stuart, second-highest nonvolcanic summit in the Cascades and highest in the eastern section of the Alpine Lakes Wilderness, and in the other to 7899-foot Mt. Daniel, highest summit in King County and the western section of the Alpine Lakes. Look below to the green valley of Spinola Creek and, at its head, under the slopes of Daniel, the blue waters of Deep Lake.

Drive to Salmon la Sac (Hike 34). Just before crossing the Cle Elum River turn right on rough dirt road No. 2405, signed Fish Lake Guard Station. Drive 12½ miles (sign says 14), passing Fish Lake (Tucquala Lake) and the guard station, to a junction near the road-end. The right spur goes a few dozen yards to the Hyas Lake-Deception Pass trailhead. Take the left spur a similar distance to the Deep Lake trailhead, elevation 3350 feet.

The trail crosses the Cle Elum River on a bridge and ascends steadily but moderately in cool forest, at 1 mile passing a small creek and a junction with the old, abandoned trail to Deep Lake. At 2½ miles the new trail emerges into marshy meadows around the shores of little Squaw Lake, 4841 feet, a pleasant picnic spot and a good turnaround for an easy afternoon.

The way continues up in alpine forest and patches of flowers and growing views, traverses heather gardens along the ridge slopes, and at 4¼ miles, 5500 feet, reaches Cathedral Pass nearly at the foot of Cathedral Rock, at this point intersecting the new Pacific Crest Trail coming from Deception Pass.

To descend or not to descend—that is the question. The views from the saddle make it a satisfying destination, and parkland on the crest of the ridge invites wandering; in early summer, snowmelt ponds permit delightful camps.

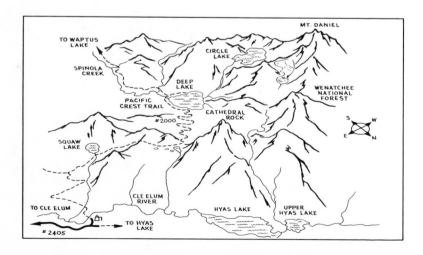

90

Spinola Creek and shoulder of Mt. Daniel

If the lake is chosen, descend 1200 feet on the Crest Trail, which drops into forest in a long series of switchbacks, at 7¼ miles arriving on the east side of Deep Lake, 4382 feet. Campsites here and elsewhere along the shores. If time allows, explore to broad meadows at the lake outlet and to flowers and waterfalls at the inlet.

The Crest Trail proceeds down the lake to horse camps, the broad meadows, and onward along Spinola Creek to Waptus Lake.

CLE ELUM RIVER

36 Marmot Lake

Round trip 18 miles
Allow 2 days
High point 4900 feet
Elevation gain 2400 feet
Best July through October
USGS Mt. Daniel and The Cradle

Sample the variety of the Alpine Lakes: begin with a close-to-the-road and extremely-popular valley lake, climb to a cirque lake ringed by cliffs and talus parkland and fishermen, and wander on to a lonesome off-trail lake colored jade green by meltwater from a small glacier. Go from forests to heather meadows to moraines. Look up at the peaks from below, then out to the peaks from high viewpoints.

Drive from Salmon la Sac to the Hyas Lake-Deception Pass trailhead, elevation 3350 feet (Hike 35). Hike to Hyas Lake at 1½ miles, 3448 feet. The occupants of most of the scores of cars typically parked at the road-end stop here, content with the wading, swimming, fishing, camping, and scenery-watching.

Continue past the lake and along the river bottom, then up switchbacks with views back down to Hyas Lake and across the valley to Mt. Daniel and Mt. Hinman. At 5 miles the trail tops 4500-foot Deception Pass and turns north toward Deception Lakes. Turn left on trail No. 1066, signed Marmot Lake.

The path ascends gently to a 4700-foot rise, then descends moderately beside a small creek, and a short bit from the 2-mile marker (2 miles from Deception Pass) starts up again. At about 3 miles from the pass the trail crosses a nameless creek from Marmot Lake and comes to a Y. The right fork is to Lake Clarice; go left, switchbacking up, recross the creek, and at some 9 miles from the road reach Marmot Lake, 4930 feet. Cliffs of Terrace Mountain and its ridges stand high above the water. The best camps lie ¼ mile south along the shore.

For fishermen and reflective campers Marmot Lake is sufficient, but for off-trail ramblers the best is yet to come. To visit 4330-foot Clarice Lake, contour from the outlet of Marmot Lake in open forest and meadows about 1 mile around the hogback to the north.

Jade Lake is a tougher and longer trip, recommended only for experienced wilderness travelers, but is more than worth the trouble—of which there is plenty. Follow the

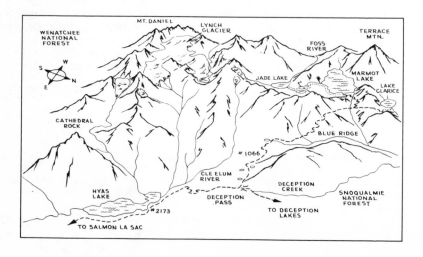

No Name Lake and Lynch Peak

rough fishermen's track around Marmot Lake to the inlet and scramble up the steep and brushy gully to No Name Lake and on to Jade Lake, 5442 feet. The jade color comes from the rock milk supplied by a little glacier. Explore upward on ice-carved rocks to the ridge crest and stunning close views of much bigger glaciers on Mt. Daniel.

Deception Pass and Marmot Lake can also be approached from the north via the Deception Creek trail or the Surprise Lake (Hike 6).

Mt. Stuart from County Line Trail

NORTH FORK TEANAWAY

37 County Line Trail

One-way trip from Highway 97 to Teanaway
  River road about 24 miles
Allow 3-4 days
High point 6300 feet
Elevation gain 3500 feet
Best mid-June through October
USGS Mt. Stuart, Liberty

The Wenatchee Mountain crest, boundary of two counties, offers two sets of spectacular views: from the Chelan County side, to rugged peaks of the Stuart Range; from the Kittitas County side, to foothills and farmlands. Presently the trip offers solitude, at a price—about half the trail, built in the 1920s for patrol work and abandoned prior to World War II, has totally vanished and most of the rest is sketchy. This therefore is not truly a trail walk but rather a cross-country venture to be attempted only with the aid of Forest Service and USGS maps. It's not tough for experienced wilderness navigators to follow in clear weather, but a party engulfed in clouds had best beat a quick retreat. When the trail is rebuilt, as is planned for sometime in the distant future, it will form part of a splendid long journey from Blewett Pass to Stevens Pass. But don't, then, expect solitude on the county line. For that, come now.

There are several ways to start the hike from the Blewett Pass end. The easiest is Negro Creek trail No. 1210. For that, drive Highway 97 between Wenatchee and Ellensburg to .6 mile north (downstream) from the arrastra at old Blewett townsite. Find Negro Creek road No. 2308, unsigned. Park here, elevation 2200 feet. The road goes 3 miles to the trailhead but is in too poor shape to recommend for autos.

To start the County Line Trail at the beginning, drive Highway 97 toward Swauk Pass from either direction. Turn off the highway on the old Blewett Pass highway, now road No. 2208, signed "Scotty Campground" at the north end and "Park Campground" at the south. Drive to Blewett Pass and park, elevation 4064 feet.

On the west side of the pass find Blewett Summit trail No. 1226 (shown as 1225 on some maps). The first mile is on old logging road succeeded by intermittent ridge-top tread that ends 5 miles from the pass, just short of 6400-foot Miller Peak. Scramble over the peak and follow ups and downs of the ridge crest toward Navaho Peak, sometimes on surviving bits of the County Line Trail. At approximately 10 miles from Blewett Pass, on slopes of Navaho Peak, intersect Fall Creek trail and follow it westward a short mile to a saddle under Earl Peak and an intersection with trails from Stafford and Cascade Creeks.

For the next 3 air miles the trail is plainer on maps than on the ground, but even where tread is utterly gone the walking is not all that difficult. At the intersection with Fourth Creek trail the County Line Trail is maintained ½ mile to the intersection with Beverly-Turnpike trail (Hike 38).

Descend the Beverly Creek trail a short bit and find Iron Peak trail, a long-abandoned route reopened in 1977 by the Youth Conservation Corps, climbing over a saddle and dropping 4 miles to the Teanaway River road.

Walk the road upvalley 1½ miles to the road-end and take the trail up Esmerelda Basin (Hike 39) to Fortune Creek Pass—or near. At ¼ mile short of the pass, at a little creek, the old trail route turns up right into a small basin and climbs to a divide on the ridge of Ingalls Peak. Drop to tiny Lake Ann, at the foot of the peak's walls, and follow an old sheep trail to Van Epps Pass, from where the Scatter Creek trail leads down to Fish Lake Guard Station on the Cle Elum River road.

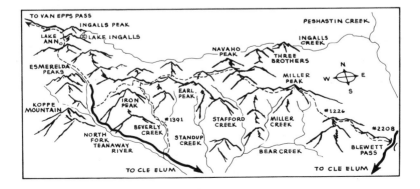

NORTH FORK TEANAWAY

38 Beverly-Turnpike

Round trip to Ingalls Creek 14 miles
Allow 2 days
High point 5800 feet
Elevation gain 2000 feet in, 1000 feet out
Best mid-July through October
USGS Mt. Stuart

Cross a high pass from the Teanaway River valley to Ingalls Creek. Climb through open forests, flower fields, rock gardens, and views, including 9415-foot Mt. Stuart, second-highest nonvolcanic mountain in the state. In proper season the flowers begin at the trailhead and never quit, climaxing in the weird, desert-like serpentine barrens for which the area is famed among botanists. A number of stream crossings can give bad trouble in high water—an argument for not doing the hike in early summer, since a little while later when the flowers are best the creeks are easy.

Drive North Fork Teanaway River road (Hike 39) 16½ miles to Beverly Creek. Just before crossing the creek, turn right on Beverly Creek road No. 232A and proceed 1.6 miles to the end and trailhead, elevation 3800 feet.

Trail No. 1391 starts steeply up a clearing, quickly passing a junction with the Bean Creek trail, and then facing the first of the high-water challenges, the crossing of Bean Creek. For ½ mile the trail sidehills high above Beverly Creek, then drops to make the first of five crossings of the stream. Some of these may have footlogs, but don't count on it. Past the fourth crossing the way switchbacks high up a rocky hillside, brilliant at the right time with the yellow of buckwheat and the scarlet of gilia, and at 2½ miles meets Fourth Creek trail, a possible alternate return. Beverly Creek is crossed the last time and switchbacks climb to 5800-foot Beverly-Turnpike Pass.

The north side of the pass is thick-forested, so if one is not going on, for views of Stuart climb the hill to the left (west) of the pass. But the really terrific side-trip from here is on the Iron Peak trail, hit just before the pass, leading up to the serpentine barrens and a superb ridge-crest stroll in crazy rocks and violent flowers and big views down to and across the Teanaway River.

From the pass the trail drops through woods, then switchbacks steeply down a barren avalanche slope to the valley bottom and a pleasant forest walk along Turnpike Creek. At 6 miles, by a nice campsite, is a crossing of the creek (again, possibly difficult). The way then climbs a bit and drops to a crossing of Ingalls Creek—unless a log (scarce) can be found, this is impossible at high water. On the far side is the Ingalls Creek trail (Hike 12). For a loop trip, follow the Ingalls Creek trail downstream 1½ miles to the junction with Fourth Creek trail, recross Ingalls Creek, and follow Fourth Creek up to its source, cross the ridge, and rejoin the Beverly-Turnpike trail.

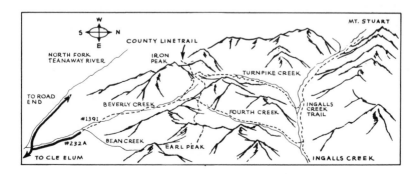

Mt. Stuart from near Beverly-Turnpike Pass 97

NORTH FORK TEANAWAY

39 Esmerelda Basin

Round trip to Fortune Creek Pass 7 miles
Hiking time 5 hours
High point 6000 feet
Elevation gain 1750 feet
Best late June through October
One day or backpack
USGS Mt. Stuart

Pass through a canyon between craggy buttes of Iron Mountain and Esmerelda Peaks into a peaceful basin of forest, streams, and, in season, a wildflower display all the more striking in contrast to the barren-seeming mountainsides. Climb to wide views above Fortune Creek Pass. This is a segment of the County Line Trail (Hike 37), a sometimes-there-and-sometimes-not path on the boundary between Chelan and Kittitas Counties.

Esmerelda Basin is splendid for day and weekend hikes, particularly when the Cascade Crest is misty-dripping and drizzling and the sun is (maybe) shining here in the rainshadow. Close-to-road camps make the basin ideal for families introducing small children to backpacking.

Drive Interstate 90 east of Cle Elum, go off on Exit 85, proceed north toward Wenatchee on US 97 for 5 miles, and turn west on Teanaway River road. At all junctions follow signs for "North Fork Teanaway." The first 13 miles are paved county road, succeeded by the dirt track of Forest Service road No. 232. At 23 miles from US 97 the road ends in a trailhead parking lot, elevation 4243 feet.

The hike starts on an old mine road, but the miners are gone these 25 years and the jeeps and motorcycles have been banned and the road is now merely a nice wide trail. A short ascent within sight and sound of the river, cascading and leaping over a series of falls, leads to the basin. The way flattens out in streamside greenery and rock gardens. At ½ mile is a junction. The trail right climbs to Longs Pass and Ingalls Lake (Hike 40). Good campsites here, though in midsummer water may have to be carried from the river.

From the junction go straight ahead, partly on bits of old mine road, mostly on new trail higher on the mountainside. The trail crosses a rocky avalanche slope, brilliant in late July with scarlet gilia. Farther along the trail skirts marshy meadows covered with pink elephanthead and white bog orchid, crosses creeks lined with violet shooting stars and blue butterwort.

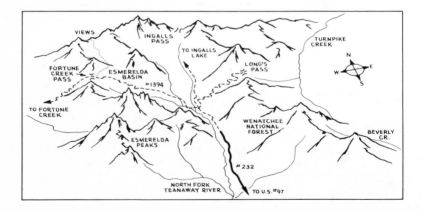

Harebell
Red columbine

Scarlet gilia
Elephant's head

These flowers were all photographed along the trail to Esmerelda Basin

At 2 miles, near the remnants of the settlement of Esmerelda (off the trail), the old mine road is left for the last time and the 10-percent grade horse trail begins its endless aimless uphill wandering around. At 3½ miles, 6000 feet, the trail tops out at Fortune Creek Pass and views over the Cle Elum River to Mt. Daniel. Close above the pass is Hawkins Mountain. Behind, above the basin, are Esmerelda Peaks.

For bigger views climb the righthand (north) skyline to a 6500-foot hilltop. Or, drop back down from the pass ¼ mile to the last creek and follow it up to a hidden basin and a pass overlooking Lake Ann, a delightful tarn (Hike 37).

NORTH FORK TEANAWAY

40 Ingalls Lake

Round trip to Ingalls Lake 7 miles
Hiking time 8 hours
High point 6500 feet
Elevation gain 2600 feet in, 600 feet out
Best mid-July through October
One day or backpack
USGS Mt. Stuart

A rock-basin lake at the foot of rugged Ingalls Peak, at the top of waterfalls plunging to Ingalls Creek, and directly across the valley from the massive south wall of 9415-foot Mt. Stuart, the highest peak between Glacier Peak and Rainier. The blend of blue lake, snowfields, ice-polished slabs of brown rock, lush green meadows, a glory of flowers, and groves of whitebark pine, larch, and alpine fir is magical. From a basecamp one can spend days of happy alpine wandering.

Drive to the end of the North Fork Teanaway road, elevation 4243 feet, and hike to Esmerelda Basin (Hike 39). At ½ mile turn right, and in ¼ mile more turn left on the old jeep road signed "Ingalls Lake-Mt. Stuart." Carry a loaded canteen; the climb can be hot and usually is waterless.

The road ascends steeply in forest, then levels out briefly and ends on a grassy flat. Now super-steep trail heads straight up, with scarcely a switchback, in fields of grass and blossoms, patches of small trees. Nearby ridges are a startling mixture of gray and brown and rusty-red rocks. South beyond Esmerelda Peaks appear Mt. Adams, the Goat Rocks, and Mt. Rainier. Higher up, the trail swings along the side of a narrow valley, winds through buttresses and flowers, and just below the pass comes to a small green bench with snowmelt (and camps) in early summer. The final stretch is a rough crawl up outcrops to Ingalls Pass, 6500 feet, about 2½ miles, and a grand view of Mt. Stuart. The way to here is mostly free of snow in late June, while slopes to the north are still white. The ridge can be scrambled in either direction for higher views.

Drop abruptly into parkland with cold streams and delightful camps and traverse headwaters of a branch of Ingalls Creek, losing 300 feet or so. (Or better, but longer, leave the trail and contour beautiful little meadows.) Meager trail regains the 300 feet in climbing a low ridge of polished brown buttresses—and at last, below, is the lake. The way down to the 6463-foot shore is short and easy, but getting around the west side to the outlet requires a ticklish scramble up and down slabs and huge boulders. As reward, there is lonesomeness even when the rest of the area is crowded. And also the choicest arctic-alpine camps. And a view of Stuart that is unsurpassed.

From the outlet one can explore to Stuart Pass (Hike 12). From the trail one can roam to private meadow basins and wide-horizon ridges.

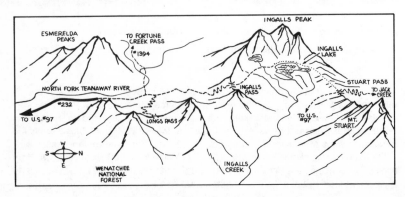

Ingalls Lake and Mt. Stuart

CARBON RIVER

41 Summit Lake

Round trip to Summit Lake 5 miles
Hiking time 3 hours
High point 5400 feet
Elevation gain 1200 feet
Best July through October
One day or backpack
USGS Enumclaw

An alpine lake, but don't be misled by the name—it isn't on the summit of anything. However, there are flower fields and a fabulous view of Mt. Rainier.

Drive US 410 to a complicated intersection at the southwest corner of Buckley, turn south on Highway No. 162-165 for 1½ miles, and turn left on Highway 165 and proceed 18 miles, passing Wilkeson and Carbonado, following signs to Ipsut Creek and Fairfax. Just before the entrance to Mount Rainier National Park, turn left on road No. 1811, cross the Carbon River on a wooden bridge, and drive about 6 miles uphill to a junction. Turn left a short bit to the end of the spur and find the trailhead, 4200 feet, to Twin Lake, Bearhead Mountain, and Summit Lake.

Going steadily east and constantly climbing, the trail starts up through a clearcut, makes a big switchback, and enters thick forest which cuts off sights and sound of encroaching logging and automobiles. At 1 mile, 4800 feet, is wooded Twin Lake; keep left here at the junction with the Carbon trail.

The path rounds the lake and heads uphill, passing subalpine ponds or marshes, depending on the season. Nearly at the top of the ridge the way turns west and traverses the slopes on a fairly level grade, at one point emerging from timber into a small meadow with a view of Rainier. At 2½ miles, 5400 feet, Summit Lake is attained. Bordering the shores are open fields covered with beargrass. On the west side is an old burn. The best camps are on the east side where the trail reaches the lake.

For the first and most essential side-trip, follow the trail around the lake, leave tread, find an easy route to the top of the 5737-foot hill, and look down at Coplay, Coundly, Lily, and Cedar Lakes. The view is grand of Mt. Rainier above—and equally broad of the network of logging operations below.

For another wandering, hike the trail past the lake a mile to the end, climb Rooster Comb Ridge, and follow the crest down to boggy meadows; if ambitious, join the Clearwater trail and go ½ mile to 4700-foot Celery Meadows.

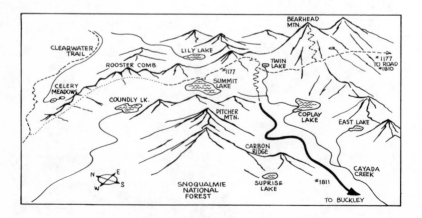

Summit Lake and Mt. Rainier (John Spring photo)

For an alternate trip, turn right at Twin Lake on the Carbon trail, keep right at all old trail junctions, and in 2½ miles from Twin Lake reach the 6089-foot summit of Bearhead, former site of a lookout, and a magnificent panorama of Rainier and the hinterland.

WHITE RIVER

42 Naches Wagon Trail

Round trip to Government Meadows from
  west side 10½ miles
Hiking time 5 hours
High point 4800 feet
Elevation gain 2200 feet
Best late June through November
One day or backpack
USGS Lester

One-way trip from east side 9½ miles
Hiking time 5 hours
High point 4900 feet
Elevation gain 1500 feet

Walk the pioneer wagon route across Naches Pass and see blazes cut by emigrants, logs they rolled out of the way, dirt they shoveled, and trees they chopped. Unfortunately, you will see more tracks of vandals than pioneers, because the Forest Service inexcusably permits motorbikes and jeeps on the route. These adventurers seeking a mechanical challenge have obliterated much of the pioneers' trail which should have been preserved for more respectful travelers with an appreciation of history. This may be the only pioneer trail left in the 48 states that hasn't been paved over or bulldozed. Yet Weyerhaeuser has twice cut the trail with roads near the famous "cliff" and the Forest Service has shortened the trail on the east side.

Highlights can be enjoyed in a day hike to Government Meadows from the west side, but for a better appreciation of the trek of 1853, start from the east side, camp overnight at Government Meadows (where the pioneers spent months), and next morning descend the west side, over "The Cliff" where wagons were lowered on rawhide ropes. In either case, allow plenty of time for leisurely exploration.

For a day hike from the west, drive US 410 east from Enumclaw 20 miles to a log-trestle overpass, turn left on road No. 197, and go 8 miles to the Greenwater River bridge. About ¼ mile beyond is a sign announcing "Greenwater Trail." Park here, elevation 2560 feet. Cross Pyramid Creek and follow the jeep track ¼ mile to the foot of a ridge. Ascend the trail (track) 3½ miles through forest to Government Meadows, 4800 feet.

For an overnight hike, leave one car at the west trailhead and drive a second to Chinook Pass and 23.5 miles east from the summit. Turn left 14 miles on Little Naches road No. 197, then turn right on road No. 1923 and go .3 mile to the trailhead, elevation 3200 feet.

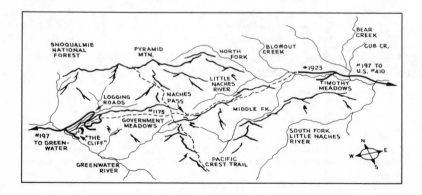

Old blaze made by pioneers

The first wagon train crossed Naches Pass in 1853. One or two others followed, but the route proved so difficult it was abandoned. In 1910 the Forest Service reopened the way for foot and horse travel. To "celebrate" the centennial of the first crossing, a group of jeepsters hacked and gouged over the pass in 1953, and since then the trail has been heavily used by motorbikes and four-wheel vehicles which have rutted the forest and churned meadows to gooey muck. Thanks to the vehicles, the trail is impossible to miss, but finding the remnants of the original wagon road requires imagination. Two clues are useful:

For one, the pioneers took the line of least resistance by detouring around big trees and logs; the jeepsters use chainsaws to make a more direct line, and thus in many places the old track is several hundred feet from the jeep ruts and relatively well-preserved. For a second clue, the wagons were top-heavy and to save shoveling on sidehills the pioneers frequently followed the ups and downs of a ridge crest; particularly on the west side, jeeps have contoured around some ridge tops.

In 6 miles from the east trailhead, reach the wooded, 4900-foot summit of Naches Pass, and in another ½ mile the Pacific Crest Trail junction and campsites at Government Meadows. The next day, at ½ mile from the west trailhead, cross switchbacks of a logging road and descend "The Cliff," where pioneers lowered their wagons.

Greenwater trail

WHITE RIVER

43 Echo Lake

Round trip 14 miles
Hiking time 7 hours
High point 4100 feet
Elevation gain 1640 feet
Best May to mid-November at lower
elevations
One day or backpack
USGS Lester

A popular walk through a cathedral of fir trees with a few giant cedars and hemlocks thrown in—outside dedicated wilderness and national parks, one of the most outstanding valley forests remaining in the state. (But for how long? Much of the best of it is owned by Weyerhaeuser and scheduled for early logging.) As an added dividend, the way passes sparkling forest lakes and climbs to a beautiful mountain lake.

Drive US 410 from Enumclaw to the same parking lot as for Naches Wagon Trail, Hike 42, and the same trailhead, signed "Greenwater Trail." Elevation, 2560 feet.

The trail, No. 1176, crosses Pyramid Creek and a clearcut and enters a climax forest where the magnificence of trees competes for attention with the rich understory of devil's club, vanilla leaf, trillium, and moss. But the tread also competes. In spots the mud is atrocious; the many boots churn it up, but have minor effect compared to the plungings of horses and the gougings of motorcycles, which between them make some stretches impassable to walkers, requiring detours in the brush. At ¾ mile the trail crosses Greenwater River, and at 1½ miles recrosses at the first of the two small, shallow Meeker (Greenwater) Lakes. The second is at 2 miles.

In the next mile the trail crosses the river twice more, and at 4 miles reaches a junction with Lost Creek trail No. 1185, a 3-mile side-trip to Lost Lake. Maggie Creek is crossed at 3½ miles and, ½ mile beyond, the Greenwater River for the last time. So far the trail has gained only 200 feet a mile, but near the 5-mile mark it leaves the valley bottom and starts climbing in earnest. At 5½ miles pass a junction with trail No. 1186. At 6½ miles cross a 4100-foot high point and drop 200 feet to the edge of 3819-foot Echo Lake, surrounded by wooded hills with a glimpse of meadows and craggy peaks of Castle Mountain.

The trail continues 6 miles to Corral Pass. The entire route, near lakes and along river, offers numerous campsites.

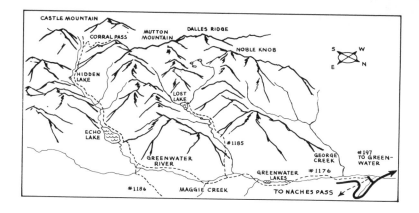

White River and Mt. Rainier from Crystal Ridge

WHITE RIVER

44 Crystal Ridge

Round trip to viewpoint 6 miles
Hiking time 3½ hours
High point 5500 feet
Elevation gain 1300 feet
Best July to October
One day
USGS Bumping Lake and White River Park

Loop trip 13 miles
Hiking time 7 hours
High point 6600 feet
Elevation gain 2400 feet
One day

Along the Crystal Mountain ridge, boundary of Rainier National Park, a Forest Service trail wanders through a series of striking views of Rainier and the White River. Flowers in one season, great huckleberries in another. Hikers who get up early enough in the morning have a good chance of seeing elk.

The trip comes in two versions, one using the feet only for a standard uphill-downhill walk, the other using the Crystal Mountain chairlift for the uphill, a trail-road combination for the downhill. Both will be described here, the "normal" version first.

From US 410 at the Park boundary near Silver Springs, turn left on the Crystal Mountain Ski Area road. Drive 4½ miles to an unmarked logging road and follow it ¼ mile to the trailhead and horse-unloading ramp, elevation 4200 feet.

Trail No. 1163 begins as a jeep track under a powerline but soon becomes legitimate, climbing gently through clearcuts, then an old burn, in loose, dusty, pumice soil. Shade is scarce and water non-existent (did you remember to fill the canteen?). Heat and thirst are forgotten when, in 3 miles, at 5500 feet, the crest of Crystal Ridge is attained and Mt. Rainier overpowers the horizon.

The ridge varies from narrow, with a cliff on the park side, to broad and rounded meadows. Below the crest are vast fields of huckleberries. And the views! Chances are a party will find ample rewards long before completing the 3 steady-climbing ridgecrest miles to the top terminal of Chair No. 2.

For a loop trip with an interesting variety of lakes, meadows, and huckleberries, descend on a service road that starts near the terminal. In ¹/₃ mile find a legitimate trail switchbacking down through Silver Queen Basin, past Henskin Lakes, to a junction with Silver Creek trail No. 1182. Follow it 1 mile to road No. 184, then go by road to the ski area parking lot, 4½ miles from the top terminal. From there walk the paved road 2½ miles back to the starting point.

Now for the all-downhill tour. (Let it be noted this version is no good for elk-watching—by the time of day the chairlifts start running, the animals have finished eating and have retired to the forest to chew their cuds.) Drive to the ski area parking lot, elevation 4200 feet, ride chair No. 2 to the top, elevation 6600 feet, and find the Crystal Ridge trail and hike either way. Both ways are so interesting and different that you may want to go back a second time for the other direction or, as we did, start early in the morning so you can see the elk and hike the whole loop at one time.

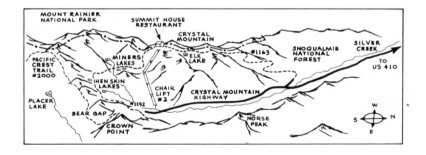

WHITE RIVER

45 Big Crow Basin- Norse Peak

Round trip to Norse Peak 8½ miles
Hiking time 6 hours
High point 6856 feet
Elevation gain 2900 feet
Best late June through early November
One day
USGS Bumping Lake

Lovely alpine meadows, one with a small lake, offering a wonderful weekend of wandering. However, the shortest way to the basin involves climbing nearly to the top of 6856-foot Norse Peak—an arduous backpack. Most hikers therefore settle for a day trip to the summit, an abandoned lookout site, and enjoy the views down to the inviting gardens and all around to panoramas extending from Snoqualmie Pass peaks to Mt. Adams, from golden hills of Eastern Washington to green lowlands of Puget Sound. The trail to Norse Peak usually is open for walking in late June; the meadow country remains under snow until mid-July.

Drive US 410 east 33 miles from Enumclaw to Silver Springs summer homes. A bit beyond, just before the Rainier National Park boundary, turn left toward the Crystal Mountain ski area. At 4 miles find the trailhead on the left side of the road. Parking is on the right, elevation 3900 feet.

The hike begins along an old logging road, passes a spring (fill canteens—this is the last sure water), and in ¼ mile enters onto true trail. The original path to the lookout was short and steep; the Forest Service recently improved the route, which now is somewhat gentler but considerably longer.

Very soon the tip of Mt. Rainier appears over the ridge to the west and every additional step reveals more of the mountain. By 2 miles the whole summit is in sight and the scene steadily expands as more elevation is gained. The route is confused here and there by crisscrossing of the old tread—take the path of least resistance, which generally is the new trail. At 4 miles, 6600 feet, the summit ridge is topped and a junction reached.

The right fork follows the ridge crest ¼ mile to Norse Peak. Look northeast into Big Crow Basin and east to Lake Basin and appealing Basin Lake. Look down to the Crystal Mountain ski area, one of the finest ski developments in the Northwest; unfortunately, winter doesn't last all year and the summer view is a hodgepodge of bulldozer tracks.

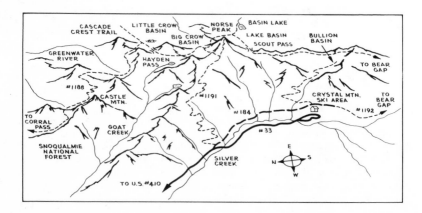

Mt. Rainier from Norse Peak

The left fork drops eastward 1 mile to join the Pacific Crest Trail, which descends ½ mile to Big Crow Basin; at about 5700 feet are a shelter cabin and good camping, though water may be scarce in late summer. Partway down find a side-trail leading over a low green ridge to Basin Lake, 6200 feet.

The meadows and peak also can be approached by intersecting the Crest Trail at Bullion Basin, or by taking the trail starting at Corral Pass, 5600 feet. The latter long and scenic route includes two descents and ascents of 800 feet each in 4 miles before joining the Crest Trail near Little Crow Basin (camps and water).

AMERICAN RIVER

46 Crow Lake Way

Round trip to Grassy Meadow 8 miles
Hiking time 7 hours
High point 6200 feet
Elevation gain 3000 feet in, 600 feet out
Best early June to hunting season
One day or backpack
USGS Bumping Lake

An extremely steep trail, with no water except that carried in canteens, climbs from valley forests to high meadows, compensating for the sweat and struggle by offering exciting views of the needle-like spires of Fifes Peaks and the meandering course of the American River. The route can be continued past pretty little Grassy Meadow to the large, boggy meadows surrounding Crow Creek Lake, a favorite haunt of throngs of elk and deer. The animals are fun to watch in summer but are best steered clear of in hunting season, what with hikers so often being mistaken for fair game.

Drive US 410 east of Chinook Pass to 1.2 miles west of Pleasant Valley Campground and find the trailhead, elevation 3400 feet.

Crow Lake Way No. 953, steep from the start and gaining 2200 feet in the first 2½ hot, dry miles, begins with ¼ mile of jeep track before turning into true trail. The way climbs 1¼ miles through forest to a hogback, which then is followed, by glimpses of Fifes Peaks, past dramatic dropoffs overlooking American Ridge, the views growing step by step, to a 5800-foot high point at 3 miles, a good turnaround for day-trippers.

The trail then descends 200 feet into Survey Creek drainage and at 3½ miles crosses a broad divide, 6000 feet, to Crow Creek drainage. West are rolling green meadows inviting a tour. At about 4 miles, 5600 feet, the trail enters Grassy Meadow, with a small creek and, half-hidden in trees, a small lake. Campsites nearby are great bases for explorations.

For the first, roam the basin at the head of Falls Creek. The unmarked trail starts at the far end of the lake, skirts a rockslide, and climbs to the basin edge at 6400 feet. The basin rim can be followed like the lip of a cup in a semicircle to cliffs of Fifes Peaks. Other explorations are the 6400-foot hill to the west and, longer, the 3 miles along Crow Lake Way, in green meadows, to Crow Creek Lake.

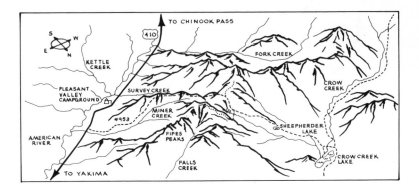

Fifes Peaks from Crow Lake Way

AMERICAN RIVER

47 Sourdough Gap

Round trip 6 miles
Hiking time 4 hours
High point 6400 feet
Elevation gain 1100 feet in, 200 feet out
Best July through October
One day or backpack
USGS Mt. Rainier and Bumping Lake

A delightful bit of the Pacific Crest Trail (probably the easiest meadow walk in this entire book) through flower gardens and grassy fields to a high pass. A good over-night hike for beginners, except that camping space is limited and very crowded on weekends. Do the trip in early August when flowers are at their peak.

Drive US 410 east from Enumclaw to the summit of Chinook Pass, 5500 feet. Find the first available parking lot—which may be around the bend in the highway. (The shortage of parking space is a serious problem on fine summer weekends. So is the vandalism of cars left overnight.) The trailhead (Pacific Crest Trail No. 2000) is near the wooden overpass.

The trail goes north, paralleling the highway, dropping slightly in the first mile, at times on cliffs almost directly above the road. At about 1½ miles the way rounds a ridge, leaves the highway, and starts a gentle climb to Sheep Lake, 2½ miles, 5700 feet—a great place to camp if not crowded. But it almost always is, and the meadows have been badly damaged. Find better camping on benches a few hundred feet away.

The moderate ascent continues through flowers, with a final long switchback leading to Sourdough Gap, 3 miles, 6400 feet. (About 500 feet below the gap the summit of Mt. Rainier can be seen briefly between two peaks to the west.)

Views from the gap are limited. For broader vistas, continue on the trail another ⅓ mile, descending a little to a small pass with looks down Morse Creek to Placer Lake, an artificial lake made by miners years ago.

For really wide horizons, ascend the 6734-foot peak west of the gap—not a difficult climb by mountaineering standards, but steep with a loose scree slope near the top. Drop a few feet north from the gap and start up along the base of cliffs, following a well-worn path. For the best footing stay off the scree. From the summit admire the huge white bulk of Mt. Rainier, peaks south to Mt. Adams, and north along the Cascade Crest. A vertical cliff falls to Crystal Lakes 900 feet below, seemingly only a swandive away.

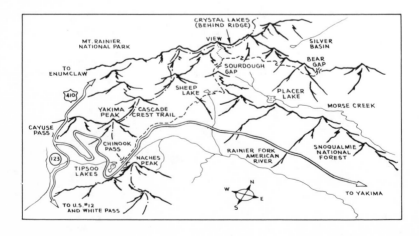

Sheep Lake

BUMPING RIVER

48 American Ridge

Round trip from Goose Prairie to viewpoint 12 miles
Hiking time 7 hours
High point 6310 feet
Elevation gain 2900 feet
Best June through November
One day or backpack
USGS Bumping Lake

One-way trip from Goose Prairie to Pacific Crest Trail 19 miles
Allow 3 days
High point 6946 feet
Elevation gain 5500 feet
Best late July through October

As the crow flies, American Ridge is 17 miles long, but with twists, turns, and switchbacks, the trail takes 27 miles to complete the traverse. The way is mostly rough and sometimes steep, but the meadowlands are beautiful and lonesome. Flowers are in full bloom at the east end of the ridge about Memorial Day (the usual time that Chinook Pass opens) and at the west end in early August. The east end makes an excellent early-season trip when other high trails are still snowed in. Look for avalanche and glacier lilies and a rare pink-and-purple flower called steer's head.

The entire ridge is worth hiking, but only the east end is free of snow in June, and by August it is dry and hot. Therefore the recommendation is to hike from Goose Prairie to an intersection with the American Ridge trail and then go east (in June) or west (in August) along the ridge crest.

Drive US 410 east from Chinook Pass 20 miles and turn right on the Bumping River road. In .6 mile is the eastern trailhead, elevation 2900 feet, signed American Ridge trail No. 958; if a complete traverse of American Ridge is planned, start here.

At 9.3 miles from US 410 find Goose Prairie trail No. 972 on the right side of the road, elevation 3360 feet. Parking space in a small camp on the left.

The Goose Prairie trail is in woods all the way, beginning in fir and pine forest typical of the east slopes of the Cascades and ascending into Alaska cedars, alpine firs, and wind-bent pines. The route climbs steadily but never steeply. At 1½ miles the path crosses several small streams and begins a series of nine switchbacks, at 2 miles recrossing the same streams, the last reliable water for a long stretch. At 4¾ miles is a spring which runs most of the summer; possible camping here. At 5 miles the ridge top

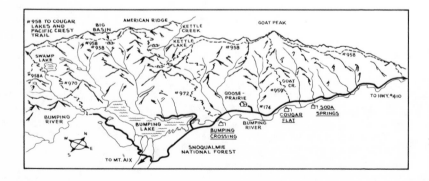

Nelson Ridge from American Ridge

is attained and the intersection with American Ridge trail No. 958, elevation 6200 feet.

Day hikers (any season) should follow the ridge west, climbing ½ mile to a point where the trail starts down into Kettle Creek drainage. Leave the trail and continue ¼ mile more up the ridge to a 6310-foot knoll with fine views of Mt. Rainier, Mt. Aix, and miles of ridges north and south.

Early-season overnight hikers should turn east, following the ridge through forest and meadows to Goat Peak at 11 miles, site of the former American Ridge Lookout, elevation 6473 feet, and a view of the spectacular cliffs of Fifes Peaks. If transportation has been arranged, a party can continue 7½ miles down to the Bumping River road and the previously-mentioned American Ridge trailhead, completing a one-way trip of 18½ miles with an elevation gain of about 3600 feet.

Midsummer and fall overnight hikers should turn west, climbing near the top of the 6310-foot knoll, then descending to campsites at shallow Kettle Lake, 6 miles, 5650 feet. (Below the lake is a small spring.) The trail contours around the head of Kettle Creek, climbing to the ridge crest at 10 miles, 6900 feet, dropping again to Big Basin at 11 miles, 6300 feet, a cirque with good campsites, bands of elk, and glorious scenery.

With some ups and more downs, the trail follows the ridge top from meadows back into alpine forest at a low point of 5500 feet, then up to meadowland at 6000 feet and a campsite near Mud Lake at 13½ miles. At 16½ miles is a junction with Swamp Lake trail No. 970, a popular route leading to Cougar Lakes in 1 mile and a steep way trail that joins the Crest Trail; No. 958 goes right, reaching American Lake at 18 miles and the Crest Trail at 19½ miles.

If transportation can be arranged, a one-way trip can be made via the Crest Trail to Chinook Pass, a total distance of 26.5 miles, or via the Swamp Lake trail to Upper Bumping road, a total of 21 miles.

Looking south along Nelson Ridge

BUMPING RIVER

49 Nelson Ridge- Mount Aix

Round trip to Mt. Aix 12 miles
Hiking time 10 hours
High point 7766 feet
Elevation gain 4000 feet
Best mid-June through October
One day
USGS Bumping Lake

High gardens in the blue sky of the rainshadow, amid views east to the brown vastness of the heat-hazy Columbia Plateau, west to the shimmering white hugeness of Mt. Rainier, and south along the Cascade Crest to the Goat Rocks and Mt. Adams. Plus closer looks over meadows and forests of the proposed Cougar Lakes Wilderness. This is not a beginners' trail—the way is steep, hot, and dry.

Drive US 410 east from Chinook Pass 20 miles and turn right on the Bumping Lake road 11 miles to a junction. Take the left fork, signed road No. 162, 1½ miles and just before a bridge over Copper Creek turn left up a steep road signed "Mt. Aix Trail." Park in a few yards, elevation 3700 feet. The rude road continues ¼ mile but this final stretch is best walked to the trailhead. Fill canteens at a creek not far from the beginning; the climb is long and can be thirsty.

The merciless trail attains highlands with minimum delay. For openers, the path ascends deep forest nearly to a branch of Copper Creek, but never gets to the water, instead switchbacking up a steep hillside. (Across the Copper Creek valley, above Miners Ridge, Rainier appears, and grows with every step.) At 2¼ miles the trail swings into open subalpine forest at the lip of a hanging valley but again never gets to the water. Switchbacks now trend out from the valley into open forest distinguished by superb specimens of whitebark pine.

At nearly 4 miles, 6400 feet, is a grassy promontory with views of Rainier, Adams, St. Helens, and the Goat Rocks. A nice campsite here in early summer, when snowmelt is available. This far makes a satisfying destination for a day hike, especially when slopes above are snowy or the party is pooped.

From the promontory the trail traverses shrubby forest and scree southward and upward to the wide-open crest of Nelson Ridge, 7100 feet, and a choice of wanderings. The up-and-down crest cries out for rambling in either or both directions. The trail contours and climbs a final rocky mile to the summit of 7766-foot Mt. Aix, one-time site of a fire lookout.

Because of their position on the east slope of the Cascades, and the mostly southwest exposures of the trail route, Nelson Ridge and Mt. Aix are free of snow weeks earlier than country a few miles distant. And if the tread at the hanging valley of Copper Creek is all white, as it may be through June, a short and simple detour up amid trees leads back to clear ground. Actually, the maximum flower display comes when patches of snow still linger. The locals consider this trail—whether to the promontory at 4 miles, to Nelson Ridge at 5 miles, or Mt. Aix at 6 miles—the best early-summer hike in the entire Bumping River area.

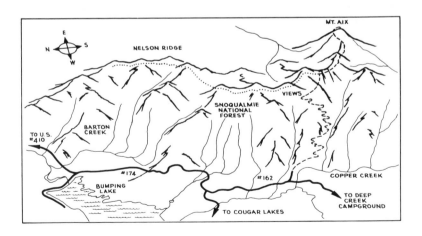

BUMPING RIVER

50 Cougar Lakes

Round trip to Cougar Lakes 12 miles
Hiking time 8 hours
High point 5300 feet
Elevation gain 1700 feet in, 300 feet out
Best mid-July through October
One day or backpack
USGS Bumping Lake

Two alpine lakes, a big one and a little one, surrounded by generous flower fields in late July and early August, blueberries in early September, and fall colors in October. From ridges above, wide views of Mt. Rainier and the Cascade Crest country.

Drive US 410 east from Chinook Pass 20 miles and turn right 10.8 miles on the Bumping River road to the end of pavement at Bumping Lake. Continue on road No. 174 to a junction at 2½ miles and turn right on the Upper Bumping road 3.6 miles to the road-end and trailhead, elevation 3600 feet.

The flat forest way leads in ½ mile to an easy ford of the broad and shallow Bumping River, which has exceptionally sharp rocks. A bit farther is a junction with the Bumping Lake trail. Go straight ahead, climbing moderately and steadily in woods and occasional openings to the outlet of Swamp Lake, 3.7 miles, 4800 feet; campsites at and near the shelter cabin.

The trail ascends several hundred feet in ¾ mile to an indistinct divide and a junction with the American Ridge trail (Hike 48). Go left ¼ mile to another junction. The righthand trail climbs past American Lake to the Cascade Crest; go left instead, rounding a ridge spur at 5300 feet and dropping into the lake basin, at 6 miles, 5015 feet, reaching the isthmus between the Cougar Lakes.

To the right is Little Cougar Lake, at the foot of the basalt cliffs of House Rock. To the left is Big Cougar Lake. The shores offer numerous camps but the sites with the most privacy and largest views are in meadows along the inlet stream feeding Big Cougar Lake. (Be sure to camp a distance from lakeshore and streams.)

For extended horizons, climb a steep and perhaps very muddy mile on the boulder-strewn path leading from the inlet of Big Cougar to the Cascade Crest at 6000 feet. Look for mountain goat, marmots, and rock conies (pikas). For maximum

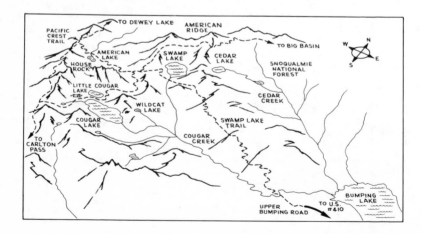

Little Cougar Lake and House Rock

scenery and garden walking, wander north on the Pacific Crest Trail and in about 1½ miles turn right on the trail down to American Lake and back to Cougar Lakes, completing a 5-mile loop.

To preserve the vegetation, campers are asked to use sites at least 100 feet from the lakeshores.

Beargrass on top of Tumac Mountain

BUMPING RIVER

51 Tumac Mountain

Round trip 9 miles
Hiking time 5 hours
High point 6340 feet
Elevation gain 2100 feet
Best July through October
One day or backpack
USGS Bumping Lake and White Pass

Hike through alpine meadows by myriad lakes and ponds to the most fascinating view of vulcanism in the Washington Cascades. Tumac itself is no simple cone but rather, built of both cinders and lava and having two craters (both lake-filled), an infant stratovolcano standing on a broad lava plateau. This is how mighty Rainier began.

The summit presents a panorama of stratovolcanoes of other ages: Spiral Butte, another infant, at the south end of the lava plateau; youthful St. Helens, expected by geologists to grow a lot more; bulky, mature, deeply-dissected Rainier and Adams; and the old old Goat Rocks, remnant of a once-mighty volcano now reduced to mere roots. Do the climb in mid-July when upper slopes are covered with red and white heather plus a peppering of bright red paintbrush. The trip can be one day or overnight, camping at one of the lovely Twin Sisters Lakes. Carry water; except for the lakes, the way can be quite dry.

Drive US 410 east from Chinook Pass 20 miles and turn right 10.8 miles on the Bumping River road to the end of pavement at Bumping Lake. Continue on road No. 174 to a junction at 2.5 miles and turn left on road No. 162, going 7 miles to the road-end at Deep Creek Campground, elevation 4300 feet.

Find Twin Sister trail No. 980 on the south side of the campground. In a few hundred feet turn right at a junction and drop to a crossing of Deep Creek. On the far side the trail climbs steeply, with only a few short level spots, gaining 800 feet in a little over 1½ miles (all in woods) to Little Twin Sister Lake, 5100 feet. Just before the lake is an old mine tunnel filled with water.

The "little" lake (only a comparison, for both are quite large) has numerous bays and rocky points. To see it at its best, climb open slopes of the 5733-foot hill rising above the shores. To reach Big Twin Sister Lake, follow trail No. 980 westward ½ mile. Both lakes are outstanding and have beautiful campsites.

From Little Twin Sister Lake turn left on trail No. 1104, which in ½ mile turns toward Blankenship Meadows. Keep straight ahead on the Tumac Mountain trail, which aims at the peak. The way climbs steadily in open meadows 1 mile. Note how small trees are taking over the meadowland, a phenomenon which only recently has received attention. Are the trees just now growing after the Ice Age, or are they returning after catastrophic forest fires, insect invasion, or uncontrolled stock grazing of years ago? Whatever the reason, alpine meadows all over this portion of the Cascades are rapidly changing to forest, especially here and at Mt. Rainier.

The final mile is steep and badly chewed up by horses, but the views get steadily better and become downright exciting on the 6340-foot summit. The most striking is northeast, down to Blankenship Meadows and the three Blankenship Lakes (Hike 54). To the west are many tree-ringed lakes, a few of which can be seen, including Dumbbell Lake (Hike 52). Mt. Aix and neighbors dominate the northeast horizon. In other directions are the volcanoes.

To protect the vegetation, campers are asked to use sites at least 100 feet from the lakeshores. At Big Twin Sister, the only permitted camps are on the north side.

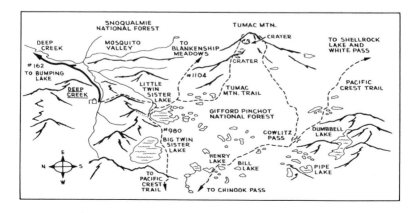

TIETON RIVER

52 Dumbbell Lake

Round trip to Sand Lake 6 miles
Hiking time 4 hours
High point 5295 feet
Elevation gain 900 feet
Best mid-July through November
One day
USGS White Pass

Round trip to Dumbbell Lake 13 miles
Hiking time 7 hours
High point 5600 feet
Elevation gain 1200 feet in, 500 feet out
Best mid-July through November
One day or backpack

If you like alpine lakes, this is certainly the trail—there are dozens of them, large and small. If you like tall, picturesque alpine trees, this is the trail—there are thousands of lovely specimens. And if you like fall hiking through the bright red leaves of huckleberry bushes, this is the trail—there are miles of color. The hike along a delightful section of the Pacific Crest Trail can be done as a day trip to Sand Lake or an overnight to Dumbbell Lake. The trail is a bit rough from heavy horse use and there are practically no distant views.

Drive US 12 east from White Pass .7 mile, turn left into White Pass Campground, and continue about ¼ mile to the trailhead near Leech Lake, elevation 4412 feet. This is Pacific Crest Trail No. 2000. A new and very confusing system of signing gives trail numbers rather than destinations. There is no problem so long as a party stays on the Crest Trail but any deviation requires a Forest Service map to decipher the signs.

The trail starts in forest, climbing 800 feet in 2½ miles to Deer Lake, 5206 feet, still in woods. Many people lose the trail here; while the most-used path heads for the lake, the Crest Trail turns sharply right and skirts a large, wet meadow.

At 3 miles is Sand Lake, 5295 feet, with numerous arms surrounded by meadows and alpine trees. Though the water is very clear, the shallow lake seems to have neither inlet nor outlet, so the water should be boiled before drinking. Sand Lake is an excellent turnaround for day hikers.

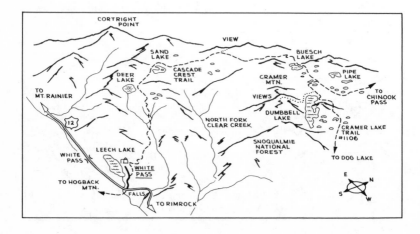

Fog blowing over Sand Lake

Now the trail wanders past numerous small lakes, climbing to 5600 feet at 4 miles. Several places offer glimpses southward of Mt. Adams and the Goat Rocks; Spiral Butte can be seen through the trees to the east.

At about 5 miles the trail switches from the east side of the crest to the west and descends in forest, losing 500 feet in ¾ mile. Now and then Mt. Rainier can be partly viewed through trees; for a better look walk off the trail 100 feet onto a low, rocky knoll located on the left side of the path soon after passing two small ponds.

At 6 miles the way skirts Buesch Lake, 5081 feet, and reaches a junction with Cramer Lake trail No. 1106. Follow this a short ¼ mile to Dumbbell Lake, 5091 feet. Much of the lake is shallow; the rocky shoreline is very interesting. To appreciate its unusual shape, beat through a patch of brush and scramble to the bald summit of 5992-foot Cramer Mountain—and views much broader than merely the lake.

For an alternate return, follow Cramer Lake trail No. 1106 down to within ½ mile of Dog Lake, turn west on Dark Meadow trail No. 1107, and finish with a last mile on the Crest Trail. The distance is about the same but most of the way is in forest.

Shoe Lake and Pacific Crest Trail

TIETON RIVER

53 Shoe Lake

Round trip from trailhead east of White
  Pass 14 miles
Hiking time 7 hours
High point 6600 feet
Elevation gain 2200 feet in, 500 feet out
Best mid-July through October
One day
USGS White Pass

Round trip from top of White Pass chairlift
  8 miles
Hiking time 4 hours
Elevation gain 900 feet in, 600 feet out
Forest Service wilderness permit required

Meadows and parklands along the Cascade Crest, grand views of the Goat Rocks and Mt. Adams, and a beautiful lake in a green basin. All this on an easy day from the road.

Drive US 12 east from White Pass .7 mile to the parking lot and trailhead (Pacific Crest Trail) in Leech Lake Campground, elevation 4400 feet.

(Alternatively, for a shorter hike, park at White Pass ski area, 4400 feet, climb the ski hill 1½ miles, and take a short path which intersects the Pacific Crest Trail at a point 3 miles from the trailhead described above. For an even quicker trip, some hikers ride the chairlift to the top.)

From the formal trailhead east of White Pass, the way traverses and switchbacks open forest, touching a ski run at one point, and at 3 miles, 5900 feet, intersects the ridge crest and the path from the top of the chairlift.

Now the trail ascends into gardens and scattered alpine trees on the slopes of Hogback Mountain and swings onto the west side of the crest, with a great view of Mt. Rainier. Attaining a 6400-foot saddle, the route contours steep, broad shale slopes on the east side of 6789-foot Hogback (an easy scramble from the trail to the summit) above the basin containing little Miriam Lake, and climbs to a 6600-foot saddle, 6½ miles, in a spur ridge—and commanding views of the Goat Rocks and Mt. Adams. And below, the bright waters of Shoe Lake.

Drop ¹/₃ mile to the lake, 6200 feet, and fields of flowers. However, due to damage done by past overuse, camping has been banned that the meadows may have a chance to recover.

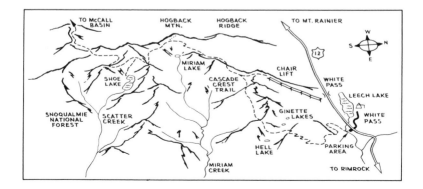

TIETON RIVER

54 Blankenship Lakes

Round trip to Blankenship Lakes 12 miles
Hiking time 6 hours
High point 5200 feet
Elevation gain 2000 feet in, 200 feet out
Best mid-July through October
One day or backpack
USGS White Pass

Pocket-size meadows, vast grasslands, and beautiful mountain lakes make this country unique in the Cascades. The map calls the area "Mosquito Valley," and rightly so. Though the meadows are magnificent when bright green, the bugs are then numbered by the billions; the hike is much more enjoyable in late summer and fall.

Besides a USGS map, a party **must carry** a Forest Service map, because the local signing system gives only trail numbers instead of place names, guaranteed to confuse and lose anyone who forgets his map.

Drive US 12 east from White Pass 8.3 miles. A few hundred feet before Indian Creek Campground, turn left on road No. 1410, signed "Bootjack Summer Homes." Drive .8 mile to a junction and keep left, still on road No. 1410; at 3 miles from the highway is the parking lot by the trailhead sign, Indian Creek trail No. 1105, elevation 3400 feet.

The first 2 miles of "trail" lie along a very rough mining road best walked. Just before the end of the road, find the start of true trail, which drops steeply 200 feet into a canyon, crosses Indian Creek, and climbs very steeply out of the canyon. At about 2½ miles listen for a waterfall; the canyon edge and a view of the lovely falls are just a few feet off the path, though one may have to try a couple spots before finding the only really good vantage point.

The trail crosses Indian Creek again at about 3 miles, recrosses at 4 miles, and at 4½ miles enters the large (⅓-mile-long) Indian Meadows. Stay on trail No. 1105, passing trail No. 1148 to Pear and Apple Lakes. The tread is faint as it traverses the meadow and heads west, but becomes distinct again beyond the grass. At 5 miles pass trail No. 1148 to Apple Lake, and at just under 6 miles take a short side-trail to the first of the three Blankenship Lakes, 5200 feet, a fair spot for a basecamp.

The first thing to do is explore the other two lakes, a stone's throw from each other. Next comes the ascent of 6340-foot Tumac Mountain, a small volcano rising over the lakes and offering superb views; two trails lead to the top from other sides (Hike 51)

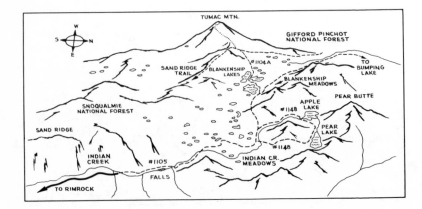

Blankenship Lake and Tumac Mountain

but a path really isn't needed. Follow trail No. 1104B between the lakes, climbing to its junction with the Sand Ridge trail. Continue uphill, offtrail, to the summit, avoiding soft cinder slopes.

Another ½ mile along trail No. 1105 are Blankenship Meadows—many little clearings and one huge expanse. As is true of many other meadows in this portion of the Cascades, young trees are invading the grass. There are strangely few flowers in the meadows, but beargrass and lupine grow in the woods, and bog orchids and elephantheads in wet places. (Blankenship Meadows can also be reached by a 4-mile hike from road No. 162, near Bumping Lake.)

A 2-mile side-trip to Pear and Apple Lakes is a must. This can be done as a one-way walk, going first to shallow Apple Lake on trail No. 1148, then continuing on the same trail to deep Pear Lake, and returning to the main route on trail No. 1148.

Good camps at Indian Meadows, Blankenship Lakes, and Pear Lake.

55 Devils Horns

Round trip to Tieton-Conrad divide 16 miles
Allow 3 days
High point 5800 feet
Elevation gain 1900 feet
Best mid-July through October
USGS White Pass (part only)

Round trip to trail's end under Devils Horns 24 miles
Allow 3 days minimum
High point 5800 feet
Elevation gain 1900 feet
Forest Service wilderness permit required

Miles and miles of alpine rambling, on and off the trail, in the ultimate meadows of the Goat Rocks Wilderness. The entry through horse country is long and can be hot and dusty, with 50-100 animals on the trail every summer weekend; the hoof-churned tread alternates between deep, choking powder and boot-sucking quagmire, and unless the wilderness ranger is on hand to control thoughtless riders, campsites often reek with horsedroppings. Once above timberline, however, the horses are mostly left behind and quickly forgotten in the magnificence.

Drive US 12 east from White Pass about 18 miles, considerably past Rimrock Lake, and turn right on South Fork Tieton road No. 143 heading back along the east side of the lake. Don't be confused by a campground road; drive 4½ miles from the highway and turn left on road No. 133, signed "Graycreek Campground." At all of the half-dozen subsequent junctions stay with 133. At 17 miles the road is gated at the edge of

A shoulder of Gilbert Peak

private property. Park here and find the trailhead (No. 1120) beyond the gate, elevation 3900 feet.

The first 1½ miles traverse some of the prettiest subalpine meadows in the state. They would be, that is, if not cow-cropped and cow-flopped.

At about 2 miles the way comes to a logged area and a private logging road. Turn left on it, cross the bridge over the South Fork Tieton River, following trail No. 1120 signs through a clearcut to a resumption of forest trail.

At about 2½ miles ford the now-small river and, at the end of the last logging, at 3 miles, enter the Goat Rocks Wilderness. At a little over 4 miles, 4200 feet, the trail for the last time crosses the Tieton River—now merely a jump wide—and starts climbing very steep and badly-eroded tread, gaining 700 feet in ¾ mile. The way moderates and in the next ¾ mile ascends 200 feet to Surprise Lake, 6 miles, 5300 feet.

The lake, surrounded by forest and with only a small view of snowy mountains, is the destination of most horsemen and all fishermen. Camping can be miserable if horses have been picketed in the few sites level enough for a tent. Nobody but a fanatic fisherman would walk so far on such poor trail simply to get to the lake.

The trail skirts the north shore and about ¼ mile beyond enters meadows; horses have churned the moist greenery into big gooey mud pies. The way traverses a lovely basin and climbs to the low point of a ridge at about 8 miles, 5800 feet. Here the horse trail climbs a few feet to the ridge crest and starts down. (This trail completes a loop, rejoining trail No. 1120 at the 4-mile ford. It is very steep, rough and dry—a better way to go out than in.) Hikers take an old abandoned trail which heads left into a vast, park-like meadowland, the headwaters of Conrad Creek, and the best alpine roaming in the Goat Rocks. For unexplained reasons, relatively few horses enter these meadows.

The views! Amid a semicircle of high summits, to the west rises 8201-foot Gilbert Peak. The big reddish-yellowish one to the northwest is Tieton Peak. Devils Horns is the lower, ragged peak with a topping of red rock. Farther northeast lies Bear Creek Mountain.

The abandoned trail strikes off toward Tieton Peak, going from one meadow to another. About ½ mile from the main trail is a somewhat difficult crossing of the fork of Conrad Creek coming from the Meade Glacier. At 2 miles is the crossing of another fork, milky from rock flour milled by Conrad Glacier. Beyond here the trail is easily lost, but little matter—the country is open, the going easy, and the trail likely will be picked up again—to finally peter out at 4 miles, about 5800 feet, under Devils Horns.

Explorations are unlimited. View the glaciers that feed Conrad Creek. Visit secluded basins on the east side of Gilbert Peak. Look for Warm Lake.

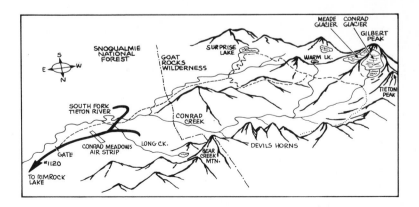

COWLITZ RIVER

56 Trails End (Purcell Mountain)

Round trip via Purcell Mountain trail 16 miles
Allow 2 days
High point 5442 feet
Elevation gain 4500 feet
Best July through November
USGS Randle

Round trip via lookout trail 7 miles
Hiking time 6 hours (unless maintained)
Elevation gain 2600 feet
Best mid-June through November
One day or backpack

A forest basin topped by 5442-foot Purcell Mountain, once the location of Trails End Lookout. Nothing left now but a pile of rubble, two heliports, and a panoramic view. The basin and peak are surrounded by logging activities and the Forest Service plans eventually to build a permanent road and log this basin too. Due to hikers' complaints, unstable soil, and a Sierra Club lawsuit, the road has not yet been built. However, permanently saving this hike will require a lot more letters to the forest supervisor.

Whalehead Ridge and Mt. St. Helens from Purcell Mountain

There are two approaches, the long Purcell Mountain trail which traverses the entire length of the basin, and the lookout trail climbing directly to the summit. Snow remains in the basin until the first of July, but the direct route can be hiked in mid-June with only a few snowpatches up high. The first 3½ miles of the Purcell Mountain trail, going along the south slopes of Prairie Mountain, are open to travel in early June.

Drive US 12 east from Randle toward Packwood. For the Purcell Mountain trail, at 5.6 miles turn left, then immediately right, and within 300 feet find the trailhead.

The trail starts from the valley bottom at an elevation of 920 feet and switchbacks upward in a 160-year-old stand of timber, gaining 2500 feet in 3 miles. The trees provide shade but the slope faces south and has no dependable water, so carry loaded canteens. At 3 miles the trail passes "The Gate"—a local landmark though the gate has been gone a long time—and makes a big switchback. The way is still up, but the views improve. At 3½ miles is a junction with a path to springs and open meadows, 4400 feet, under Cockscomb Mountain. Now the trail levels off, still in timber, ascending slightly under 5065-foot Prairie Mountain. At approximately 5 miles is Little Paradise, 4800 feet, a small meadow surrounded by tall trees; water and camps can be found a bit below the meadow.

What to do now? One choice is to wander the short distance up Prairie Mountain; all but the summit and steep south side are wooded. The other choice is to continue 3 more miles to the top of Purcell Mountain and the panoramas.

For the lookout trail, continue .3 mile past the Purcell Mountain trailhead, turn left on an unmarked paved road (the old highway), and in 1 mile turn left on road No. 1303. In a mile look over the side of the Davis Creek bridge into a spectacular canyon. At 4½ miles from the paved road (11½ miles from Randle) turn left on road No. 1303C and in ½ mile park at the end, elevation 2800 feet.

The trail follows an abandoned road. In 500 feet cross a collapsed bridge, turn right, recross the small creek on another collapsed bridge, and continue on the overgrown road about 500 feet to a trail sign. The trail, an abandoned skid road, zigzags almost to the top of the clearing and then enters forest with more zigzags. At 2½ miles the way reaches meadows and proceeds upward. At 3 miles, 5000 feet, just before the junction with the Purcell Mountain trail, is a possible camp. A final ½ mile climbs to the summit.

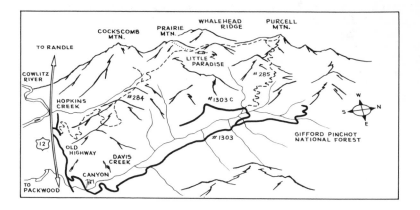

COWLITZ RIVER

57 Klickitat Trail

One-way trip 16 miles
Allow 2-3 days
High point 5400 feet
Elevation gain 4000 feet
Best mid-July through October
USGS Tower Rock, Steamboat Mountain

Tradition says this is part of the trail followed by the Klickitats on trading excursions from their homes east of the Cascades, climbing from the Klickitat River to Cispus Pass (Hike 63), then descending to Puget Sound country. Though there may have been easier valley-bottom paths, the trail probably has been in use for many centuries, white settlers picking up where the Indians left off. Today, the route offers one of the most lonesome walks in the state, winding along ridge crests for 17 miles, mostly in forest with occasional tantalizing glimpses of mountains and valleys, but offering marvelous views from high points (and clearcuts). Tread often is so faint one must pay close attention to stay on the track; the sense of remoteness is thus reinforced, and a feeling of kinship with the people who owned the land for thousands of years—or rather, in their ethic, were owned **by** the land.

But the white man has come, and though the trail is lonesome, seldom is it beyond sight or sound of logging. The way is paralleled by logging roads, cut once by a road (near Jackpot Lake), and hacked by several clearcuts. Only time will tell whether the Forest Service will adopt true multiple-use and preserve this rewarding trail, or strip off the trees and leave a wasteland of little interest to hikers.

To reach the west terminus of the trail, turn south in Randle, cross the Cowlitz River, and in 1 mile keep left on road No. 123. At 6 miles turn left on road No. 121 and in 15 miles (from Randle) turn left on road No. 1216B and in 1 mile find the trailhead on the left side of the road, elevation 4000 feet.

To reach the east terminus, drive State Highway 12 south from Packwood 2½ miles, turn east on Johnson Creek road No. 1302, and in 16 miles (from Packwood) find the trailhead opposite the junction of road No. 1302 and road No. 1104, elevation 4000 feet.

Signs at both ends call it "Klickitat Trail No. 7." By consulting a current Forest Service map, hikers can intersect the trail by climbing clearcuts from logging roads, but in doing so would lose a lot of the fun. The mileages and elevations given here are estimates; there are some mile markers along the route, but no indication where the counting starts.

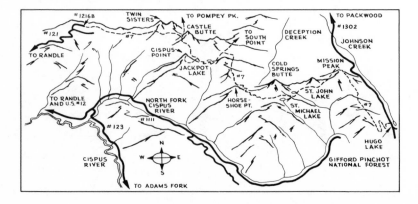

Mt. Rainier from Cispus Point

From the west terminus, the trail climbs 500 feet, follows the ridge top, and in a bit more than a mile drops steeply to a clearcut. Once beyond this, the way passes under 5805-foot Twin Sisters and at about 4 miles, 5200 feet, comes to a junction with the Pompey Peak trail.

The next 1½ miles are a glorious combination of alpine meadows and forest groves. Castle Butte towers above. At Cispus Point, 5½ miles, are campsites. An absolute must is the ½-mile side-trip to the site of the old lookout and wide views of Rainier, Adams, St. Helens, Hood, and ridge upon forested ridge.

Now the trail descends into timber, dropping almost 1000 feet to Jackpot Lake, 6 miles, 4500 feet, and another logging mess. A traverse near the top of a 5500-foot butte offers more views. At 8 miles the route drops into headwaters of Deception Creek, crosses clearcuts, and at 9 miles contours under Horseshoe Point and gradually ascends to a saddle below 5733-foot Cold Springs Butte. Along here the tread is particularly faint and appears unwalked in years. The short side-trip to the summit of the butte is well worth the effort.

The path drops through forest to campsites at St. Michael Lake, 10½ miles, 4700 feet, contours past tiny St. John Lake, climbs nearly over the top of 5683-foot Mission Mountain, and goes downward in trees, passing a junction with the Elk Peak trail at 15¾ miles and at 17 miles reaching the east terminus on road No. 1302.

COWLITZ RIVER

58 Packwood Lake

Round trip to Packwood Lake 9 miles
Hiking time 5 hours
High point 3100 feet
Elevation gain 400 feet, loss 300 feet
Best June through November
One day or backpack
USGS Packwood

Round trip to Lost Lake 18¼ miles
Allow 2 days
High point 5165 feet
Elevation gain 2300 feet
Best July through October

A tree-ringed lake on the edge of the Goat Rocks Wilderness. From the outlet, look up to 7487-foot Johnson Peak. From the inlet, look back to Mt. Rainier. A wooded island punctuates the picturesque waters.

Unfortunately, man has left his disastrous mark on this scenic treasure. Washington Public Power Supply System was allowed to dam the outlet to gain a small amount of "peaking" power and the Federal Power Commission mysteriously gave permission for the dam to be built 3 feet higher than specified in the agreement with the Forest Service. So far the power company has not been permitted to raise the lake above the natural level; if it ever is, the shore will be ruined.

Additionally, the trail was built so wide and flat and easy that every weekend the lake is overwhelmed by 200-300 people—little children, old folk, motorbikers, horsemen, all jumbled together. Near the outlet are a small resort and a few campsites—terribly overcrowded. To avoid standing room only, visit the lake on a weekday; otherwise, pause amid the crowds to enjoy the view, then hike onward to Lost Lake.

Thanks to an easy trail, the lake is heavily used by hikers and horses. Though motorcycles are forbidden on the trail, they race up and down the adjoining pipeline road.

From Packwood, next to the Packwood Ranger Station, drive east on road No. 1320, in 6 miles coming to a steel tower and, nearby, a large parking lot and the trailhead, elevation 2700 feet.

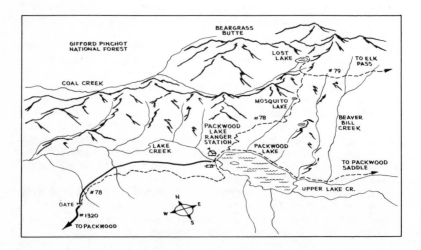

Trail No. 78 goes gently through big trees with occasional views over the Cowlitz valley toward Rainier, passing several springs in the first half—but the second half is dry, so carry water. As the lake is neared, the snowy, craggy Goat Rocks can be seen at the valley head. With ups and downs grossing 400 feet but netting a gain of only 100 feet, at 4¼ miles the trail reaches Packwood Lake, 2867 feet.

For less jammed-up camping, continue 4¾ miles to tiny Mosquito Lake, 4800 feet, or Lost Lake, 5165 feet, surrounded by alpine trees and flowery meadows.

Hikers seeking a special treat should try the Coyote Ridge trail, first climbing from Lost Lake, then contouring 7 airy miles along a 6700-foot ridge to the Pacific Crest Trail at Elk Pass (Hike 63). About half the distance is through steep mountain meadows high above timberline. The way is little traveled, very odd considering the superb scenery.

Packwood Lake and Johnson Peak

COWLITZ RIVER

59 Lily Basin-Heart Lake

Round trip to viewpoint 8 miles
Hiking time 5 hours
High point 5700 feet
Elevation gain 1300 feet
Best late July to mid-October
One day
USGS Packwood

Round trip to Heart Lake 13 miles
Hiking time 8 hours
High point 6100 feet
Elevation gain 1700 feet in, 400 out
Backpack

Hike a forest ridge to a spectacular view of Packwood Lake and Mt. Rainier, then contour Lily Basin, a high cirque under Johnson Peak, and continue to Heart Lake and views of Mt. Adams. Logging roads to 4500 feet have ripped up the wildland and taken most of the work out of visiting this once-remote corner of the Goat Rocks.

Drive US 12 from Packwood Ranger Station west toward Randle 1.6 miles, passing the Packwood Lumber Company, and approximately opposite a small power substation turn left on road No. 132. Follow it 9 miles and turn left on road No. 1323 another 1.2 miles to the trailhead, on the right side of the road. Park on a wide shoulder just beyond, elevation about 4400 feet.

The trail is signed "Lily Basin Trail No. 86." Climbing through timber to an old burn, at ½ mile the way enters Goat Rocks Wilderness and at 1½ miles reaches the crest of a wooded ridge, 4900 feet. The path follows ups and downs of the crest, more ups than downs, occasionally contouring around a bump. At 4 miles, 5700 feet, begin heather and flower meadows with a spectacular view of Packwood Lake and Rainier. At 4½ miles the trail dips under cliffs and regains the ridge top, following to its very end at Johnson Peak.

Now a mile-long contour around the head of Lily Basin leads over several creeks (the first water of the trip) and a large rockslide. At 6 miles, 6100 feet, the path tops a ridge with magnificent views of Mt. Adams. Here, joined by the Angry Mountain trail, it contours a steep slope and drops to Heart Lake, 5700 feet, 6½ miles, the first logical campsite.

The trip can be extended—trail No. 86 continues to Jordan Basin, Goat Lake, and Snowgrass Flat (Hike 61).

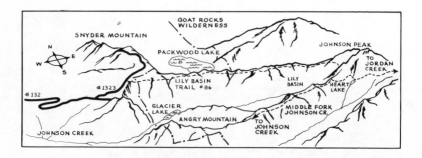

Packwood Lake and Mt. Rainier

Tatoosh Lake and Mt. Rainier

COWLITZ RIVER

60 Tatoosh Ridge

Round trip to viewpoint 6 miles
Hiking time 4 hours
High point 5400 feet
Elevation gain 2600 feet
Best July through September
One day; possible camping at lake
USGS Packwood

A long ridge with flower meadows and a beautiful lake lies under the dominance of Mt. Rainier, giving views not only of The Mountain but the backside of the Tatoosh Range, whose peaks are familiar as seen from Paradise but except for Pinnacle are difficult to recognize from here. On the highest point is the site of the Tatoosh Lookout made famous in the 1940s by Martha Hardy's bestselling book, **Tatoosh**, the story of her years as a fire lookout. "Belonging" to Rainier National Park but outside the boundaries, the ridge has been proposed for addition to the Park by both the Forest and Park Services, but to date nothing has been done about it.

The trail covers the full length of the ridge, starting in the south near Packwood and ending in the north on a logging road near the Park boundary. If transportation can be arranged, the entire distance can be done on one trip. It is described here from a north-end start because that way has 1000 feet less elevation gain.

From Packwood Ranger Station at the north end of Packwood, drive west on Skate Creek road No. 152. In ½ mile cross the Cowlitz River. (To start on the south end of the ridge, cross the bridge and turn left on Cannon road which eventually becomes road No. 1412. Follow this upriver 9 miles and turn right on road No. 1412A for 1.2 miles to the trailhead.) Continue on Skate Creek road 4 miles from the ranger station (sign says 3), turn north on road No. 1411, and drive 5.8 miles to a junction, and there continue ahead on No. 1411B for 1.5 miles to the trailhead, elevation 2800 feet.

Trail No. 161 sets off at a steep grade, gaining about 1800 feet in 2 miles, climbing from Douglas fir forest to Alaska cedar and mountain hemlock. At about 2½ miles begin steep alpine meadows, covered in season with colorful blossoms. The trail makes three short switchbacks up a small stream, the only water on the main route—and maybe none here late in summer. Shortly beyond is an unmarked junction. Proceed straight ahead but keep the junction in mind for later reference. Tread may be lost in lush greenery and soft pumice; just keep going and eventually gain a ridge shoulder, 5400 feet, and a spectacular view of Mt. Adams, St. Helens, and the Cowlitz valley. To the north Mt. Rainier looks down like a benevolent old lady, very fat.

After soaking up views, there are things to do, more to see. For one, continue on the trail another 1½ miles and find the mile-long spur trail climbing to the Tatoosh Lookout site at 6310 feet, highest point on the ridge outside the park. Second, retrace steps to that unmarked junction and follow an old trail to the park boundary. Or, if experienced in wildland navigation and possessed of the USGS map, try to find Tatoosh Lakes, a small one and a large one, both frozen most of the year. The lakes are on the east side of Tatoosh Ridge. From the aforementioned junction an unmarked trail of sorts switchbacks up, crosses a 5500-foot saddle, and drops to the lakes near the outlet. But the trail can be hard to follow and cliffs make cross-country travel tricky.

There is a new urgency in including this ridge in the sanctuary of a national park. Starting in 1977, the Forest Service has been allowing cattle to graze the lush flower fields. In addition to trampling and killing some of the more fragile flowers, the cattle are causing serious erosion problems in the soft soil.

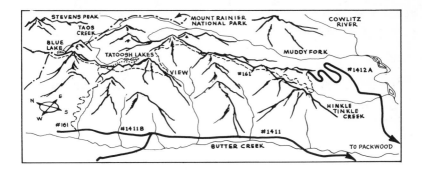

Mt. Adams and Pacific Crest Trail near Snowgrass Flat

CISPUS RIVER

61 Snowgrass Flat

Round trip to Snowgrass Flat 8 miles
Hiking time 5 hours
High point 5700 feet
Elevation gain 1100 feet
Best July through November
One day or backpack
USGS none
Forest Service wilderness permit required

One of the most famous meadows in the Cascades, a riot of color during flower season. But when the flowers are gone the vast parklands higher up, with views of Adams, St. Helens, and of course, the Goat Rocks, still make the trip a genuine spectacular.

Drive US 12 south from Packwood 2.5 miles and turn east on Johnson Creek road No. 1302. At 15.7 miles turn left on road No. 1104 and at 18.5 miles keep right on road

No. 1118, in 19 miles from Packwood coming to Berry Patch and the trailhead, elevation 4600 feet.

Set out in the woods on Snowgrass Flat trail No. 96A, contouring the slopes of Goat Ridge to a junction with trail No. 96 and then a crossing of Goat Creek, 4700 feet. Especially in early summer, stop at the bridge to apply insect repellent, lots of it, because from here the trail passes for ¼ mile through marshy forest where one may expect heavy attack by swarms of mosquitoes.

At 2 miles the trail begins climbing from the valley bottom, leaving behind the hordes of hungry bugs. At Bypass Camp, 3½ miles, cross Snowgrass Creek and continue up, emerging occasionally from trees into small meadows, and at 4 miles finally entering the open expanse of Snowgrass Flat, 5700 feet.

Because of overgrazing by horses and punishment by heavy foot traffic, and to give nature a chance to repair the damage, camping is no longer permitted in the Flat; however, Bypass Camp is only minutes below and makes a fine base for exploratory walks. From the Flat take either of two trails, northward or eastward (the latter unmarked), and hike another ½ mile and about 400 feet higher to join the Pacific Crest Trail. Campsites in the meadows here offer wide views, including all three southern volcanoes.

What to do now? For one choice, hike 2 miles south on the Crest Trail into the vast meadows of Cispus Basin and take the unmarked old path ¼ mile to Cispus Pass, 6473 feet, and superb views down the Klickitat River and out to 8201-foot Gilbert Peak.

Alternatively, hike the Crest Trail north to its 7600-foot high point on the side of Old Snowy (Hike 63). Or, for a loop trip back to Berry Patch, total distance 13 miles, traverse to 6500-foot Goat Lake (sitting in a cold cirque and frozen most of most summers) and return by way of Goat Ridge.

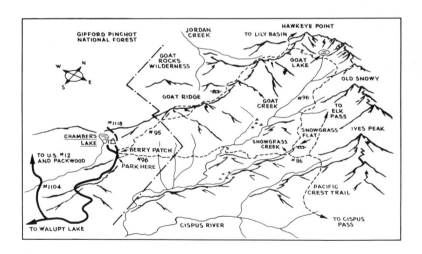

CISPUS RIVER

62 Nannie Ridge

Round trip to Nannie Peak 7 miles
Hiking time 4½ hours
High point 5800 feet
Elevation gain 1800 feet
Best July to October
One day
USGS none

Round trip to Sheep Lake 12 miles
Hiking time 8 hours
High point 5700 feet
Elevation gain 2300 feet
Best late July through September
One day or backpack
USGS none
Forest Service wilderness permit required

A long hike through meadowland to a small lake, then on to views into the head of the Klickitat River and up to the rugged pinnacles of 8201-foot Gilbert Peak, highest in the Goat Rocks; or an easy day hike to Nannie Peak, overlooking meadows and summits of the Goat Rocks.

Drive US 12 south from Packwood 2.5 miles and turn east on Johnson Creek road No. 1302. At 18.5 miles (from Packwood) turn left on road No. 1114. At 20.5 miles the good logging road turns off and the very rough and dusty recreation road (still No. 1114) continues to Walupt Lake at 24 miles, elevation 3927 feet. Find the trailhead in the Walupt Lake Picnic Area.

Start on trail No. 101 and in a few yards turn left on Nannie Ridge trail No. 98 and begin to climb. The first 1½ miles are through timber, passing two small streams—the last water for 3 miles. At about 2 miles the trees thin out; the next mile is miserably rutted. At about 3 miles the way tops a 5600-foot ridge. On the very crest an unmarked, unmaintained, but quite decent trail climbs in ½ mile to Nannie Peak, 5800 feet, site of a former lookout. The summit is a ¼-mile ridge of heather, grass, alpine trees, and rocks. Be sure to explore the full length—from the south end are views of Adams and St. Helens and from the north end views of Gilbert Peak and vast meadows.

Those who choose the longer trip now must lose a discouraging 300 feet as the main trail drops under cliffs. At 3½ miles is a pond (which may dry up in late summer)

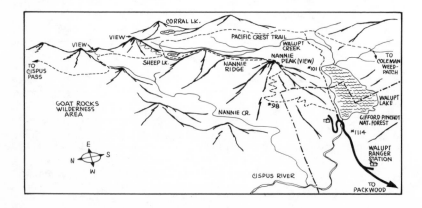

Sheep Lake and Mt. Adams

and another trail, also unmarked, switchbacking to the summit of Nannie Peak. A short bit beyond the pond look down on a small lake, about 500 feet below the trail, a tempting place to camp. After passing below more cliffs of Nannie, the way regains the ridge and meadow country and follows ups and downs of the crest to lovely little Sheep Lake, 5¾ miles, 5600 feet, surrounded by grass and flowers, an ideal camp. The best sites are on the ridge to the west beside a row of protecting trees. Walk around the shore for views of Adams and St. Helens.

A visit to a viewpoint above the Klickitat River is mandatory. There are two choices. For one, hike the ridge almost directly north a long mile to its summit at about 6200 feet. The other alternative is the pass at the head of Nannie Creek and Cispus Pass. For this follow the ridge trail a short ¼ mile to an intersection with the Pacific Crest Trail and go left and north on the Crest Trail, contouring around the 6200-foot ridge to where the Crest Trail crosses into the Klickitat drainage and the Yakima Indian Reservation; there are some steep ups and downs but the walking is pleasant. For a return follow the Crest Trail south and take trail No. 101 back to the starting point.

Gilbert Peak from the Pacific Crest Trail

CISPUS RIVER

63 Goat Rocks Crest

One-way trip 30 miles
Allow 3-4 days
High point 7600 feet
Elevation gain 5300 feet
Best July through September
USGS White Pass
Forest Service wilderness permit required

Walk between heaven and earth through a rock garden along a narrow, 7000-foot ridge dividing Eastern and Western Washington. This spectacular section of the Pacific Crest Trail is popular with horseriders, so try it in the first half of July, when the tread is free enough of snow for safe hiking but not yet passable to horses; tiny alpine flowers are then in bloom, too. The climax portion can be done as a round trip of about 8 miles from Snowgrass Flat (Hike 61), but the route is described here in its full length from White Pass to Walupt Lake.

Drive to White Pass, elevation 4400 feet, and hike 7 miles south on the Pacific Crest Trail to Shoe Lake (Hike 53).

From Shoe Lake the trail crosses a low ridge and drops 900 feet into timber offering an occasional view out, then ascends and contours to Tieton Pass, 12 miles, and a junction with the North Fork Tieton River trail. Going only slightly up and down, the way swings first along west side of the crest, then the east, above McCall Basin, 14 miles, 5200 feet. (**Note:** Construction is in progress on a new Pacific Crest Trail route from McCall Basin to Yelverton shelter. When complete, the present trail will be maintained for hikers only.) Now the route is up, some of it very steeply up, climbing 2 long miles to Elk Pass, 6600 feet. One great compensation for the energy output is that the entire way is in open country with views of Mt. Rainier and miles of meadow-land on the slopes of Coyote Ridge to the west. The last campsites for 3½ miles are in flat meadows before the final drag to the pass, at which is a junction with the Coyote Ridge trail (Hike 58).

Views broaden at the pass—down to Packwood Lake and across the immense depth of Lake Creek to rugged Johnson Peak. The trail follows the ridge several hundred feet higher and then descends. From here one senses the quality of the route ahead. The tread can be seen—blasted out of cliffs, gouged in scree slopes; in some places the crest of the ridge has actually been leveled off to give walking room.

The next 2 miles are mostly above 7000 feet, the highest Washington section of the Crest Trail, and also the most dangerous. Meeting a horse party is bad business, because the horses cannot be turned around and thus hikers must backtrack to a safe turnout. Snowstorms can be expected in any month. Two parties of recent years have lost a member from hypothermia (exposure) and there have been several narrow escapes. Don't attempt this section in poor weather.

The trail first contours and climbs to a 7100-foot point with a view of weird-shaped towers and small glaciers on 8201-foot Gilbert Peak, highest in the Goat Rocks. There is also a fine view of Old Snowy, 7930 feet. Nooks and crannies hold the superb rock gardens, which are in full bloom during early July.

The way now follows ups and downs of the narrow crest, sometimes on the exact top and other times swinging around small knobs. From a spot a little beyond the lowest portion, it is possible to avoid a climb by contouring across the Packwood Glacier and rejoining the trail where several signs can be seen in a saddle on the skyline. The glacier crossing is easy in July, but by late August may involve hard ice; the best plan is to stay with the trail on its ascent to the highest elevation at 7600 feet on Old Snowy, a short side-trip away from the 7930-foot summit.

The trail now descends. At 6900 feet is a sturdy rock shelter built by the Bellevue Presbyterian Church in memory of Dana May Yelverton, who died of exposure on the crest August 4, 1962.

From the cabin the path drops into parkland, at 21 miles intersecting the Snowgrass Flat trail (Hike 61), then contouring into the glory of Cispus Basin. The route continues in meadows to the Nannie Ridge trail at 24 miles, and then by this trail 6 miles to Walupt Lake, as described in Hike 62.

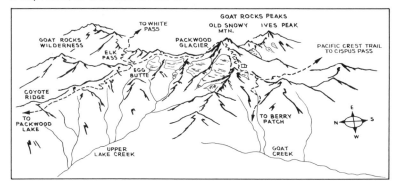

CISPUS RIVER

64 Adams Glacier Meadows

Round trip 11 miles
Hiking time 7 hours
High point 6900 feet
Elevation gain 2300 feet
Best mid-July through mid-October
One day or backpack
USGS Green Mtn.; Mt. Adams West
Forest Service wilderness permit required

Parklands, meadows, waterfalls, and moraines, close views of lava cliffs, cinder cones, and glaciers, distant views of St. Helens and Rainier, all this and more in a paradise for wandering high on the slopes of Mt. Adams. The hike leads to a magnificent alpine camp used by summit climbers, a place variously called Mountaineer Camp, Adams Glacier Camp, or High Camp. Snow still covers some of the meadows in early July, but tiny alpine flowers are then blooming in the highest gardens and beargrass down lower. Later in the summer more of the meadows are open for roaming and the country is superb in every month on through autumn.

Drive south, then east from Randle 32 miles on road No. 123 and turn left on road No. 101, a narrow and dusty track that must be traveled with care. In 2 miles from the junction pass Taklakh Lake and at 5.7 miles (37.7 miles from Randle) find the parking area and trailhead, elevation 4600 feet.

Killen Creek trail No. 113 ascends toward the mountain in subalpine forest on a wide ridge. Occasionally the crest steepens and the path does likewise. At about 3 miles, 5800 feet, the way enters meadowland with the first dependable creek and remains of an old cabin. The camping here, just inside the Mt. Adams Wilderness, is wonderful, but there is better to come. In 3½ miles cross abandoned tread of the Pacific Crest Trail; a short bit farther is a reflecting pond and a junction with the new Crest Trail, elevation 6100 feet.

Beyond the junction the trail continues upward sometimes in alpine trees, sometimes in grassy meadows dotted in season by paintbrush, hellebore, and avalanche lilies, generally following slopes of a prominent ridge trending toward the peak. The tread soon becomes faint and in ½ mile one may be tempted by the wide-open terrain to forget the sketchy path and roam at will. Do so if desired, but be sure to take careful visual "fixes" on landmarks so the trail can be found again on the way out—from up high one ridge looks like the next and it's easy to get confused.

At 5½ miles the trail ends at High Camp, 6900 feet, near a saddle in the main ridge and not far above the green flats and meandering streams of Adams Glacier

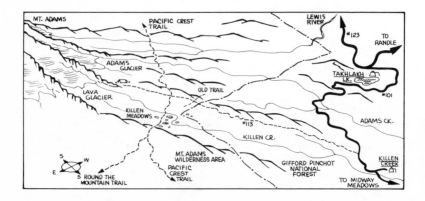

Mt. Adams and meadow

Meadows. The camp area lies along a snowmelt stream bubbling through gardens decorated with lava boulders and wind-sculpted clumps of trees. And the views! St. Helens, Rainier, and the Goat Rocks rise above forests and ridges of the Cispus River. Look north into the crater of Potato Hill, an old cinder cone, and out over ancient lava flows covered by scrubby trees. Especially look up to steep ice of the Adams Glacier cascading from the summit. Sunsets from this camp are beyond words—and also the dawns.

Spend a day or weekend or longer. Follow a waterfall down to the delights of Glacier Meadows. Follow the ridge up past lava cliffs, waterfalls, meadows, moraines to the edge of the Adams Glacier. Climb higher onto the crest of the northwest ridge of Adams and look down to the Lava Glacier, and look up to the summit of the great volcano and out to far horizons.

Much of the way back to the road the trail points straight at Rainier, some compensation for having to leave these heavenly meadows.

CISPUS RIVER

65 Juniper Mountain

Round trip to Juniper Peak 8 miles
Hiking time 5 hours
High point 5593 feet
Elevation gain 2000 feet
Best mid-June through November
One day
USGS McCoy Peak

Round trip to Boundary Trail 26 miles
Allow 3 days
High point about 5788 feet
Elevation gain 2300 feet, plus ups and
**   downs**
Best July through October

Dramatic views up the Cispus River to Mt. Adams, out to Mt. Rainier and Mt. St. Helens, and over endless forested hills and valleys—all while walking a long ridge, sometimes on open hillsides covered with huckleberries, sometimes in second growth timber just getting established after the tremendous Cispus fires of 1902 and 1929. The route provides a variety of trips: an easy afternoon stroll to a 4500-foot

Beargrass on Juniper Peak, Mt. Adams in distance

saddle (the trail this far generally is free of snow in early or mid-June); a day hike to Juniper Mountain; an overnight backpack; or a long approach to the Boundary Trail (Hike 66). Sorry to say, cattle graze the ridge, eating most of the flowers; also, the east side is being logged all the way up to the 5000-foot timberline.

Turn south in Randle, cross the Cowlitz River, and drive 1 mile. Turn left on road No. 123 and in 9 miles (from Randle) turn right on road No. 112. At 10 miles leave pavement and keep straight ahead on road No. 111. In 14 miles turn left on road No. 1106 and at 18 miles find the trailhead, elevation about 3500 feet.

The trail goes a few hundred feet through a clearcut, enters second-growth forest, and climbs under two prominent knolls, ascending steadily, with frequent views, 2¼ miles to a 4500-foot saddle. The trail continues climbing, gaining 1100 feet to within a few feet of the top of 5593-foot Juniper Peak (4 miles, a good turnaround for day hikers), then, dropping about 400 feet, goes under cliffs. At 5½ miles is a super-great huckleberry patch—outstanding even in an area famous for huckleberries. At 5¾ miles pass a tiny lake and campsites; the water is drinkable in early summer but later becomes murky.

At 7 miles is the Sunrise Peak trail, a ¼-mile side-trip up a steep stairway with handrails to the 5880-foot site of a former lookout; by the junction are a waterhole and a fair camp. At 7¾ miles, on a big saddle in the ridge, is Old Cow Camp with water and scenic camping. The trail again drops several hundred feet and passes under cliffs of 5788-foot Jumbo Peak, 9 miles, then descends to Dark Meadows, 12 miles, 4300 feet, offering plenty of water and campsites. From here a trail drops 3½ miles to road No. 123; a new logging road soon will shorten the distance to about 1½ miles.

From Dark Meadows the trail proceeds ¾ mile to good campsites in a large basin and in ¼ mile more reaches the Boundary Trail at a point 2 miles from the road at McCoy Pass.

Note the many sawn stumps along the ridge to Juniper. These are not from logging operations, but from the cutting of old snags, which make prominent targets for lightning strikes and then may flame like torches, sending sparks for long distances. Probably the snags were felled in the 1930s.

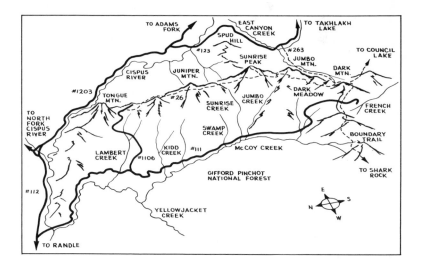

CISPUS RIVER

66 Boundary Trail

One-way trip 45½ miles
Allow 4-6 days
High point 5000 feet
Elevation gain about 4700 feet
Best July through October
USGS Spirit Lake, French Butte, McCoy
   Peak, and Steamboat Mountain

A ridge trip that eventually will start at Mt. Adams, follow the crest of the Lewis River-Cispus River watershed (the boundary between the Lewis and Randle Ranger Districts, and thus the name), and finish at Mt. St. Helens. Currently, part of the way near Adams lies along roads, but 41 miles are complete. At six places roads cut the route, which therefore can be traveled in small sections if desired. For a good sample of the country, hike from McCoy Creek to Elk Pass.

The trail seldom drops below 4000 feet and just as seldom climbs above 5000 feet, mostly going through forest with frequent views. Parts are snow-free in mid-June but some steep north slopes hold dangerous snow patches several weeks later, so those intending to do the whole trip should wait until early July.

The hike can be taken in either direction, depending on whether one prefers to watch Adams or St. Helens grow larger and the other smaller. The east-to-west direction is described here.

Turn south in Randle, cross the Cowlitz River, and drive 1 mile. Turn left 33 miles on road No. 123 to Council Lake, 4200 feet, and find the head of trail No. 1. (Some trail, somewhere, had to be No. 1!)

The way starts with a steep climb up the abandoned Council Bluff road, then gradually drops to a stream crossing at 4½ miles and again goes up. At 6¾ miles round Table Mountain, at 8½ miles pass Prairie Mountain and a good camp, climb a few hundred feet, and drop to campsites at Dark Meadows. Climb again to a 4000-foot saddle at 12 miles and descend to McCoy Creek road No. 111, 14½ miles, 3800 feet. At 15½ miles are more camps in a basin south of the trail, which then rises steadily to 16½ miles. A bit beyond, keep left on new tread ascending to a 4800-foot viewpoint, 17 miles, then skirting below impressive cliffs of Hat Rock while dropping to 4000-foot Yellowjacket Pass; campsites here a few feet to the south.

At 21½ miles pass under 4800-foot Craggy Peak, next under Shark Rock, and with little change in elevation contour slopes of 5659-foot Badger Peak to Badger Lake,

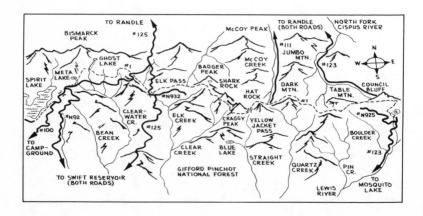

152

Mt. Adams from side of Hat Mountain

25½ miles; numerous good camps. At 30½ miles cross Randle-Lewis River road No. 125 at Elk Pass, 3900 feet. The trail enters timber but soon emerges into a clearcut and follows a spur road ¼ mile before reverting to footpath and trees. At 33½ miles the route again strikes a road and goes along it almost 2 miles, partly on forest road and partly on a jeep track, crossing a stream at 34½ miles and at 35½ miles intersecting Spirit Lake road No. 100 and traversing a large clearcut. At 36½ miles re-enter forest; the tread here is cut into soft pumice—easy on the feet but slow walking, like mushy snow. At 37 miles pass three small streams (but no possible camps) and at 38 miles reach a ridge. There switchback up a slope burned in 1961, and at 39½ miles cross road No. 100 and pass an undeveloped path to Ghost Lake, a ½-mile side-trip. At 40 miles top the ridge and start down into Green River drainage, at 41½ miles reaching Meta Lake, 3600 feet, and campsites. At 42½ miles reach Independence Pass, 4000 feet, from which the trail drops to Spirit Lake, 3188 feet, 44½ miles. Walk the lakeshore trail 1 mile to Duck Bay boat launching area and the road.

SKYKOMISH RIVER

67 Deception Creek

Round trip to Deception Pass 20½ miles
Allow 2-3 days
High point 4500 feet
Elevation gain 3400 feet in, 900 feet out
Best July through October
USGS Scenic and Mt. Daniel
Round trip from road No. 2605 to Deception Lakes
9½ miles
Elevation gain 2900 feet in, 600 feet out

There is no deception about Deception Creek except to those who believe river routes are always the easiest type. The trail gains and loses elevation constantly, and nears the creek only to cross to the far side — which it does four times in less than 6 miles. The maddening ups and downs and the tricky footlogs and all-summer mud may be discouraging; however, the valley offers the fullest and finest experience of virgin forest and wild water remaining in this portion of the Cascades.

Hikers may still enjoy the difficult valley trail. However, "multiple use" has removed the challenge. The Forest Service has built a logging road that allows a party to bypass the first 5 miles of the creek trail and quickly enlarge the mob already crowding Deception Lakes.

Drive US 2 east from Skykomish 7.8 miles to Deception Falls Picnic Area and to a road signed "Deception Creek Trail." Turn right ½ mile on the powerline service road to the trailhead, elevation 2000 feet.

For the shorter route, follow directions for Tonga Ridge (Hike 3). Drive road No. 2605 11 miles beyond the Tonga Ridge trail turnoff to where the road intersects trail No. 1058. The trail drops 600 feet in ¾ mile to join the Deception Creek trail near the 5-mile mark.

The hike begins with a down and a short but steep up, then levels off for ½ mile to a footlog crossing of Deception Creek. Now the way climbs above the stream and sidehills up and down through forest. At approximately 2 miles is a crossing of Sawyer Creek; the footlog is a lot higher in the air than the many others on the route; the creek rushes from a waterfall overhung with bushes and trees and gurgles over stones beneath.

At 3 miles Deception Creek is recrossed on a log. A nice campsite here. The stream is close for the next ½ mile to the third footlog crossing of Deception Creek. After more ups and downs, at 5 miles is the junction with the trail from Sawyer Pass (Hike 3, and see note below). A bit farther is another good camp and in ¼ mile the trail crosses Deception Creek the fourth time, elevation 3200 feet. By now there are occasional views of Mt. Daniel at the valley head.

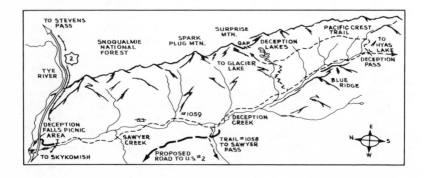

Trail crossing Deception Creek

From this crossing the trail continues briefly in the valley bottom and then quits messing around and starts UP — climbing steeply from the stream, gaining 1200 feet to the Deception Lakes trail junction, 7 miles from the road, 4400 feet.

Here the hiker has a choice. He can stay on the Deception Creek trail, which drops 500 feet back to the creek and then climbs to 4500-foot Deception Pass, 10¼ miles from the road, and a junction with the Pacific Crest Trail; this low route winds through a string of subalpine meadows offering flowers and glimpses of peaks. Or, he can detour to Deception Lakes, climbing 700 feet in 1¼ miles, and follow the Pacific Crest Trail from there to Deception Pass; this route contours high on ridges with larger views of mountains and of Lake Clarice across the valley.

For multiday trips, Deception Creek can be combined with Tonga Ridge (Hike 3), Surprise Lakes (Hike 6), or Marmot and Hyas Lakes (Hike 36).

Lake Josephine

SKYKOMISH RIVER

68 Lake Josephine

Round trip to Lake Josephine 9 miles
Hiking time 7 hours
High point 5500 feet
Elevation gain 1600 feet in, 850 feet out
Best mid-July through October
One day or backpack
USGS Stevens Pass

Roam fields of heather and blueberries on the Pacific Crest Trail. Linger at small lakes and large. Enjoy alpine trees and flowers and talus and streams and views over deep valleys. However, the trip is not all pure pleasure: the trail is partly obscured by ski slopes and the clearcut swaths of power transmission lines.

Drive US 2 to Stevens Pass. On the south side of the highway find a dirt road just east of the Forest Service guard station and drive 500 feet to a parking lot hidden from the road, elevation 4100 feet. Pick up the Pacific Crest Trail on the far side of the parking lot and follow it through the ski area.

Past the ski slopes the way ascends steadily in trees and rockslides to Tye Mill Pass at 1 mile, 5100 feet, and then descends the east side 100 feet to the powerline clearcut and a service road. (A somewhat shorter approach can be made by driving the Mill

Creek road, which takes off from US 2 at 3 miles east of Stevens Pass, and hiking up the steep powerline maintenance road to intersect the Crest Trail.)

Cross the road, watching for trail markers leading away from the road into a traverse through bits of forest, patches of well-watered meadow, and open talus with views out Mill Creek to Nason Creek valley and Nason Ridge.

At 3 miles is 4595-foot Lake Susan Jane, a picturesque tarn (good camps) bounded by forest on one side and steep mountainside on the other.

From here shift into low gear and gain 400 feet to heather-and-berry meadows. Traverse gardens to the edge of a cliff and a 5000-foot junction, 3½ miles, with the Icicle Creek trail. Look down to the rock-and-forest cirque of Lake Josephine, 4681 feet, and beyond to the Stuart Range. Take the Icicle Creek trail and descend gently around the basin 350 feet to the lake and campsites near the outlet, 4½ miles from Stevens Pass.

The blue, sparkling lake is appealing, but so too are the high wanders. Before dropping to the shores, ascend heather slopes southwest to the 5500-foot ridge and long views. Or find the two small tarns in the meadow a few hundred feet west of the junction. Or follow the Crest Trail a mile from the junction to a view of Swimming Deer Lake.

If pickup transportation can be arranged, a one-way hike can be made south on the Crest Trail to Surprise Lake (Hike 6), exiting at Scenic on US 2.

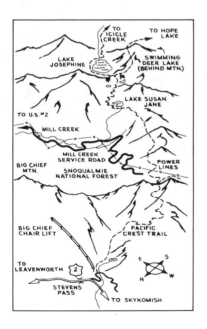

157

Cultus Lake and Lemei Rock

TROUT LAKE

69 Indian Heaven

Short loop trip 10 miles
Hiking time 6 hours
High point 5237 feet
Elevation gain about 1700 feet
Best July through October
One day or backpack
USGS Lone Butte and Wind River

A fascinating portion of the Pacific Crest Trail, with 17 lakes big enough to have names, 6 more on a short side-trail, and almost 100 smaller lakes, ponds, and tadpole pools, all in an area of around 5000 feet elevation, a mixture of forest, groves of alpine trees, and flat, grassy meadows, the foregrounds complemented by occasional glimpses of glaciered volcanoes. The Forest Service is comtemplating designating the country from Red Mountain to the Berryfields as a wilderness area.

The region can be sampled by taking a one-day, 10-mile loop hike (described here), an overnight 18-mile loop, or by spending several days in order to include a visit to the Indian Race Track, where the rut made by racing horses still indents a meadow used for centuries as a tribal gathering place. The lakes melt free of snow early in July, but since Indian Heaven has been appropriately called "Mosquito Heaven," the trip is recommended for late August or September when the bugs are gone, and incidentally, the blueberries are ripe.

The starting point is Cultus Creek Campground, elevation 3988 feet. To get there from Trout Lake, drive north 16 miles on road No. 123. To get there from Randle, drive south 33 miles on road No. 123, turn left on road No. N84, to N85 to N852 to N88. Follow signs first to Trout Lake, then Trout Lake Creek Camp, then Berryfields, and at 48 miles from Randle rejoin road No. 123, reaching the campground in 61 miles. (Mileages given here may not be accurate; the signs do not always agree.) The trailhead is in the back of a charge camp with no provision for hikers' cars, so park either at the guard station or the woodshed, making sure to leave the Forest Service access to its buildings.

Whatever the chosen trip, start on trail No. 33, thus avoiding a very steep and hot ascent of 1200 feet on trail No. 108, which is better used for the return leg of the loop.

Trail No. 33 begins in forest, climbing 600 feet in the first mile. At 1¾ mile make the short side-trip on trail 33A to Deep Lake with a view of Mt. Adams rising over tree tops, then on to Cultus Lake at 2 miles, 5050 feet, a body of water typical of many of the lakes, having trees around half the shore, meadows around the rest. To the southeast is 5925-foot Lemei Rock, and the northwest, 5706-foot Bird Mountain; one or the other of these peaks can be seen from a number of the lakes. The way climbs 100 more feet, then descends in ½ mile to meet Lemei Lake trail No. 179. Keep right, staying on trail No. 33; in ½ mile pass within a few yards of Clear Lake, coming to Bear Lake at 4 miles. Cross the outlet (no problem) to join the Crest Trail on the far side, the return route for the longer loop. Head north on the Crest Trail, passing Deer Lake and numerous ponds. At about 7½ miles turn right on trail No. 108, climb 100 feet over a 5237-foot saddle in Bird Mountain, and drop steeply 1½ miles to Cultus Creek Campground.

Don't be fooled by the seemingly-flat terrain—the paths have many short ups and downs. Campsites are numerous, some by lakes and others by streams. The pumice soil is very fragile, so camp in the forest or in already established campsites. The lakes and streams have a very small flow of water so to avoid contamination keep camps far away from the water's edge.

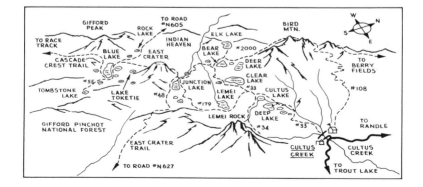

70 Mount Adams Highline Trail

One-way trip to trail-end 25 miles
Allow 3 days
High point 7000 feet
Elevation gain approximately 3000 feet
Best mid-July through September
USGS Mt. Adams (East and West);
      Green Mtn.; Glaciate Butte

The classic trek of the Mt. Adams region, hiking a timberline route with ever-changing views of the huge, glacier-draped volcano, standing 12,326 feet high in the sky.

The missing link for a complete around-the-mountain loop is a 12- to 15-mile section in the Yakima Indian Reservation between Avalanche Camp and Ridge of Wonders. There is no trail and two glacier streams are serious problems, during July and August being raging torrents. Don't bother to look for logs—there aren't any. The only hope of crossing them is in early fall when melting has slackened and before heavy rains start. Hikers contemplating this section would do best to start at Bench Lake and learn the first day if the streams can be negotiated. Coming the other way, with time and food running short, one might be tempted to risk a dangerous ford on the last day of a hike.

From State Highway 141 at Trout Lake, drive north on the paved logging road No. FH17, signed "Mt. Adams Recreation Area." In 1½ miles keep right and follow road No. N700 signed "Bird Creek Meadows." At 5 miles pavement yields to gravel. At 11 miles the excellent logging road veers left; follow, instead, recreation road No. N80, which is extremely poor the rest of the way to Bird Creek Meadows, 17 miles, elevation 6500 feet.

The Mount Adams Highline Trail starts on trail No. 9, traverses 3 easy miles of glorious views and flower fields to the Timberline Camp road, 6300 feet, and contours on. At about 8¾ miles cross Salt Creek; the water tastes fine but crusted vegetation along with the banks testifies to the mineral content. The way climbs gently and at 9 miles, 6500 feet, joins the Pacific Crest Trail. To this point campsites, some with broad views, are numerous, but for the next 6 miles good drinking water may be hard

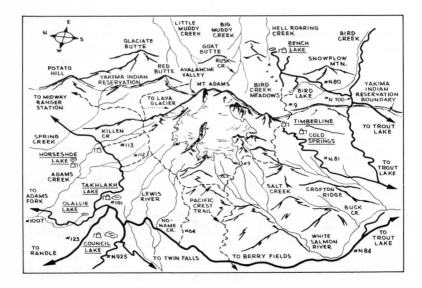

Camping near Foggy Bottom, Mt. Rainier in distance

to find—the streams flow from glaciers and tend to be excessively thick with rock milk; camping is possible, however, if one can tolerate the silt.

The Crest Trail swings under Pinnacle and Adams Glaciers. At 16 miles is a junction with trail No. 112, 3 miles distant from road No. 101. At about 18 miles, 6100 feet, is a junction with Killen Creek trail No. 113 (Hike 64), 3½ miles from road No. 101. At 18½ miles cross Killen Creek; campsites here.

At 1 mile from the junction with Killen Creek trail (¼ mile after crossing Killen Creek) turn right on trail No. 114, signed "Highline Trail." Follow 114 approximately 2 up-and-down miles to Foggy Bottom, a lovely meadow traversed by a clear brook. The trail may be lost in the meadow in a confusion of paths leading to campsites.

The trail crosses the brook and from here on the way is up, first through forest to a boulder-hopping crossing of a milky stream from Lava Glacier (the stream may be impossible during heavy melting periods). It then continues up—through an endless, shadeless moraine of pumice and lava, passing Red Butte to a 7000-foot saddle between Goat Butte and Mt. Adams. The trail is marked with huge cairns. The way is rough and made more difficult because one's eyes are more likely to be on the tremendous view of Adams than looking out for rocks in the trail.

From there the way drops to Avalanche Valley and the end of the trail at 25 miles. The valley is named for the ice which periodically drops from a mile-long hanging glacier onto the Rusk and Klickitat Glaciers.

For exploring, hike to the top of 7484-foot Goat Butte. For more exploring, go back to Foggy Bottom and follow the stream bed upward about 1 mile, close to the toe of Lava Glacier. From here try to find wind caves and lava formations to the west. It is also possible to contour to Adams Glacier Meadows (Hike 64).

If Avalanche Valley alone is the goal, start on trail No. 113 for a hike of 10 miles each way.

Mt. St. Helens from Observation Peak

WIND RIVER

71 Observation (Trapper) Peak

Round trip from Government Mineral
Springs 12 miles
Hiking time 7½ hours
High point 4207 feet
Elevation gain 2900 feet
Best June to October
One day
USGS Lookout Mountain, Wind River

Round trip from road N63 6 miles
Hiking time 3 hours
Elevation gain 1600 feet in, 300 feet out

A former lookout site with a commanding view of the Wind River valley. Two ways lead to the summit, a long trail from the valley floor, mostly in forest, and a shorter ridge route partly in woods and partly in big-view meadows. Sadly, the Forest Service has given this scenic route to motorcyclists so the walk can be sickening.

For the long way, drive to Government Mineral Springs via any of several approaches: from the south (Columbia River) at Carson, 15 miles up Wind River road No. 30; from Berryfields, road No. N73; from the Lewis River, road No. N714. However the approach is made, at the junction of roads No. 30 and No. N73 turn west, cross the Wind River, and in ¼ mile turn north (right) on road No. N528 and drive 1½ miles to the road-end and trailhead, elevation 1300 feet.

Trail No. 132 starts steep and stays that way, climbing the south side of Howe Ridge through forest with fleeting views. In 2 miles cross a small creek, maybe the only water. At 3½ miles switch to the north side of the ridge. At 5½ miles is a junction with the motorcycle "trail." Keep climbing a final ½ mile to the peak—and views, views, and more views.

For the short and dirty way, drive No. N73 north from the junction with road No. 30 for 2 miles, turn left on No. N64 for 8 miles, turn left on No. N63 for 10 miles, and find the trailhead on the left side of the road. Elevation, 3200 feet.

Trail No. 132 sets out in virgin forest of Sister Rocks Research Natural Area, gaining 800 feet. Then, at about 1 mile, it enters an old burn grown up in huckleberries and flowers and drops 300 feet along the ridge connecting Sisters Rock to Observation (Trapper) Peak. At 1¾ miles is Observation Camp (water is sometimes to be found in a spring on the north side of the ridge). At 2½ miles is the junction with the trail from Government Mineral Springs. The Forest Service requires motorcycles to be left here, so the last ½ mile theoretically is wheelfree.

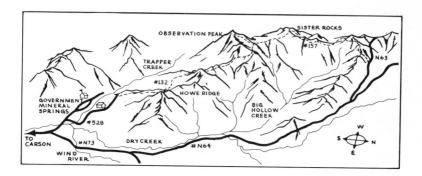

Mt. St. Helens — the Old and the New

The human tragedy of St. Helens, the loss of property and life, dwarfs the sorrow of climbers and hikers at the destruction of an elegant volcanic cone, a hauntingly beautiful lake, and miles of trails through forests and meadows. Yet memories of the lost places long will stir pangs of nostalgia — pangs almost as painful as those felt through the years while watching clearcuts climb the mountain to timberline, destroying in the peak's hinterland a hundred times more trail miles than the big blow did.

Still, no person who has lived intimately with volcanoes of the Northwest and in mind's eye recreated their violent pasts can but have been excited to *be here* when *something happened.* Just ask any hiker where he or she was May 18 — everybody's got a story.

If less elegant, the new St. Helens is more dramatic, and will so continue, and by employing what conservationists call the "Lassen Gambit," has earned the national attention required to achieve some sort of protected status. However, public enjoyment of the spectacle must be, for some time, at arm's length. (In fact, the best vantage point is the south side of Mt. Rainier!)

The eruption buried five popular trails. For safety, the Forest Service has declared Red and Blue Zones around the mountain which for now bar parts of five more trails to recreational use.

The five lost trails may be gone forever but the status of trails in the Red and Blue Zones will change for better or worse depending on how active the mountain remains. In this printing of *102 Hikes* the lost trails have been replaced by old favorites. Since trails in the Blue Zone still exist, they have been left in this printing even though years may pass before they can be hiked again. Trails entirely or partly affected by the Red and Blue Zones are:

Trail 66   Boundary Trail (western half)
Trail 69   Indian Heaven (western approaches)
Trail 71   Observation (Trapper) Peak (from Road N-63)
Trail 75   Shark Rock and Craggy Peak (entire trail)
Trail 76   Lewis River Trail (entire trail)

Before planning any hikes in Gifford Pinchot National Forest, it is advisable to contact the Supervisor's office and learn the current status of the trail you want to hike. Write or call Gifford Pinchot National Forest, 500 West 12th Street, Vancouver, WA 98660, phone (206) 696-7500. The office is open from 7:45 a.m. to 4:30 p.m. weekdays during the summer season. Someone generally will answer the phone on weekends at Randle Ranger Station (206) 497-7565, Packwood Ranger Station (206) 494-5515, and Wind River Ranger Station (509) 427-5645.

Mt. St. Helens as it was, from Coldwater Peak

SO. FORK SNOQUALMIE RIVER

72 Commonwealth Basin-Red Pass

Round trip to pass 10 miles
Hiking time 5 hours
High point 5400 feet
Elevation gain 2400 feet
Best mid-July through October
One day or backpack
USGS Snoqualmie Pass

Those who have watched the degradation of Snoqualmie Pass over the past quarter-century generally ignore the area when the ski season is over. However, the wilderness of Commonwealth Basin remains intact. Here one can find a peaceful subalpine forest, cold creeks, a perfect place for hiking with a family.

Drive Interstate 90 to Snoqualmie Pass and take Exit 52. Follow the Alpental signs and within 500 feet of the highway find the Pacific Crest Trail parking lot, elevation 3004 feet.

The original trail took only 1 mile to reach Commonwealth Basin. The new way takes 2½ miles. Unfortunately, the old trail crossed private land and when this was logged the path became so badly eroded it was abandoned. The new way is on the Pacific Crest Trail which makes a wide detour around the private land, climbing 700 feet and then losing 300 feet in the process.

From the parking lot follow the Pacific Crest Trail (Hike 25) approximately 2½ miles. Before starting up the side of Kendall Peak the trail dips down to within 100 feet or so of Commonwealth Creek near the entrance to the basin. Find a trail dropping to the creek (if vandals, porcupines, and bears haven't destroyed it, the junction will be signed) and pick up the old Commonwealth Basin trail.

The trail follows Commonwealth Creek upward another mile to the end of the valley

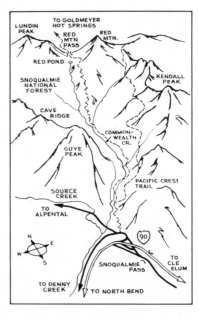

Mt. Thompson from near Red Pass

and views of Red Mountain towering above, a good place for lunch and turning back. But the trail goes on and the views get better.

From the basin the trail ascends the crest of an open-forested ridge in numerous short switchbacks, with steadily growing views, the rough, hot way finally flattening out in heather gardens and alpine trees of a cirque basin at the foot of Red Mountain. A few steps away on a side-trail is Red Pond, 4½ miles, 4900 feet. Eat a picnic lunch, tour the bouldery and flowery shores, listen for marmots whistling, walk to the edge of the cirque and look over the valley and the rimming peaks and south to Mt. Rainier. Campsites are overused but pleasant; carry a stove and don't hack the shrubbery.

The trail swings up talus and rock buttresses almost but not quite to the saddle and follows the ridge west to Red Mountain Pass, 5 miles, 5400 feet, and views to the deep Middle Fork Snoqualmie valley, the sharp tower of Mt. Thompson, the rugged Chimney Rock group, and far horizons.

Sprite Lake

CLE ELUM RIVER

73 Paddy Go Easy Pass

Round trip to pass 6 miles
Hiking time 4 hours
High point 6100 feet
Elevation gain 2700 feet
Best mid-July through October
One day or backpack
USGS The Cradle

A short, steep climb to a high pass with views out to great peaks and down to Fish Lake (Tucquala Lake) and the marshy valley of the Cle Elum River, and then an easy meadow-roaming walk to a lovely little lake. Flowers bloom here in mid-July but the lake is generally frozen until the end of the month. Thanks (no thanks) to the archaic

1872 Mining Laws, both the pass and lake are private lands — one more reason to change the outmoded law.

Drive to Salmon la Sac (Hike 34). A few yards past the ranger station keep right on rough dirt road No. 2405 for 11 miles. About ¾ mile after passing Fish Lake Guard Station, find the trailhead, elevation 3400 feet, on the right side of the road behind a group of private cabins along a stream.

Paddy Go Easy Pass trail, signed French Creek Trail No. 1595, starts in woods and in ½ mile passes a creek, the last water for 2 miles. At 1 mile is a junction with an abandoned trail going to the guard station; keep left. The way now steepens, switchbacking up through dense timber to small meadows with views to the valley and to Cathedral Rock and Mt. Daniel. At about 2½ miles the trail forks (unmarked). The left fork switchbacks directly to the pass. The right fork detours by an old mine and a stream, rejoining the main trail ¼ mile below the pass. The final stretch traverses under red cliffs of a 6500-foot peak to Paddy Go Easy Pass, 3½ miles, 6100 feet.

The east slopes of the pass are mostly meadowland. Contour south along the ridge ¼ mile to a point directly above 5900-foot Sprite Lake and descend to the shores. Delightful campsites but no wood, so carry a stove. The tiny lake provides a striking foreground for The Cradle, the impressive 7467-foot peak across the valley.

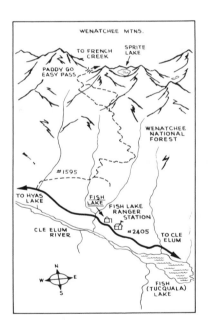

TIETON RIVER

74 McCall Basin

Round trip to McCall Basin 15 miles
Allow 2-3 days
High point 5000 feet
Elevation gain 1800 feet
Best July through November
USGS White Pass

McCall Basin-Shoe Lake loop trip 23 miles
Allow 3 days
High point 6200 feet
Elevation gain 3200 feet
Best July through November
Forest Service Wilderness Permit required

Climb for miles in forest with scarcely a window out, enjoying woodland flowers growing from what has been, since May 18 of 1980, an ash-gray floor. Join the Pacific Crest Trail and continue more miles in forest. Then walk out into the big sky and wide lawns of McCall Basin. Explore onward into Glacier Basin, below the McCall Glacier and Old Snowy.

Drive US 12 east from White Pass 7.5 miles and turn right on Tieton Road No. 143. In 3 miles, just before crossing the Tieton River, keep right on the North Fork Tieton River road and go 5 miles to the end at Scatter Creek, elevation 3300 feet.

Beware of confusion at the start. Do not take the Tieton Meadows trail. Also, do not take the old route of North Fork Tieton trail No. 1118, still shown on many maps. Instead, a few steps from Scatter Creek turn right on new trail No. 1118 and begin a long, sidehilling ascent of the valley wall. Tieton Meadows is glimpsed and then the impressive cliffs of Devils Horns and Tieton Peak. But mainly there are nice creeks to sample and spirea, collomia, ocean spray, Indian pipe, and the like to admire. At about 5 miles, 4800 feet, is Tieton Pass and the Pacific Crest Trail, which Gifford Pinchot National Forest thinks is very dangerous.

If it can be done so legally, turn left on the Crest Trail 2 miles, passing little Lutz Lake, to a Y. The new Crest Trail goes right; go left on the old Crest Trail, now the McCall Basin trail, ½ mile to the entry into parkland, 7½ miles, 4800 feet.

Though McCall Basin is a delicious green meadow coursed by swift, milky waters of the Tieton River, a person who sat himself down in the over-camped grass (camping is

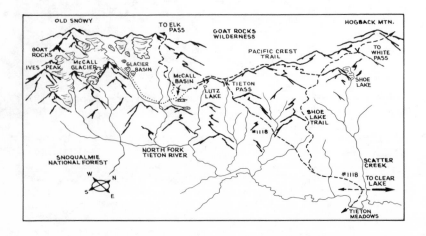

McCall Glacier and Old Snowy Mountain

restricted now) and wandered no farther would wonder why it's so famous. Actually it's not. Glacier Basin is.

To get there, cross the flats to the far side and find an obscure but much-used path climbing a low ridge to bypass a slot canyon of the river. Here is what's famous — a basin nearly a mile long and a half-mile wide, the glacial stream rushing through carpets of flowers and thickets of willows. Though boisterous waters may limit explorations by folks unable to long-jump 8 feet and unwilling to get wet to the knees, a week's roaming would not exhaust the riches. Buttresses and moraines and waterfalls below McCall Glacier call. Old Snowy, 7930 feet, may not beckon but it certainly poses handsomely for the camera.

A 3-day loop trip can be done by returning on the Crest Trail to Shoe Lake (Hike 53). Retrace the way as far as Tieton Pass, follow the Crest Trail northward, contour north around the west side of a knoll to a couple of small lakes, cross to the east side of the crest, and climb to a junction with trail No. 1117 at 6¾ miles. (This is the return leg of the loop.) Another mile leads to Shoe Lake, 6200 feet, at 7¾ miles from McCall Basin, with an elevation gain of 1600 feet. To complete the loop, backtrack south 1 mile on the Crest Trail and take trail No. 1117 for 4 miles to North Fork Tieton trail No. 1118 and a final mile to the road.

Blue Lake and Mt. Adams

LEWIS RIVER

75 Shark Rock and Craggy Peak

Round trip to Boundary Trail 13 miles
Hiking time 5 hours
High point 5200 feet
Elevation gain 1800 feet
Best mid-July to early November
One day or backpack
USGS Spencer Butte, Quartz Creek, and
　McCoy Peak

Follow a wooded ridge to a mountain lake, 2 miles of alpine meadows, and views, and views, and views. Nowhere else in the State of Washington can one see so vast an expanse of solid virgin forest as in the vista over Straight Creek and Quartz Creek to Mt. Adams; only a few distant clearings far to the south break the solid green. Try this trip early in July; if conditions are right there may be miles of beargrass in bloom.

The trail is harassed by machines and jeopardized by logging, including a proposed timber sale ¼ mile from Blue Lake. That the path has survived until now is due solely to a Sierra Club lawsuit. Logging at these high elevations is particularly shocking because the timber has relatively little commercial value—a quarter or more of the trees are left on the ground to rot after being cut and a new forest may be 150-300 years growing.

From Lewis River Ranger Station on Swift Reservoir, drive north on road No. 125 (passing a junction with road No. N92). At 5.6 miles turn right on road No. N920. Watch all intersections carefully; during logging operations some sideroads are used more than the main road. At 18 miles is a junction of road No. N923 (a possible shortcut) and at 18.7 miles find the trailhead, elevation 3400 feet.

The way starts as trail No. 80, part of the old Spirit Lake—Guler trail. In 1½ up-and-down miles reach an intersection (only ¼ mile from road No. N923, a possible shortcut) with trail No. 3, signed "Blue Lake." Follow this trail uphill. At 2½ miles pass close to a clearcut which offers another shortcut. (To reach this alternative starting point from the trailhead, drive road No. N920 another 1.3 miles to an unmarked spur and find your way across the clearing.)

In the next 2 miles the trail climbs gently, eventually ascending a wide ridge. At a little over 4½ miles the ridge becomes quite narrow and at times the route is steep. But the vista begins. At 5200 feet the way contours around a high point and drops to a view of Blue Lake at 5 miles. (To get to 4553-foot Blue Lake hike the trail to the point where the lake comes clearly in sight and find a unmarked way trail down to the shore.)

The timber thins, the trail enters meadows, and at 5½ miles, 5200 feet, is a short side-trail to a campsite—water is scarce after the snow melts. At 6 miles pass a side-trail leading ¼ mile southeast to Basin Camp. After contouring slopes of a knob, at 6½ miles, 5200 feet, join trail No. 1, the Boundary Trail (Hike 66).

For the widest views along the route, wander up either of the grassy knolls at 3½ or 4 miles. Shark Rock at the head of Clear Creek is the most impressive rocky peak on the Boundary Ridge.

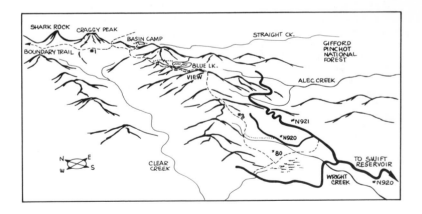

LEWIS RIVER

76 Lewis River Trail

One-way trip 9½ miles
Hiking time 5 hours
High point 1600 feet
Elevation gain 1000 feet upstream, 600 feet
    downstream
Best March through November
One day or backpack
USGS Burnt Peak and Spencer Butte

A forest of huge firs, cedars, and maples serves as a canopy to a green and varied carpet of Oregon grape, vanilla leaf, moss dotted with oxalis, and shoulder-high brush. The Forest Service has promised to preserve in a natural condition a wide corridor along the Lewis River, keeping this trail, perhaps the last low-elevation valley path remaining in Gifford Pinchot National Forest, as a 9-mile sample and reminder of the many, many miles of such splendor that we inherited and have now mostly squandered.

The trail can be hiked in either direction, and parties which can arrange transportation to allow a one-way trip would be well-advised to start at the top, which is 400 feet higher than the bottom. However, parties making a round trip should start at the bottom and thus be sure to cover at least the lower 3 miles, where the best trees are; for this reason the bottom-to-top direction is described here.

From Lewis River Ranger Station on Swift Reservoir drive .3 mile north and turn right on road No. N90. At 5.5 miles from the ranger station turn left on road No. N836, and at 6.2 miles cross the Lewis River bridge. At 6.6 miles find the lower trailhead, elevation about 1100 feet.

To reach the upper trailhead, from the junction of roads Nos. N90 and 836 continue on No. N90 (avoiding side-roads that may be used more than the main one) to a concrete bridge over the Lewis River at 14.5 miles from the ranger station. A few yards from the west end of the bridge find the trailhead, elevation about 1400 feet.

From the lower beginning, trail No. 31 immediately drops to river level, about 1000 feet, and magnificent forest. The way winds along bottomland flats, climbs a small bank, and emerges into a clearcut at 1 mile. To somewhat beyond 1½ miles the path follows the margin of the logging show before re-entering virgin trees. After a few steep ups and downs, at just under 2½ miles is Bolt Camp; the shelter here is amazingly well-preserved considering it was built in the early 1930s. At 4 miles the valley narrows to a canyon, a good turnaround for round-trip hikers, since from this

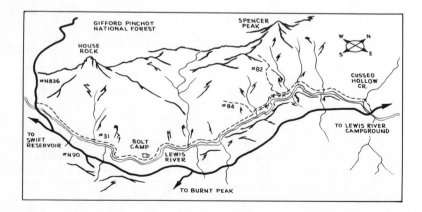

Lewis River trail

point the trail goes up and down a lot but never again reaches river level—though there are several spots where one can easily drop to the stream.

At 7 miles the trail climbs a 300-foot bluff. At 7½ miles find a viewpoint a few feet off the tread and look down to the canyon sliced in columnar basalt. From here on the river is unseen and old forest yields to young forest dating from the Spencer Butte fire which swept the area in the 1920s; because snags are considered a major fire hazard, most were cut many years ago. At 9 miles cross Cussed Hollow and climb over the last bump to the upper trailhead at 9½ miles, 1400 feet.

LEWIS RIVER

77 Pacific Crest Trail

One-way trip from Columbia River to White
    Pass about 120 miles
Hiking time 13 days minimum
High point 7620 feet
Elevation gain about 18,000 feet
Best in May the first 27 miles, mid-July for
    the rest
USGS Hood River, Wind River, Willard,
    Steamboat Mtn., Mt. Adams, and White
    Pass
Forest Service Wilderness permits
    required in Mt. Adams and Goat Rocks
    Wildernesses

The Pacific Crest National Scenic Trail which extends from Mexico to Canada, is most commonly called in the northernmost 470 miles by its older name, the Cascade Crest Trail. The 286-mile portion between the Columbia River and Stevens Pass traverses highlands past three grand volcanoes and penetrates the heart of two spectacular masses of high alpine peaks. The way isn't all pure fun because it also goes through lower, forested sections of the Cascade Range where logging roads and clearcuts have savaged the wilderness solitude. However, the feeling of accomplishment gained by traveling the full length of the crest cannot be spoiled even by the worst of the messed-up parts.

Few hikers complete the route in a single effort; most do the trail in short bits over a period of years. Those taking the whole trip at once can start at either end; the south-to-north direction is described here.

At many places the trail is being relocated for the sake of easier grades or better scenery. For example, to bring Crest hikers closer to a crossing of the Columbia River, the trail will be re-routed toward the Bridge of the Gods. A temporary starting point may be established at Panther Creek on road No. 605 (near Wind River Ranger Station). Until this trailhead is established use the one described below. For current information, contact Engineer Department, U.S. Forest Service, Randle, WA.

The following brief summary is intended merely to provide a general impression of the route. For details of mileages and campsites, consult the Forest Service map and log of the Pacific Crest Trail, available from any Forest Service office.

Columbia River to White Pass

Begin beside the legendary "River of the West," skirt the slopes of giant Mt. Adams, enjoy views to graceful Mt. St. Helens, and walk the airy crest of the Goat Rocks Wilderness—the most difficult, as well as one of the most dramatically beautiful, segments of the entire Crest Trail.

Drive US 180 east from Vancouver, Washington to the town of Stevenson and some 9 miles beyond to the parking lot and trailhead (adjacent to small cafe in parking lot) on the north side of the highway, elevation 186 feet.

Hike through forests, lava flows, and occasional views—the route interrupted by logging roads, clearcuts, powerlines, and pipelines. Go steeply up and down several times, passing Dog Mountain, Grassy Knoll, and Big Huckleberry Mountain to road No. N60 near Race Track Campground. **Distance from Columbia River to Race Track Campground about 27 miles; elevation gain about 5500 feet; hiking time 3 days.**

From road No. N60 climb miles of woods to Red Mountain and Blue Lake and the pond-dotted meadows and famous huckleberry fields of Indian Heaven (Hike 69).

Johnson Peak, Egg Butte in lower right

Pass near Bear Lake, go almost over the top of Sawtooth Mountain, cross road No. 123, and continue through Huckleberry Meadows to Mosquito Creek. Cross the road again and traverse the east side of Steamboat Mountain to a third crossing of road No. 123. **Distance from Race Track Campground to road No. 123 about 26 miles; elevation gain about 2900 feet; hiking time 3 days.**

The next stage is climaxed by the alpine gardens and glacial streams on the flanks of Mt. Adams. From road No. 123 cross road No. N88, Trout Lake Creek, and road No. N85, climb to Dry Meadows and Grand Meadows, cross road No. N84, traverse Swampy Meadows, and at 12 miles join the Mount Adams Highline Trail (Hike 70). At 22 miles leave the Highline Trail and at 23½ miles leave the Mt. Adams Wilderness at Spring Creek and proceed to road No. 101 at Midway Meadows. **Distance from road No. 123 to Midway Meadows about 29 miles; elevation gain about 3500 feet; hiking time 3 days.**

Now starts the first long stretch of roadless country, most of it in the Goat Rocks Wilderness, including a couple miles which can be dangerous. From Midway Meadows go a short bit along a rough road, round a lava flow, and at 6 miles enter the Wilderness. Proceed past Coleman Weed Patch, intersect the Walupt Lake trail, and pass above Snowgrass Flat (Hike 61). Carefully, bewaring of hazards, climb the ridge above Packwood Glacier and traverse the shoulder of Old Snowy to Elk Pass (Hike 63). The route crosses above to McCall Basin, Tieton Pass, and Shoe Lake (Hike 53), at 34 miles leaving the Wilderness and descending to White Pass. **Distance from Midway Meadows to White Pass about 38 miles; elevation gain about 6100 feet; hiking time 4-5 days.**

177

Pacific Crest Trail (Cont'd.)

One-way trip from White Pass to Stevens Pass about 166 miles
Hiking time 19 days
High point 6500 feet
Elevation gain about 20,400 feet
Best mid-July through October
USGS White Pass, Bumping Lake, Lester, Snoqualmie Pass, Big Snow Mountain, Mt. Daniel, The Cradle, Scenic, and Stevens Pass

White Pass to Stevens Pass

North from White Pass extend miles of marvelous meadows and lakes and large views of Mt. Rainier, then a lower and more wooded (and road-marred) section of the crest leading to Snoqualmie Pass, and finally the splendid assemblage of forests and cliffs and glaciers and flowers and waters constituting the Alpine Lakes Wilderness. This scenic segment of the Crest Trail is close to population centers and extremely popular.

The first stage rarely leaves meadows and panoramas for long and passes numerous small lakes—too many to name here. From the White Pass Highway at Leech Lake (Hike 52) hike to Sand Lake, Cowlitz Pass, Fish Lake, and the Mount Rainier National Park boundary at 15½ miles. Weave in and out of the Park, following the crest by Two Lakes, Dewey Lakes, and around the side of Naches Peak to Chinook Pass and US 410; here leave the National Park. **Distance from White Pass to Chinook Pass about 25 miles; elevation gain about 2400 feet; hiking time 3 days.**

The opening third of the next part lies in alpine terrain as before, and the remainder in woods broken by roads. Climb from Chinook Pass to Sourdough Gap (Hike 47), traverse to Bear Gap and around Pickhandle Point and Crown Point, with views to the Crystal Mountain Ski Area, ascend the crest, contour below the summit of Norse Peak, and drop into Big Crow Basin (Hike 45). Proceed to Little Crow Basin, a junction with the Arch Rock trail, Arch Rock Camp, and Rod's Gap—where a Forest Service road cuts the trail. Pass Government Meadows and cross the Naches Wagon Trail (Hike 42), contour under Pyramid Peak, and reach road No. 195 at Windy Gap. **Distance from Chinook Pass to Windy Gap about 27 miles; elevation gain about 2500 feet; hiking time 3 days.**

Now comes a portion with few views except in clearcuts. From Windy Gap follow the crest nearly to the top of Blowout Mountain, descend in woods and clearcuts to Tacoma Pass and a logging road, and travel onward under Snowshoe Butte to Lizard Lake and the road at Stampede Pass. **Distance from Windy Gap to Stampede Pass about 27 miles; elevation gain about 1100 feet; hiking time 3 days.**

More forest travel—but much of the private land is being logged so the path is not always easy to find and not always pleasant, despite increasingly mountainous views northward. From Stampede Pass hike to Dandy Pass, Mirror Lake, contour Tinkham and Silver Peaks (Hike 23) to Olallie Meadow and Lodge Lake, climb to Beaver Lake, and drop down ski slopes to Snoqualmie Pass Ranger Station. **Distance from Stampede Pass to Snoqualmie Pass about 18 miles; elevation gain about 1400 feet; hiking time 2 days.**

From this point north no roads mar the route, which now traverses the superb Alpine Lakes Wilderness. From Snoqualmie Pass the trail climbs high on Kendall Peak and ridge-runs in meadows to Ridge Lake (Hike 25) at 6 miles, then contours headwaters of Gold Creek under avalanche-scoured walls of Chikamin Ridge to a green pass above Park Lakes (Hike 28) at 14 miles. It enters the Cle Elum River watershed, passes Spectacle Lake junction (Hike 31) at 17 miles, and drops to a crossing of Lemah Creek at 21 miles. It climbs past Escondido Lake at 27½ miles and descends to a crossing of the Waptus River at 32 miles. The trail rounds the shore of Waptus Lake (Hike 33) and climbs Spinola Creek to Deep Lake (Hike 35) at 39 miles. It switchbacks to Cathedral Pass at 42½ miles and proceeds down and up to Deception Pass (Hike 36) at 47½ miles. From there the way is fairly level to Deception Lakes (Hike 6), then up to Piper Pass, down to Glacier Lake, over another pass to a viewpoint above Lake Josephine, and finally down to Stevens Pass at 68 miles. **Distance from Snoqualmie Pass to Stevens Pass about 68 miles; elevation gain 10,600 feet; hiking time 6 days.**

From Stevens Pass the Pacific Crest Trail continues 185 miles to Allison Pass in Canada. See **101 Hikes in the North Cascades.**

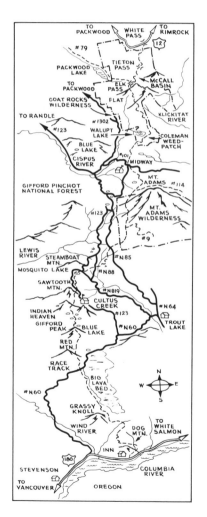

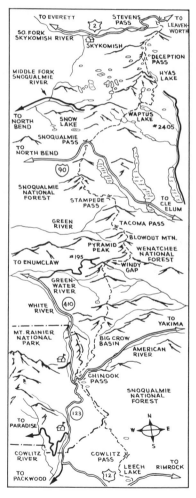

78 Mount Ellinor

Round trip to timberline 3 miles
Hiking time 2 hours
High point 5200 feet
Elevation gain 1700 feet
Best July through October
One day
USGS Mt. Steele and The Brothers

From 1853 to 1857 George Davidson surveyed Puget Sound, working from the brig **R. H. Fauntleroy,** named for his superior, the head of the U.S. Coast and Geodetic Survey. Needing names for the maps he was making, he drew upon the Fauntleroy family, calling the southernmost prominent peak on the Olympic skyline Ellinor, for the youngest daughter, the double-summited peak for her Brothers, and the highest point for her older sister Constance. Later, Davidson and Ellinor were married. However, subsequent mappers shifted Ellinor to a lower peak, replacing her with Mt. Washington.

A century and more later, hikers look from Ellinor over a panorama of the Cascades from Mt. St. Helens to Glacier Peak, and of the Olympics from neighboring Mt. Washington, whose profile can be imagined to resemble that of the general and president, to the distant white mass of Mt. Olympus.

Drive US 101 along Hood Canal to Hoodsport. Turn west 9 miles on the Lake Cushman road to a junction. Turn right 1.6 miles on road No. 245, then left 4.9 miles on Big Creek road No. 2419 to the signed trailhead. Though the trail will be kept open from this start, for a shorter hike continue on the road to the first Y, take the left fork to the end, and there find an unsigned trailhead, elevation about 3500 feet. Carry a full canteen; the slopes are dry.

Find a boot-built path climbing to the ridge top. At 1½ miles, about 5200 feet, is timberline and the trail-end, and for inexperienced hikers, the proper turnaround. The vistas of lowlands and Cascades are as good here as from the summit—and there is no danger of getting lost, as there may be on the final slopes.

The temptation to go on is overwhelming; to the inexperienced eye, the gully from trail-end to summit looks simple. It's not. The gully is steeper than it appears and the rocks are sometimes slippery and always loose—terrain for an experienced rock-

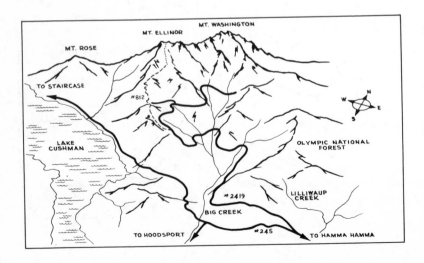

Hood Canal and Mt. Rainier from trail's end on Mt. Ellinor

scrambler. Should the fog roll in, one easily can stray into the wrong gully and get lost. If a person wants to go for the top of the mountain, he should choose a quiet weekday rather than a mobbed weekend, or come in early summer when the road is still snowbound.

Upper Mildred Lake and Sawtooth Range

79 Mildred Lakes

Round trip about 8 miles
Hiking time 7 hours
High point 4100 feet
Elevation gain 2300 feet in, 600 feet out
Best mid-July to mid-October
Backpack
USGS Mt. Steel

Three mountain lakes beneath the startling basalt spires of Sawtooth Ridge, well worth a visit—as they'd darn well better be, after the struggle. The trail (way), not recognized by the Forest Service as part of its system, and on certain wooded slopes so obscure the hiker may not recognize it either, has been hammered into hillsides and over countless logs by generations of fishermen, hikers, and climbers. The distance is only 4 miles (or is it 5?), but that doesn't include detours around wooden barricades. Nor does the figure given here for elevation gain include the ups and downs over logs and rocks and bumps. These are just extra dividends. But don't complain—they keep out the motorcycles.

Drive 14 miles up Hamma Hamma road No. 249 to the end at a concrete bridge over the Hamma Hamma River, elevation 1900 feet. Find the trail, signed by the Forest Service even if not recognized, at the far side of the bridge.

On the first mile a little work has been done—logs cut, the tread occasionally graded. Such gestures end in the second mile as the way climbs steeply over a 3200-foot ridge and drops 300 feet to a delightful camp beside a brook, approximately 2½ miles. The trail is easily lost here amid false paths made by mixed-up hikers.

Cross the creek, stay level several hundred feet, then climb—and climb, with only an occasional respite, 1000 feet, mostly straight up. At 4100 feet is a ridge top of heather and alpine trees and great views that tempt a party to call it quits. Don't. The end is near. Drop 300 feet to Lower Mildred Lake, follow the shore to the lakehead, and near the inlet find the trail (again, amid many false paths) climbing a bit more than 300 feet in ⅓ mile to the upper lake and great views and great camps.

The third lake, about the same elevation, is off toward Cruiser Peak. The path starts from the outlet of the upper lake.

If time permits, ascend (with some bushwhacking) a 5000-foot knoll below Mt. Lincoln. The effort is repaid with a view of Mt. Washington, Mt. Pershing, and a score of other Olympic peaks.

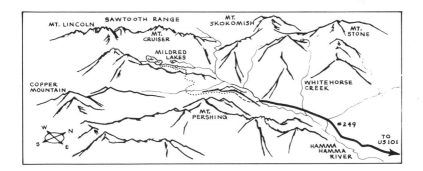

80 Flapjack Lakes

Round trip to lakes 15.6 miles
Hiking time 10 hours
High point 4000 feet
Elevation gain 3100 feet
Best July through October
One day or backpack
USGS Mt. Steel
Park Service backcountry use permit
   required

Two subalpine lakes set side by side like flapjacks in a frying pan. Above the waters and the forests rise sharp summits of the Sawtooth Range, a group of peaks noted among climbers for the odd texture of the rock, which largely consists of "pillow lava" erupted under the surface of an ancient sea and now eroded into weird shapes.

Drive US 101 along Hood Canal to Hoodsport. Turn west to Lake Cushman and follow the North Fork Skokomish River road to Staircase Ranger Station and the trailhead, elevation 800 feet.

The trail follows an abandoned road the first 3.7 miles, then ascends moderately but steadily in cool forest to a junction at 7 miles. From here a faint way trail goes left to Black and White Lakes in 1¼ miles, Smith Lake in 1½ miles.

The right fork reaches Flapjack Lakes, 4000 feet, in a short mile. One lake, quite shallow, is well along toward becoming a marsh, while the other is deeper and ringed by rock buttresses; the two are separated by a narrow isthmus. The most striking Sawtooth summit from the lake is The Horn—known to a party of hikers who saw it on an autumn night years ago with the full moon (made of green cheese, then) touching its yearning snout, as "The Mouse."

Actually, the trip only just begins at the lakes. For high and wide meadows and broad views, walk the Mt. Gladys trail 1½ more miles up a lovely valley of rocks and flowers and bubbling water to Gladys Pass, 5000 feet, between a rounded garden peak and a vicious finger of lava. Roam the gardens to the 5600-foot summit of Mt. Gladys. Stare at the frightening walls of 6104-foot Cruiser ("Bruiser") Peak, whose tower is visible from Seattle, standing like a boundary monument on the southeast corner of Olympic National Park.

Popularity has forced stringent restrictions on camping: a nightly limit of 30 persons at the lakes and above; stoves only at the lakes and above (wood fires permitted below Donahue Creek). Alternative campsites are at Smith Lake.

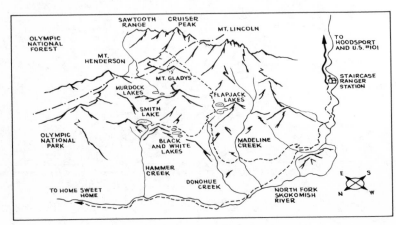

Upper Flapjack Lake and Mt. Lincoln

HOOD CANAL

81 Home Sweet Home

Round trip to Camp Pleasant 13 miles
Hiking time 8 hours
High point 1600 feet
Elevation gain 800 feet
Best May through November
One day or backpack
USGS Mt. Steel

Round trip to Home Sweet Home 26 miles
Allow 2 days
High point 5688 feet
Elevation gain 4000 feet in, 500 feet out
Best mid-July through October
Park Service backcountry use permit
required

In early May, when a small elk herd is still in the Skokomish valley and trillium and calypso orchids are in bloom, walk the gentle trail to Nine Stream. In summer, climb from the valley to First Divide and broad views, then drop to Duckabush River drainage and the lupine meadows of Home Sweet Home.

Drive US 101 to Hoodsport and turn west to the end of the North Fork Skokomish River road (Hike 80), elevation 800 feet.

The North Fork Skokomish River trail follows an abandoned road 3.7 miles, then enters forest to Big Log Camp, 5½ miles, a spacious area beside the stream. At 6 miles the way crosses the river on a bridge over a deep, quiet pool. Immediately beyond is a junction; go right. The trail climbs slightly to Camp Pleasant, 6½ miles, 1600 feet, on a large maple flat. This appropriately-named spot makes a good overnight stop for springtime backpackers.

At 9½ miles, 2091 feet, is Nine Stream and the end of level walking. In the next mile the trail ascends at a comfortable rate through a big meadow, then forest. After that the way is continuously steep and often rough. Flower gardens become more frequent. Mt. Stone appears to the south.

At about 12 miles the trail reaches a meadow below Mt. Steel, turns sharply right, and climbs to the crest of 4688-foot First Divide, 12½ miles, and views across the Duckabush valley to Mt. LaCrosse, White Mountain, and the greenery of LaCrosse Pass.

The path descends ½ mile to Home Sweet Home, 4198 feet. Even from a bunk in the shelter one may enjoy the blossoms of avalanche lilies or lupine, depending on the season. The view is superb of 6233-foot Mt. Steel.

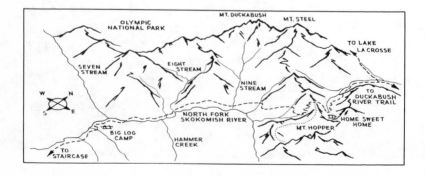

*Mt. Steel from near Home Sweet Home. Picture was
taken in early July when the meadows were still
covered with snow*

From First Divide a faint way trail goes around the south side of Mt. Hopper, but the route is rough and best left to very experienced travelers.

Many hikers continue from Home Sweet Home to Lake LaCrosse (Hike 99), 7 miles farther, with a loss of 2000 feet followed by a stiff gain of 2500 feet to the lake. From there they either proceed onward around O'Neil Pass to the Enchanted Valley trail or over Anderson Pass to the Dosewallips trail.

A few hikers drop from Home Sweet Home to the Duckabush River, hike 1½ miles downstream, and climb over 5566-foot LaCrosse Pass to Honeymoon Meadows on the Dosewallips (Hike 85). Only the vast meadows at the pass make this grueling 3000-foot ascent on a waterless, south-facing slope worth the effort.

82 Upper Lena Lake

Round trip to upper lake 14 miles
Hiking time 12 hours
High point 4600 feet
Elevation gain 3900 feet
Best to lower lake April through November
Best to upper lake July through October
One day or backpack
USGS The Brothers
Park Service backcountry use permit
    required

Hike an easy trail, free of snow most of the year, through splendid forest to popular and often crowded Lower Lena Lake, surrounded by tall trees. Continue on steeper, rougher trail to the subalpine country of Upper Lena Lake.

Drive US 101 along Hood Canal to Eldon. Turn west on the Hamma Hamma River

Upper Lena Lake and Mt. Bretherton

road about 9 miles to Phantom Creek and ½ mile beyond to the trailhead, elevation 685 feet.

The wide "super-trail" switchbacks gently and endlessly in forest shadows, crossing beautiful Lena Creek and soon thereafter reaching Lower Lena Lake at 2¾ miles, 1800 feet. The way passes a popular camp area and rounds the west shore ½ mile to other campsites near the head of the lake.

Shortly beyond the head of the lake is a junction. The path to the right follows East Fork Lena Creek into the Valley of Silent Men, crossing and recrossing the stream many times, toward The Brothers, a principal summit of the Olympic horizon seen from Seattle. This boot-built track is mainly used by fishermen and climbers, but is well worth exploration by hikers who enjoy loitering beside cold water frothing and sparkling through rapids, swirling in green pools, all in the deep shade of old forest.

The left fork—no supertrail—follows West Fork Lena Creek, entering Olympic National Park at 4 miles. At approximately 5 miles, 2700 feet, the trail crosses a small creek and becomes steep and badly eroded. The present trail was built in the late 1930s. It was steep then, but the tread was smooth and wide. Subsequently a few windfalls have been cut but otherwise there has been no maintenance. Floods, slides, and fallen trees have taken their toll and only remnants of the original tread remain.

As the trail climbs, the vegetation changes from fir to subalpine forest. Heather and huckleberry appear along with Alaska cedar. There are occasional views down the valley toward The Brothers. The steepness ends abruptly at Upper Lena Lake, 4600 feet, 7 miles. A rough up-and-down way trail rounds the north side.

Camps are inviting (no wood fires, stoves only) and the shore demands roaming, as do the meadows and screes ringing the cirque. For more ambitious explorations scramble to the summit of 5998-foot Mt. Lena, or ascend the creek falling from little Milk Lake, tucked in a quiet pocket and generally frozen until late summer, or follow a boot-worn track over a 5000-foot ridge near Mt. Lena to Scout Lake, or follow the ridge with its numerous tarns toward Mt. Stone and Lake of the Angels.

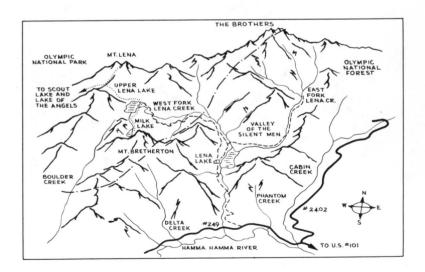

The Brothers from Mt. Jupiter trail

HOOD CANAL

83 Mount Jupiter

Round trip 14 miles
Hiking time 10 hours
High point 5701 feet
Elevation gain 3600 feet
Best June through October
One day
USGS Point Misery and The Brothers

Look from Seattle across Puget Sound to the Olympic horizon; right smack between The Brothers and Mt. Constance is Jupiter. Actually, the peak does not deserve inclusion in such distinguished company, but stands so far out in the front of the range as to seem bigger than it really is. And in fact, old Jupe offers unique combination views of lowlands and mountains. The summit ascent, however, is long and strenuous and usually dry and hot. Most hikers are content to climb the trail to the views and leave the summit to peakbaggers.

Drive US 101 along Hood Canal to a short mile north of the Duckabush River bridge. A bit south of the Black Point road, turn west 3½ miles on unsigned Mt. Jupiter road No. 262 to a junction. Turn left on the fork (sometimes) signed "Mt. Jupiter Trail" and drive 3 steep and tortuous miles to the trailhead, elevation 2150 feet.

The first mile switchbacks up south slopes of the ridge dividing the Duckabush and Dosewallips Rivers. At 1 mile, 2850 feet, the trail reaches the ridge crest, and here leaves state land and enters Olympic National Forest. The hike to this point, with splendid panoramas, can be done in late May and early June, when the trip is really the most pleasant, especially since rhododendrons are then in bloom along the lower trail.

However, the way goes on for those willing, following the ridge crest up and down, up and down, with more views, and finally climbs a very steep final mile to the summit, 7 miles, 5701 feet.

From the summit, or from the trail, the views are glorious—and thought-provoking. North beyond the Dosewallips is Mt. Constance, and south beyond the Duckabush are The Brothers. See the logging, steadily encroaching on state and Olympic National Forest lands. Westward is the protected grandeur of Olympic National Park. Eastward across Hood Canal and the Kitsap Peninsula are Seattle, the Space Needle, suburbia, smog, civilization.

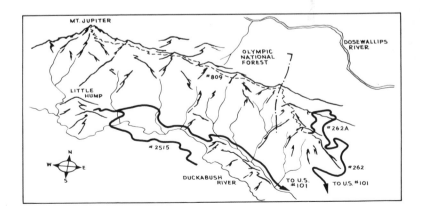

HOOD CANAL

84 Lake Constance

Round trip to the lake 4 miles
Hiking time 7 hours
High point 4750 feet
Elevation gain 3300 feet
Best August through October
One day or backpack
USGS The Brothers and Tyler Peak
Park Service backcountry use permit
required

A classic tarn, the deep blue waters ringed by alpine trees and heather gardens and sheer cliffs of Mt. Constance. Mountain goats wander the precipices by day—and at night visit campfires to scavenge goodies. But hikers must earn their passage to the secluded cirque the hard way, climbing 3400 feet in only 2 miles. The trail is super-steep, somewhat dangerous in spots, and is not recommended for beginners or small children or the fainthearted.

Drive US 101 along Hood Canal to the Dosewallips River road just north of Brinnon. Turn west 14 miles to ½ mile inside the Park boundary and several wide spots that serve for the trailhead parking area at Constance Creek, elevation 1450 feet.

The first mile is brutal, virtually without switchbacks, gaining some 2000 feet to a short level stretch, and good forest camp, at the 1-mile marker. The second mile seems even steeper, though this is purely an optical illusion caused by the ladder-ways of tree roots and the short rock cliffs. Feet must be placed with care and hands used for balance. Caution is especially essential on the descent. At 2 miles, 4750 feet, the trail flattens into the cirque. Camping restrictions forced by popularity include a nightly limit of 20 campers and a ban on wood fires.

Impressive as is the lake, the truly awesome scenery lies higher, beyond the portals of what oldtime Boy Scouts, feeling spooky, used to call "Dead Man's Gap." Follow a boot-beaten climbers' track above the lake, up talus, through the gap into Avalanche Canyon, a mile-long glacier trough between the east and west peaks of Constance. Solemn and spectacular it is, a place of crags, cliffs, and screes, snowfields and moraines. Hikers can walk safely to the canyon head at about 6000 feet. Those with ice axes and experience in snow travel can climb easily to Crystal Pass and views down the glacier in Tunnel Creek.

The geology adds fascination. The weird, bumpy-looking walls of the canyon consist of "pillow lava" formed by molten rock erupting under the sea and cooling into

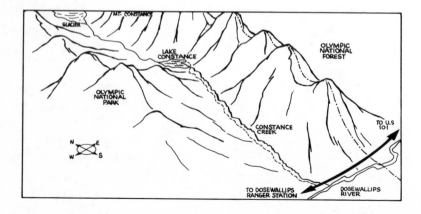

Lake Constance

these odd, rounded shapes. Heat and pressure metamorphosed limestone into pastel-colored rocks, often in variegated fault breccias of striking beauty. Hot mineralized solutions deposited green crystals of epidote intermixed with quartz and calcite.

The goats that tour the campsites by night and occasionally by day (such as on a Monday morning, after the weekenders have gone home) often can be spotted on cliffs, little kids gamboling about the airy rocks, older folks moving more deliberately.

85 Anderson Glacier

Round trip to Anderson Glacier 22½ miles
Allow 3 days
High point 5200 feet
Elevation gain 4000 feet
Best mid-July through October
USGS The Brothers and Mt. Steel
Park Service backcountry use permit
   required

Follow a long trail to the edge of one of the largest glaciers in the eastern Olympics. Enjoy glorious views down the Dosewallips River to Mt. Constance, over Anderson Pass to Mt. LaCrosse and White Mountain, down into the Enchanted Valley at the head of the Quinault River, and of course, across the Anderson Glacier to the summits of Mt. Anderson. In early August a wild array of flowers bloom, including small fields of lupine and paintbrush that stand out dramatically against the rugged background.

Drive US 101 along Hood Canal to just north of Brinnon and turn west on the Dosewallips River road, coming to the end of pavement in 4¾ miles, Elkhorn Campground junction at 10¾ miles, Constance Creek at 13½ miles, and at 15 miles the road-end and trailhead, elevation 1540 feet.

The trail starts in deep forest with a showing of rhododendrons in late June, and after going up and down a bit reaches a junction at 1½ miles. Turn left to Dose Forks Camp and cross the river. At about 2½ miles the way again crosses the river, now the

Anderson Glacier on Mt. Anderson

West Fork Dosewallips, this time on a bridge perched spectacularly some 100 feet above the water. The trail climbs steeply to dry forests high above the stream, which flows in so deep a gorge that often it cannot be heard.

The trail descends a bit to a welcome drink of water and campsites at 5 miles, then climbs high again and with minor ups and downs reaches the small opening of Diamond Meadow at 6¾ miles, 2692 feet. Pleasant campsites by the stream. At 7¼ miles the trail once more crosses the river and begins a steady ascent, at about 8 miles climbing steeply beside the raging torrent as it tumbles through a narrow gorge. At 8¾ miles, 3627 feet, the valley opens into the broad, flat expanse and good camps of Honeymoon Meadows, named years ago by a Seattle couple who long since have celebrated their golden wedding anniversary. (Here and above, stove-only camping.) One final time the trail crosses the river, here only a jump wide (a big jump), and ascends a rough path to Anderson Pass Shelter ("Camp Siberia") at 10 miles and Anderson Pass at 10½ miles, 4464 feet.

The Anderson Glacier trail climbs steeply from the north side of the wooded pass, emerging from trees and in ¾ mile ending at a small tarn amid boulders and meadows. A few feet farther lead to the 5200-foot edge of an old moraine and the views.

The West Fork Dosewallips trail to Anderson Pass often is included in longer trips: a 27-mile one-way hike down Enchanted Valley (Hike 98); a 49-mile one-way hike to O'Neil Pass and out the Duckabush River (Hike 99); a 36½-mile one-way hike out the North Fork Skokomish River; and a 41-mile loop trip via O'Neil Pass and the upper Duckabush, returning to the Dosewallips with a grueling 3000-foot climb to LaCrosse Pass.

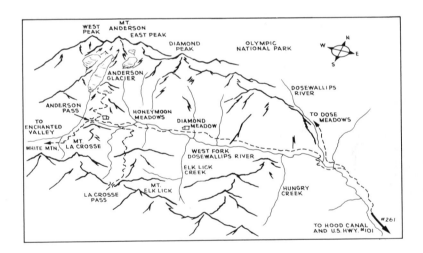

86 Hayden Pass

Round trip to Hayden Pass 31 miles
Allow 3-4 days
High point 5847 feet
Elevation gain 4250 feet
Best July through October
USGS Tyler Peak, The Brothers, and Mt. Angeles
Park Service backcountry use permit required

Miles of marvelous forest, then alpine meadows waist-deep in flowers, where fragrance makes the head swim on warm days, where a quiet hiker may see deer, elk, marmots, bear, and perhaps a goat on a high ridge. All this and impressive views too, plus numerous fine campsites at short intervals along the trail. The pass makes a superb round-trip destination, or can be included in an across-the-Olympics journey to the Elwha River, or in a 10-day giant loop over Low Divide and returning via Anderson Pass.

Drive US 101 along Hood Canal to the Dosewallips River road just north of Brinnon. Turn west 15½ miles (the final 2 miles in the National Park are steep and rough) to the road-end campground and trailhead, elevation 1540 feet.

A gentle 1½ miles through open forest with a dense groundcover of salal and rhododendron (the latter blooms in early July) lead to Dose Forks. A bit beyond is a junction with the trail to Anderson Pass (Hike 85); take the right fork and start climbing. At 2 miles note animal prints at a soda spring. Cross many little streams, nice spots for resting and drinking. At 2½ miles a side-trail heads up to supremely-scenic but far-above Constance Pass.

As the path ascends, Diamond Mountain appears across the river; from a well-marked point, see Hatana Falls. At about 8 miles the valley widens and the trail crosses a series of meadows. At 9 miles pass the Graywolf sidetrail and continue in steadily more open terrain, with wider views, to Dose Meadows at 13 miles, 4450 feet.

Beyond the meadows is a small canyon, crossed on a bridge; the creek-size river has a lion-size roar. At 13½ miles, 4600 feet, the way enters the vast garden basin of the headwaters, surrounded by high peaks. The trail crosses the river one last time and switchbacks to Hayden Pass, 15½ miles, 5847 feet. In early summer a large, steep snowbank blocks the tread; be cautious.

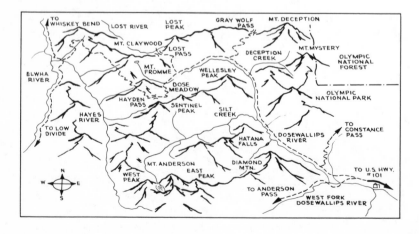

Avalanche lilies on Hayden Pass (John Spring photo)

Hayden Pass is the low point on the narrow ridge connecting Mt. Fromme and Sentinel Peak. North is Mt. Claywood, east are Wellesley Peak and the Dosewallips valley, south is glacier-covered Mt. Anderson, and west are the Bailey Range and distant Mt. Olympus.

Down from the pass 1 mile on the Elwha River side, just before the trail enters forest, find a delightful campsite by a bubbling creek.

For the across-the-Olympics hike, continue 9 miles and 4200 feet down from the pass to the Elwha River trail and then 17 miles more to the Whiskey Bend road-end (Hike 91).

Warrior Peak and Mt. Constance from Marmot Pass

HOOD CANAL

87 Marmot Pass

Round trip to Marmot Pass 12 miles
Hiking time 9 hours
High point 6000 feet
Elevation gain 3400 feet
Best July through mid-November
One day or backpack
USGS Tyler Peak

Before World War II, in an era when Boy Scouts were perhaps the principal wanderers of the Olympic wilderness, the "Three Rivers Hike" was among the most popular trips from old Camp Parsons. Thousands of Scouts now middle-aged vividly recall their introduction to highlands on the grueling "Poop Out Drag," climbing steeply and endlessly upward along a sun-baked south slope, arriving in late afternoon at Camp Mystery, then taking an after-dinner walk through flower gardens and broad meadows to Marmot Pass and thrilling evening views down to shadowed forests of the Dungeness River, 3000 feet below, and beyond to Mt. Mystery, Mt. Deception, second-highest in the Olympics, and the jagged line of The Needles, all etched in a sunset-colored sky.

Drive US 101 along Hood Canal to ½ mile north of the Quilcene River bridge, .9 mile south of the Quilcene Ranger Station, and turn west on the Quilcene River road, a paved but unmarked county road that soon is numbered road No. 2812. Stay with that number at the many junctions and at 10.7 miles from the highway turn left on road No. 272. At 15.3 miles, just beyond 10 Mile Shelter and Wet Weather Creek, find the start of Big Quilcene trail No. 833, elevation 2500 feet.

The trail follows the river bottom through cool forest, crossing numerous step-across creeks, passing many close-up looks at the lovely river. At 3 miles is Shelter Rock Camp, 3600 feet, and the last water for more than 2 miles.

Now the way turns steeply upward into the hot, dry scree, alternating with flowers, of the famous (or infamous) Poop Out Drag, so named because on these slopes in years past many a little 12-year-old Scout tottering under a big pack beneath the brutal sun abruptly fell on his face and thought he could never rise again.

At a bit past 5 miles the suffering ends as the trail abruptly turns into Camp Mystery, 5400 feet, with a delightful spring and campsites in alpine trees. Except for snowmelt there is no water above, so this is the spot to camp.

The trail continues upward, passing under a cliff and opening into a wide, flat meadow—which, sad to say, has become a race track for the motorbikes the Forest Service allows here. At 6 miles, 6000 feet, the way attains Marmot Pass and panoramas westward.

The legendary Three Rivers Hike descended the trail 1½ miles to Boulder Shelter, followed Dungeness trail No. 833 to Home Lake and Constance Pass in Olympic National Park, climbed Del Monte Ridge, and plunged down the interminable short switchbacks of the Sunnybrook trail to the Dosewallips River trail, and thence to the road.

Fine as the views are from Marmot Pass, nearby are even better ones. For a quick sample, scramble up the 6300-foot knoll directly south of the pass. For the full display, turn north of the pass on trail No. 840, leading to Copper Creek, follow it 1½ miles to just short of Buckhorn Pass, and find a path climbing to the 6950-foot west summit of Buckhorn Mountain. Especially striking are the dramatic crags of 7300-foot Warrior Peak and 7743-foot Mt. Constance.

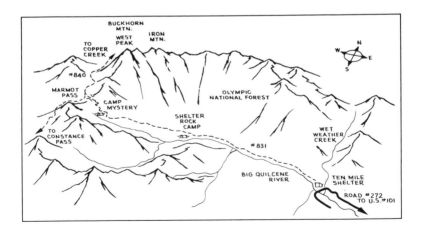

Headwaters of Silver Creek from Mt. Townsend

HOOD CANAL

88 Mount Townsend

Round trip 11 miles
Hiking time 6 hours
High point 6280 feet
Elevation gain 3500 feet
Best June through November
One day or backpack
USGS Tyler Peak

Climb to a northern outpost of the highlands. Look down to the Strait of Juan de Fuca, Puget Sound, Hood Canal, and across the water to Mt. Baker, Glacier Peak, and faraway Mt. Rainier. In the other direction, of course, see the Olympic Mountains. The steep southeast slopes of the trail route melt free of snow in early June, and usually only a few easy patches are encountered then. Mid-June is best, though, when the entire forest road is lined with rhododendron blossoms, spring flowers are blooming in the lowlands, and summer flowers on the south-facing rock gardens higher up.

Two popular trails lead to the summit of Mt. Townsend. The one from Townsend Creek, ascending the southeast side, is described here. The other, the Little Quilcene trail from Last Water Camp, is slightly longer but perhaps cooler walking in midsummer.

Drive US 101 south from the Quilcene Ranger Station .9 mile. Turn west on a paved, unsigned road that eventually is revealed as road No. 2812. At all junctions stay with that number. At 13.6 miles turn left on road No. 2764. In ½ cliff-hanging mile is the road-end and trailhead, elevation about 2800 feet.

For the alternate trail, drive road No. 2812 another 5 miles and turn left on road No. 2909 for 2 miles, then left on road No. 2892 for 3 miles to the Little Quilcene River trailhead, elevation 4000 feet.

The Townsend Creek trail ascends steadily in timber 1½ miles, then opens out and steepens somewhat to Windy Camp, 2½ miles, about 5000 feet. Pleasant camping around little Windy Lake.

The way continues upward in parkland with a scattering of small flower gardens. At just under 3 miles is an unmarked junction. The left fork climbs over a saddle, drops into Silver Creek, and climbs again to campsites at Silver Lakes, a side-trip of 2½ miles each way; one small lake is on the trail and the other is hidden. The right fork heads up the mountain, topping the ridge at 4 miles, 6000 feet, then following the crest, passing 100 feet below the first summit at 4½ miles, and running to the most northerly part of the ridge and the second summit, connecting there with the Little Quilcene trail and a trail down to Silver Creek.

Which summit is the higher? They are so evenly matched—with only 50 feet difference—you must try both to know. Wander to the summit of your choice and soak up the view over the waters to the Cascades, and over the rolling meadow ridges of the Olympics. The rugged peaks to the south are Mt. Constance and its neighbors, and farther away, The Brothers.

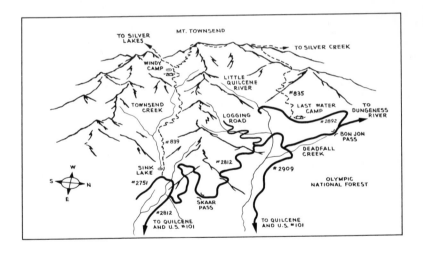

STRAIT OF JUAN DE FUCA

89 Mount Angeles

One-way trip 10 miles
Hiking time 5 hours
High point 5900 feet
Elevation gain 1200 feet
Best mid-July through October
One day
USGS Mt. Angeles and Port Angeles
Park Service backcountry use permit
  required

Once upon a time this was a challenging hike from lowland forests to alpine meadows, then along a craggy peak to some of the most glorious views of Olympic National Park. Forests, meadows, and views remain, but the challenge accepted by those who start at the bottom is like a big balloon, punctured, when greeted on top by people in street shoes walking paved trails. Most hikers, therefore, prefer to forget the challenge—they begin at the top and work down to the tall timber. (Such a plan, of course, requires either two cars or a pickup below by a non-hiking friend.)

The trail, which does not go to the actual summit of Mt. Angeles, is rough in spots. For an alternate trip with almost the same views and better tread, take the Lake Angeles trail. Both routes have the same start and finish and are approximately the same length, but the lake trail has more people.

Drive 18 miles from Port Angeles to Hurricane Ridge and find the Lake Angeles-Klahhane Ridge trail at the east end of the Big Meadow parking lot, elevation 5225 feet.

The first few hundred feet of paved pathway lead east around a low green hill. Soon the trail becomes gravel and in ½ mile narrows to normal mountain tread winding 2 miles along Sunrise Ridge, sometimes on the crest and sometimes contouring small knolls. Just before crossing the south slope of Mt. Angeles, pass a meager boot-beaten path leading upward, the climbers' route to the summit. At 2½ miles is a junction with the Switchback trail, a steep ½-mile shortcut from the highway which saves the "bother" of hiking 2 of the best alpine miles of the whole trip. From the junction the main trail switchbacks up 900 feet to 5900-foot Heather Pass at 3½ miles and the junction of the Lake Angeles and Mt. Angeles trails.

The views here are superb, with Mt. Olympus in one direction and, in the other, Port

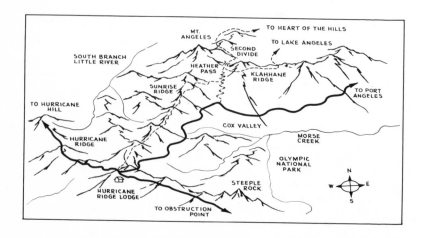

Mountain goat on Klahhane Ridge

Angeles, the Strait of Juan de Fuca, the San Juan Islands, Vancouver Island, and Mt. Baker. If mountain goats have not been seen before, look around carefully; there are many in the vicinity, as evidenced by their wool on trees, rocks, and thistles and by their numerous paths crossing shale slopes. (Warning: Goats may be harmful to your health. Remember they are wild animals with sharp horns. Stay 20 feet away. If you want closeup pictures, use a telephoto lens.) This side of Mt. Angeles is geologically unusual, having vertical erosion lines in tilted sedimentary strata.

From the junction the Lake Angeles trail follows along Klahhane Ridge about another 1½ miles and then descends meadows into woods, reaching Lake Angeles at 6½ miles, 4196 feet, and continuing down in timber to the trailhead behind the ranger's quarters at Heart of the Hills, 10 miles, 1817 feet.

From the junction the Mt. Angeles trail drops 300 feet into the head of Ennis Creek, traverses shale slides, and climbs over Second Divide at 4½ miles, about 5800 feet. The way through the shale is hard to follow; don't be misled by certain goat trails which look better than the people trail.

From Second Divide the path descends rapidly, traversing more shale and crossing a spur ridge to Heather Park at 6 miles, 5500 feet, featuring a meadow at the foot of an avalanche slope, some flowers, lots of heather, and great gobs of views. The remaining 4 miles are in trees, passing Halfway Rock at 8 miles, and finishing at the Heart of the Hills trailhead in 10 miles.

Fog near Moose Lake

STRAIT OF JUAN DE FUCA

90 Grand Valley

Round trip to Moose Lake 8 miles
Hiking time 6 hours
High point 6450 feet
Elevation gain 300 feet in, 1000 feet out
Best July through October
One day or backpack
USGS Mt. Angeles
Park Service backcountry use permit
   required

A grand valley it surely is, with a string of lakes in glacier-scooped basins, meadows to roam and waterfalls to rest by, high ridges to ramble and broad views to admire. Popular though the lakes are with fishermen, the valley has plenty of room and alpine hideaways for getting away from crowds.

Drive US 101 to Port Angeles and turn south 17 miles on the Olympic National Park highway to Hurricane Ridge. Just before the lodge turn left on a narrow and scenic dirt road through parklands along the ridge crest. In 8½ miles, on the side of Obstruction Peak, is the road-end, elevation 6200 feet.

The drive is beautiful and so is the trail going south along the meadow crest of Lillian Ridge a mile, with views over Elwha River forests to Mt. Olympus, then swinging around rocky slopes of a small peak to a notch in the ridge, 6450 feet. Now the way drops steeply down slate screes and lush flowers to open forest on the floor of Grand Valley, and a junction at 3½ miles, 5000 feet.

The left fork leads in ¼ mile to a shelter beside Grand Lake, 4750 feet, then descends Grand Creek to 4000 feet and climbs through Badger Valley to Obstruction Peak, reached in 5 miles from the junction. (The "badgers" actually are marmots; listen for their whistles.) This route makes an excellent loop-trip return to the road.

The right fork ascends ½ mile to Moose Lake, 5100 feet, and another ½ mile to little Gladys Lake. Good camps at all the lakes and elsewhere in the valley; no need to stick close to the throngs of fishermen. (The minimum distance from lakes for camps is 100 feet. No wood fires, stoves only, in Badger and Grand Valleys.)

The supreme wandering lies above the lakes. The trail climbs to Grand Pass, 5½ miles, 6400 feet, and drops to Cameron Creek. But an even better exploring direction is off the trail to the valley head, loitering amid flowers, cold streams, meltwater ponds, and snowfields, then scrambling easily to a 6701-foot peak with views west to the Bailey Range and Mt. Olympus, south to Mt. Anderson, east to Mt. Deception, The Needles, and Graywolf Ridge, and infinitely more wildland peaks of Olympic National Park.

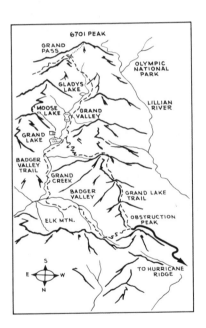

Olympic marmot

91 Whiskey Bend
To Low Divide

Round trip to Low Divide 57 miles
Allow a week or more
High point 3602 feet
Elevation gain about 2500 feet plus many
    ups and downs
Best June through October
USGS Mt. Angeles; Mt. Steel and Mt.
    Christie
Park Service backcountry use permit
    required

No whiskey, but a lot of waterfalls and forest scenery, can be found on the 28-mile Elwha River trail from Whiskey Bend to Low Divide. The valley is very heavily traveled in summer, especially below Elkhorn, by horses and hikers, including large groups of Scouts, but the natural beauty and historical interest more than compensate for crowds. Spend a day or weekend on the lower trail—or spend a week hiking the complete trail, loitering at lovely spots, taking side-trips. Before setting out, be sure to read Bob Wood's delightful book, **Across the Olympic Mountains: the Press Expedition, 1889-90.**

Drive US 101 west from Port Angeles 8 miles and turn left on the paved Elwha River road 2 miles to the National Park boundary. At 2.1 miles from the boundary, just past the Elwha Ranger Station, turn left on the Whiskey Bend road and drive 5 miles (sometimes rough and steep) to the road-end parking area, elevation 1100 feet.

The trail is wide and relatively level, with occasional glimpses of the river far below, to Cougar Mike's Cabin at 1½ miles. Here a ½-mile side-trail descends to the old homestead of Humes Ranch, where elk may sometimes be seen, mainly from late fall to spring.

At 4½ miles, 1273 feet, is Lillian Camp beside the Lillian River. Pause for refreshment, because the next stretch is the toughest of the trip, climbing 700 feet from the hot, dry Lillian Grade through an old burn, then dropping for the first time to the Elwha River at about 8 miles, 1242 feet. The trail goes up and down, never near the river very long, to Mary Falls Shelter, 8¾ miles, and a nice view of the falls. Now the way climbs again, passing a ¼-mile side-trip to secluded Canyon Camp, and at 11½ miles, 1400 feet, reaches Elkhorn Guard Station and Shelter. (About ¼ mile beyond is another small shelter at Stony Point.)

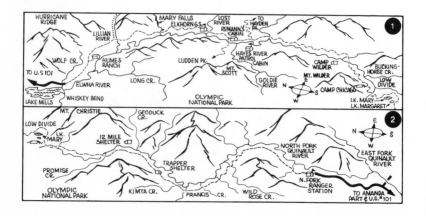

Forest floor

The trail crosses an alder bottom where elk or deer may be seen and passes two old summer-home cabins of pre-park days—Drum's Cabin (12 miles) and Remanns' Cabin (13 miles, 1450 feet) and climbs again and drops again into Press Valley. At the upper end of the valley, 16¾ miles, 1685 feet, are Hayes River Camp and Hayes River Patrol Cabin, built in 1969 by 40 volunteer boys enrolled in the Student Conservation Program. Here is a junction with the Hayden Pass trail (Hike 86).

At 21 miles, 1900 feet, is a shelter at Camp Wilder. Easily cross a footlog over Buckinghorse Creek and at 26 miles reach Chicago Camp, 2099 feet, a jumping-off point for Mt. Olympus climbers. The trail now leaves the valley bottom and switchbacks in forest to the meadows of Low Divide, 28¾ miles, 3602 feet, and there meets the North Fork Quinault River trail.

To complete the classic cross-Olympics journey, continue from the pass 18 miles down the valley to the North Fork Quinault River road-end, for a total of 46 miles.

Mt. Olympus from near Oyster Lake

STRAIT OF JUAN DE FUCA

92 Appleton Pass

Round trip to pass 10½ miles
Hiking time 7 hours
High point 5000 feet
Elevation gain 3000 feet
Best mid-July through October (or until road is closed)
One day or backpack
USGS Mt. Carrie
Park Service backcountry use permit required

One of the most popular trails in Olympic National Park climbs to green meadows sprinkled with flowers, to views of High Divide and Mt. Carrie, and to possible extensions of the route to near and far places.

Drive Highway 101 west from Port Angeles about 9 miles and turn left on Upper Elwha River road, paved all the way, 12½ miles to the end at Boulder Creek Campground (site of Olympic Hot Springs), elevation 2000 feet.

From the upper end of the campground the trail sets out in nice big trees growing from a groundcover of moss. At a junction in ½ mile, keep straight. The first mile is a breeze with only minor ups and downs. Then the trail crosses West Fork Boulder Creek and the work begins, the way climbing past two waterfalls to South Fork Boulder Creek, crossed on a shaky log, scary enough to turn back some hikers. Apart from that the path presents no problems but steepness until about 4000 feet, where mud grows deep and lush vegetation crowds in. At 5 miles are snowpatches that may last all summer (ice axes advised for early-summer hikers). At 6 miles the trail tops 5000-foot Appleton Pass.

Views from here being limited, take an unsigned way trail on the east side of the pass and follow the ridge crest upward, through alpine forest past tiny Oyster Lake, into green meadows, and in 1½ miles to a 5500-foot viewpoint overlooking Cat Creek to glacier-draped Mt. Carrie.

The first 3 miles of the trail have several small camps. Camping is superb along the ridge, though there is only snow for water and stoves should be used.

From Appleton Pass the trail descends in 2¼ miles to the Soleduck River trail, reached at 6½ miles from Sol Duc Hot Springs.

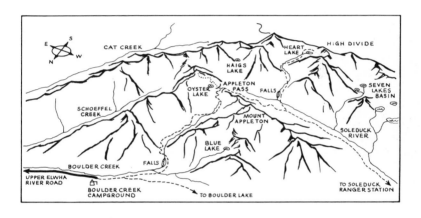

STRAIT OF JUAN DE FUCA

93 Pyramid Mountain

Round trip 7 miles
Hiking time 4 hours
High point 3100 feet
Elevation gain 2400 feet
Best late May to November
One day
USGS Lake Crescent

From Lake Crescent a delightful trail ascends magnificent forest to the 3100-foot site of a World War II airplane spotter's post. No enemy aircraft to watch for now except our own playboy-jockeyed military jets, screaming over the ridges and scaring the wits out of hikers, but there are views of lake and mountains. A delightful trip, yes, but marred by a logging road to the very boundary of Olympic National Park. Ignore it, if you can.

Drive Highway 101 from Port Angeles to the west end of Lake Crescent and turn right on the road signed "Fairholm Campground." Drive 3.2 miles to a spacious parking lot, elevation 700 feet. Walk the road back a couple hundred yards to find the trail on the uphill side.

After a moderate start, gaining only 400 feet in the first mile, at 1½ miles the way steepens, crosses several small streams (perhaps dry by late summer), and goes through beautiful fir trees. The tread is mostly well-graded and wide but on crossings of steep shale narrows to meager inches.

At 2½ miles the trail switchbacks to a saddle in the ridge marking the boundary between Olympic National Park and Olympic National Forest. A logging road here is a jolting reminder of the different objectives of park and forest. It also is shocking evidence of a contempt for wilderness—the road could just as well have been built farther below the ridge crest, out of sight, not disturbing the mood. Even though the forest probably will be clearcut to the Park boundary, there was no need to put a permanent road that close—the logging could be done from temporary roads that afterward are put to bed. As it is, some hikers surely are going to feel so disheartened they'll drive the road and throw away the best part of the trip, making it a mere stroll.

From the saddle the trail stays on the National Forest side of the ridge, generally a few feet from the crest. At 3½ miles, 3100 feet, it ends at an abandoned cabin perched atop a cliff dropping off on three sides. Here and in many other places in the Olympics, during World War II, spotters lived the year around, watching for Japanese aircraft coming to attack Seattle and Bremerton. The view must have been better then; now greenery has encroached and one must peek around trees and shrubs to look down on the lake. On a sunny day the waters are dotted with boats. Directly across the valley is Storm King Mountain but trees make it hard to see.

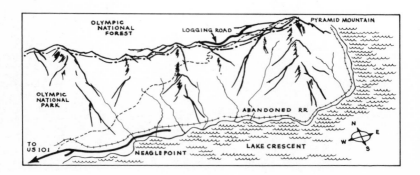

Lake Crescent and Storm King Mountain from Pyramid Mountain

211

94 High Divide

Loop trip 20 miles
Allow 3 days
High point 5474 feet
Elevation gain 4000 feet
Best August through October
USGS Bogachiel Peak and Mt. Carrie
Park Service backcountry use permit
    required

Soleduck forests, tarns and gardens of Seven Lakes Basin, meadows of the High Divide, and views across the green gulf of the Hoh River to glaciers of Mt. Olympus and far west to the Pacific Ocean. The trail is busy and the lakes crowded—sad to say, some are actually polluted—but the country is big and beautiful and offers a variety of wanderings short and long. By planning only to **look** at lakes and not to camp by them—alternative sites are numerous—hikers can enjoy solitude even now, when the fame of the area draws thousands of visitors annually. A loop trip is recommended as a sampler of the riches. (Actually, the bio-welfare of Seven Lakes Basin and the High Divide demands that the amount of camping in the fragile terrain be reduced, with more emphasis on day visits from camps in the valley forests.)

Drive US 101 west from Lake Crescent (Fairholm) 2 miles to the Soleduck River road. Turn left 14.2 miles to the end and trailhead, elevation 2000 feet.

The trail ascends gently in splendid old forest 1 mile to the misty and mossy gorge of Soleduck Falls. Close by is the junction, 1950 feet, with the Deer Lake trail—see the concluding segment of the clockwise loop described here.

The Soleduck trail continues up the valley of gorgeous trees, passes the Appleton Pass trail (Hike 92) at 5 miles, 3000 feet, and soon thereafter crosses the river and climbs steeply to grasslands and silver forest of Soleduck Park and Heart Lake, 7 miles, 4800 feet.

Shortly above, at 8½ miles, the way attains the 5100-foot crest of the High Divide, and a junction. The left fork runs the ridge 3 miles to a dead-end on the side of Cat Peak, offering close looks at the Bailey and Olympus Ranges.

Turn west on the right fork into a steady ridge-top succession of views and flowers. At 10½ miles a side-trail descends 1½ miles left to 4500-foot Hoh Lake, and from

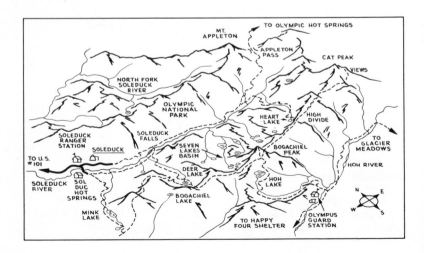

Avalanche lilies on High Divide, Mt. Olympus in distance

there to the Hoh River (Hike 96). Here, too, a path climbs a bit to the 5474-foot summit of Bogachiel Peak and the climax panoramas. Plan to spend a lot of time gazing the full round of the compass.

The route swings along the side of the peak, at 11½ miles passing the side-trail to Seven Lakes Basin, and traverses Bogachiel Ridge above the greenery (and often, a band of elk) in Bogachiel Basin. Snowfields linger late on this stretch and may be troublesome or dangerous for inexperienced hikers who try the trip too early in the summer.

The trail contours the ridge above the Bogachiel River almost 2 miles, then in subalpine trees drops to Deer Lake at 3500 feet and a junction with the Bogachiel River trail (Hike 95) at 15½ miles. Past the lake, the trail descends in lush forest to Soleduck Falls at 19 miles and in another mile to the road.

95 Bogachiel River

Round trip from Park boundary to
  Bogachiel Shelter 8 miles
Hiking time 5 hours
High point 560 feet
Elevation 260 feet
Best March through November
One day or backpack
USGS Olympic National Park or Spruce
  Mountain

One-way trip to Sol Duc Hot Springs via
  Deer Lake 30½ miles
Allow 2-3 days
High point 4304 feet
Elevation gain 4000 feet
Best July through October
Park Service backcountry use permit
  required

A beautiful hike through large old trees, rain-forest foliage, and luxuriant mosses. In autumn, the vine maple, alder, and bigleaf maple stage a glorious color show. Elk, deer, cougar, bear, and other animals may be seen by quiet and lucky hikers. A late-fall or winter visitor usually has the forest all to himself, the only footprints on the trail those of elk.

The valley offers a superb day trip for virtually any time of year, or a weekend for more extended enjoyment of wilderness greenery and streams, or a long, magnificent approach to alpine climaxes of the High Divide.

Drive US 101 to Bogachiel State Park. Turn east on the Bogachiel River road, passing several side-roads to homesteads; keep left at each intersection. After the last homestead, at 3.6 miles the road abruptly becomes very rough and crosses a small creek. Many people prefer to park here, but adventurous drivers may be able to continue 1.4 miles to the Bogachiel River, elevation 300 feet. At this point hikers may follow the old trail to the left (unmarked) through cut-over land for ¼ mile to an old logging road or follow the road to the right. (Two fordings of side creeks are required on the latter road to reach the Park boundary at about 2 miles.)

The first 1½ miles of the old and often-muddy trail follow vestiges of a logging road dating from logging operations during the early years of World War II. Amid second-growth forest, look for giant stumps with springboard holes in both sides. Then virgin forest begins.

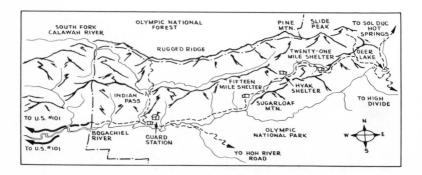

Bogachiel River (John Spring photo)

Bogachiel Shelter and the old guard station, rebuilt by the Student Conservation Program, are 4 miles from the Park boundary and make a good lunch stop and turnaround point for day hikers.

Near the shelter a branch trail climbs north over 1041-foot Indian Pass and drops to the Calawah River; at 6¼ miles another side-trail climbs over the ridge south to the Hoh River road.

The valley path continues gently in lovely forest, never far from the river and sometimes beside it, to Flapjack Camp at 8¼ miles. At about 12 miles the river forks. While the trail follows the North Fork, the narrow but pristine main river valley can be explored on a side-trip for 6 miles if you don't mind wading creeks and scrambling over high banks and fallen trees.

At 14¾ miles are Fifteen Mile Shelter and a bridge crossing the stream. At 15½ miles is Hyak Shelter, where the valley narrows to a slot, and at 18½ miles Twenty-One Mile Shelter, 2214 feet. At around 21 miles the trail abandons gentility, steeply ascends a dry hillside above the North Fork headwaters to 4300-foot Little Divide, then drops to Deer Lake at 24 miles, and climbs in parklands to the meadow crest of the High Divide. For alternative exits to Sol Duc Hot Springs, see Hike 94.

PACIFIC OCEAN

96 Hoh River

Round trip to Happy Four Shelter 11 miles
Hiking time 6 hours
High point 800 feet
Elevation gain 225 feet
Best March through November
One day or backpack

Round trip to Glacier Meadows 34 miles
Allow 3 days
High point 4200 feet
Elevation gain 3700 feet
Best mid-July through October
USGS Olympic National Park or Mt. Tom
  and Mt. Olympus
Park Service backcountry use permit
  required

From around the world, travelers are drawn to the Hoh River by the fame of the Olympic rain forest. Most of the 100,000 annual visitors are richly satisfied by the self-guiding nature walks at the road-end, but more ambitious hikers can continue for miles on the nearly-flat trail through huge trees draped with moss, and then climb to alpine meadows and the edge of the Blue Glacier.

Drive US 101 to the Hoh River road and turn east 19 miles to the Hoh Ranger Station and Campground, elevation 578 feet. The hike begins on the nature trail starting at the visitor center; before setting out, study the museum displays explaining the geology, climate, flora, and fauna.

The way lies amid superb, large specimens of Douglas-fir, western hemlock, Sitka spruce, and western red-cedar, groves of bigleaf maple swollen with moss, and shrubs and ferns. Gravel bars and cold rapids of the river are never far away, inviting side-trips. Here and there are glimpses upward to snows of Mt. Tom and Mt. Carrie. In winter one may often see bands of Roosevelt elk; were it not for their constant grazing, the relatively open forest floor would be a dense jungle.

At 2½ miles a way trail departs right, fording the river and ascending Tom Creek 1¼ miles to a dead-end far from crowds. Beside the Hoh River at 3½ miles is the Park's largest known Sitka spruce, 51½ feet in circumference; the winter of 1975 it toppled, but is impressive even lying down.

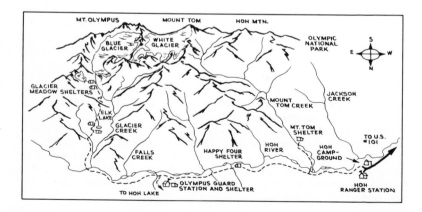

Rain forest along Hoh River

Any distance can make a full day, what with long, lingering pauses. Happy Four Shelter, at 5½ miles, elevation 800 feet, is a logical turnaround for a day hike, and also a good campsite for backpackers.

The trail remains level to the next camp at Olympus Guard Station, 9 miles, 948 feet. At 9½ miles is a junction with the trail to High Divide (Hike 94). The valley trail then climbs a bit to the bridge over the spectacular canyon of the Hoh at 12 miles, 1400 feet, leaves the Hoh valley, and climbs more to the shelters at forest-surrounded Elk Lake, 14¼ miles, 2500 feet. (Crowded camping, stove advised.)

Now the grade becomes steep, ascending through steadily smaller trees, with views across Glacier Creek of snows and cliffs, to the shelter at Glacier Meadows, 16½ miles, 4200 feet. (Stove-camping only.) Wander a short way in flowers and parkland to a viewpoint near the foot of the Blue Glacier, where torrents pour down ice-polished slabs to the forest below. Or follow the trail ½ mile to the end on the bouldery crest of a lateral moraine. Admire crevasses and icefalls of the glacier, and the summit tower of 7965-foot Mt. Olympus.

PACIFIC OCEAN

97 Colonel Bob Mountain

Round trip, north side, 14 miles
Allow 2 days
High point 4492 feet
Elevation gain 4270 feet
Best July to mid-October
USGS Quinault Lake, Grisdale, and Mt.
  Christie

Round trip, south side, 9 miles
Hiking time 7 hours
Elevation gain 3500 feet
One day

Climb to a western outpost of the Olympic Mountains, a former lookout site with views of Olympics nearby and, farther off, volcanoes of the Cascades—St. Helens, Adams, and Rainier. There's water to see, too—look down on sparkling Quinault Lake and out to the Pacific Ocean, particularly spectacular with the sun dunking into it of an evening.

There are two ways, both very steep, to Colonel Bob. The south approach, gaining 3500 feet, is better for day-tripping. The north approach, 2½ miles longer and climbing 4270 feet, is ideal for backpacking, having a good camp halfway up.

For the north side, drive US 101 to near its crossing of the Quinault River and turn east on the South Shore road. In 2½ miles pass the Quinault Ranger Station and at 6

Near summit of Colonel Bob Mountain

miles spot a sign, "Ewell's Creek Trail No. 851." Turn in on a narrow road which promptly opens to a large parking lot, elevation 270 feet.

The trail climbs through beautiful rain forest in long, sweeping switchbacks, then sidehills, still going steadily up. At 4 miles is a crossing of Ziegler Creek and soon after are campsites of Mulkey Shelter, 2000 feet. Now the way switchbacks steeply to a 3000-foot pass and drops a bit, at 5 miles reaching a junction, 2900 feet, with the trail from the south.

For the south-side approach to this junction, drive Highway 101 north 25½ miles from Hoquiam and turn east on road No. 220, signed "Donkey Creek Road, Humptulips Guard Station." Pavement ends at 5 miles. At 8.3 miles turn left on road No. 2302, signed "Campbell Tree Grove Campground," and proceed 11 miles to a sign, "Ewell's Creek Trail No. 851," near the crossing of Pete's Creek, elevation 1000 feet.

The trail starts on the uphill side of the road. The sign says it's 3½ miles to Colonel Bob; 4½ is a better guess. The way is steadily steep and in places rocky. At 1 mile is a crossing of Pete's Creek, underground here most of the year. At 2 miles is a small camp, beyond which is a slide area and then, at 2½ miles, the junction.

Signs here claim the distance is 1¼ miles to the summit; it's actually a good 2 miles, and seems longer, what with many blowdowns, brushpatches, and steep and badly-eroded stretches. But there is some drinking water and, as the trees thin, flowers. The last few feet to the top are blasted from rock.

The 4492-foot summit is littered with remains of the old lookout cabin—boards, wires, cables, broken glass. But the views are glorious. For sunset-watching, camps can be found ¼ mile back 200 feet below the trail on a wide bench covered with snow much of the summer. Bring a stove for cooking, melt snow for water.

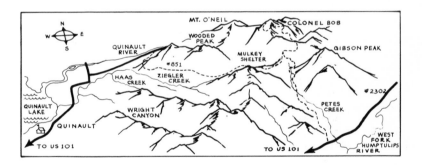

PACIFIC OCEAN

98 Enchanted Valley

Round trip 27 miles
Allow 2-3 days
High point 1957 feet
Elevation gain 1050 feet plus ups and downs
Best March through December
USGS Olympic National Park or Mt. Christie and Mt. Steele
Park Service backcountry use permit required

Walk beside the river in open alder and maple forest, and miles through cathedral-like fir forest where future generations of loggers will come to see what their grandfathers meant when they boasted of big trees. The climax is Enchanted Valley, a large alpine cirque ringed by 3000-foot cliffs. The trail has many ups and downs and during rainy spells is a muddy mess, but in such country, who can complain?

Drive US 101 to the south-side Lake Quinault road. Turn easterly, skirting the lake and winding up the valley. Pavement ends at 12 miles. In 13 miles pass the North Fork bridge and at 18 miles Graves Creek Campground. Continue on the final narrow road to the trailhead 18½ miles from US 101, elevation 907 feet.

The trail crosses Pony Bridge over the Quinault River at 3 miles; the lovely canyon under the bridge is worth a trip in itself. In another ½ mile climb around the canyon and drop back to the river. For the next 10 miles the way alternates, up and down, between flat bottoms (alders and maples) and terraces several hundred feet above the river (groves of tall fir and cedar). With any luck a hiker should see elk. At 7 miles pass a junction to O'Neil Creek Camp, ¼ mile off the main track.

All along are tantalizing glimpses of peaks above, but at about 10½ miles the change from lowlands to alpine is dramatic. Suddenly one leaves deep forest and bursts into the mountain world of rock and ice. To the left are cliffs of 6911-foot Chimney Peak. To the right is 6400-foot White Mountain. Both are dominated by the twin peaks of Mt. Anderson, divided by a small glacier: the sharp pyramid is 7366-foot West Peak, the highest point; the more massive peak in the middle is 7321 feet.

Coming down to earth, the valley has widened out. The lower part is floored with dense brush but farther up are flower fields. At 13½ miles cross the Quinault River, now a small creek (except in meltwater floods of spring, when the torrent may be impassable). Walk a short bit through meadows to the three-story Enchanted Valley Chalet, built in 1930 as a commercial hotel and now maintained by the Park Service

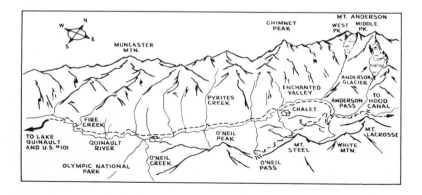

*Chimney Peak, left, and Mt. Anderson, right, above
Enchanted Valley*

as a public shelter. The structure often is full (only part of the lower floor now is open to camping) so be prepared to camp out. Be sure to carry a stove; cooking facilities are limited in the chalet and wood may be wet outside. Those unable to do the full 11 miles in a single day can stop overnight at any of a number of camps along the way.

Beyond the chalet the trail climbs 2500 feet in 5 miles to 4500-foot Anderson Pass and descends the West Fork Dosewallips River 10 miles to the road (Hike 85). Another trail leads to O'Neil Pass and Hart, Marmot, and La Crosse Lake (Hike 99).

What's the best season for the trip? Well, some winters there is little snow in the lower valley, which thus can be walked in December or March when hardly any other country is open. Early spring is wonderful, when birds are singing and shrubs and maples are exploding with new leaves, and yellow violet and oxalis are blooming, and waterfalls and avalanches tumble and slide down cliffs. So is summer, when alders and maples canopy the valley bottoms in cool green. But fall is also glorious, with bigleaf maples yellowing and the trail lost in fallen leaves. Better try it in all seasons.

PACIFIC OCEAN

99 Lake LaCrosse-O'Neil Pass

One-way trip to Lake LaCrosse:
Via Quinault River and O'Neil Pass 26½
 miles
Elevation gain 4000
By any route, allow 5 days minimum
Best mid-July through September
USGS Mt. Steel
Park Service backcountry use permit
 required

In the heart of the Olympic wilderness, 16 miles from the nearest road, a group of beautiful alpine lakes sparkle amid a wonderland of heather and huckleberries. Quicker ways of reaching the lakes are mentioned in the last paragraph, but the one described here is the classic approach, via O'Neil Pass, on one of the most spectacular trails in the National Park, traversing ridges high above the Enchanted Valley of the Quinault, with many and magnificent views and flower fields.

To reach the O'Neil Pass trail, hike 17 miles and gain 2400 feet up the Enchanted Valley (Hike 98) to the beginning at about 3400 feet (incorrectly shown as 3100 feet on the USGS map).

The O'Neil Pass trail starts from the Enchanted Valley trail beside a small torrent and heads westward and up, in a few yards going by a small camp. The way alternates between forest and wide-view meadows. At 1 mile are campsites and a crossing of White Creek; a hillside beyond gives the best look at Mt. Anderson.

At 1½ miles is a mountain hemlock with a sign saying it is 6 feet, 3 inches in diameter and 136 feet tall—a midget compared to the lowland variety but huge at this elevation. At 2 miles is an Alaska cedar identified as 7 feet, 6 inches in diameter and 114 feet tall.

The trail climbs to 4500 feet and then contours for miles, mainly in grass and blossoms. Directly across the valley is Chimney Peak, an impressive 6911 feet high. Views are breathtaking down the Quinault River to Lake Quinault and, if lucky, the ocean. The trail drops a bit, rounds a shoulder of the ridge, and ascends to O'Neil Pass, 7½ miles (25 miles from the road), 4900 feet, and close-ups of Mt. Duckabush.

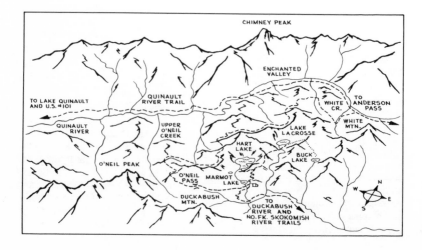

Lake LaCrosse

Still in meadows, the way descends to Marmot Lake, 8½ miles, 4400 feet. The O'Neil Pass trail ends here in a junction with the Duckabush River trail.

Scattered through higher gardens are Hart Lake, Lake LaCrosse, and Buck Lake. To get there, find the trail behind Marmot Lake Shelter and switchback upward ¾ mile to a junction. The left fork contours ½ mile to Hart Lake, enclosed on three sides by vertical cliffs; good camps. The right fork continues ¾ mile uphill to Lake LaCrosse, 4800 feet, perhaps the most splendid alpine lake in the Olympics, with views across the water to massive 6233-foot Mt. Duckabush and more graceful 6300-foot Mt. Steel. Another mile farther is Buck Lake, too small for fish and thus more private; there is no trail, but an experienced hiker can find the way from Lake LaCrosse west over a 5500-foot saddle and down to the 5000-foot shores. Camping is great at all the lakes.

The camping is stove-only, no wood fires, at Marmot, Hart, and LaCrosse Lakes and O'Neil Pass. Marmot Lake is the most crowded.

The lakes can be approached in various other ways. For one, hike the Dosewallips trail (Hike 85) and drop over Anderson Pass 1½ miles, losing 1100 feet, to the start of the O'Neil Pass trail. Or, hike directly to the lakes by way of the Duckabush River trail 20 miles to Marmot Lake, gaining 4500 feet including some major ups and downs. For another, hike the North Fork Skokomish River trail (Hike 81) 19½ miles to Marmot Lake, gaining 5200 feet counting ups and downs. The lakes can also be included in imaginative one-way and loop trips.

100 Point Of The Arches

Round trip to Point of the Arches 7 miles
Hiking time 4 hours
High point 150 feet
Good all year
One day or backpack
USGS Cape Flattery and Ozette Lake
Park Service backcountry use permit
   required

Here, perhaps, is the most scenic single segment of the Washington ocean coast, with needle-like sea stacks, caves, and arches to explore, tidal pools, and miles of sand beaches. Once threatened with roadbuilding and subdivision, in 1977 Shi-Shi Beach and the Point were added to the wilderness-ocean section of Olympic National Park.

Drive from Port Angeles on narrow, tortuous State Highway 112 to the Makah village of Neah Bay. At the west end of town turn left and follow signs to "Air Force Base and Ocean Beaches," crossing and recrossing a private logging road—stay on the public road. In 3 miles turn left over the Waatch River on a concrete bridge, again avoid the private road in favor of the public road, in about 6 miles cross the Soos River,

Point of the Arches

and pass a cluster of Indian homes on Mukkow Bay at 6½ miles. Beyond the settlement the road climbs into woods above the beach and in 1 mile deteriorates rapidly. Park either near the houses or where the road gets sloppy. Overnight hikers do best to ask at one of the houses for parking space for a fee; car-looting is a problem here.

The parking area and road are on the Makah Indian Reservation. The ocean beach and all adjacent land belong to the Makahs so private property rules apply.

The virtually-undrivable road over Portage Head is pleasant walking under a canopy of trees. During wet weather be prepared for much mud. In about 1 mile push through the roadside brush for dramatic looks down to the surf. At 1½ miles, where the road comes to the edge of the bluff for the first unobstructed views of the ocean, are two "trails," side by side. The first drops like a shot to the north end of Shi-Shi Beach and is slippery and even scary. The other, several yards away, is steep enough but descends amid trees that provide handholds and a feeling of security. (If the tide is high, follow the road, which dwindles to a jeep track and in a mile nearly touches the beach.)

A short distance from the foot of the trail is the south end of Portage Head, with spectacular sea stacks, tidal pools, and a shipwreck. Hike about 2 miles south on the beach, leaving the reservation, passing a number of good camps (the most reliable source of water in summer is Petroleum Creek), to the fabled Point of the Arches. The long string of stacks and islands can be reached and explored at very low tide; the going is rough over sharp and slippery rocks and involves some wading.

Travel south of the Point can be difficult, since there are several heads with no trails over the tops, requiring a very low tide to get around the bases or considerable bushwacking to go over the tops. Before going over, look for the thinnest salal and on top of the heads stay in the forest where there is little brush. About 6 miles from Point of the Arches is the Ozette River; a bit north of the river a road leads inland 4½ miles to Ozette Lake.

In dry spells, it may be possible for sturdy hikers to wade the knee-deep (at low tide) Ozette River and continue to Cape Alava (Hike 101).

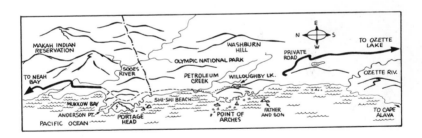

PACIFIC OCEAN

101 Rialto Beach
To Cape Alava

One-way trip 22 miles
Allow 3 days
High point 100 feet
Good all year
USGS Olympic National Park or La Push
 and Ozette Lake
Park Service backcountry use permit
 required

Olympic National Park first became famous for rain forests and glaciers set within a magnificently large area of mountain wilderness. Now, though, it is known far and wide for still another glory—the last long stretch of wilderness ocean beach remaining in the conterminous United States. North and south from the Quillayute River extend miles and miles of coastline that are now almost exactly as they were before Columbus—except that in 1492 Indians had permanent homes and temporary camps at many places along the coast now deserted.

Winter and early spring often offer the best hiking weather of the year, but storms can be hazardous. Facing a cold rain with miles of beach to hike is miserable and can lead to hypothermia (exposure).

The north section, from Rialto Beach to Cape Alava, makes a longer but easier walk than the south section described in Hike 102. There are no really difficult creek crossings, only one headland that cannot be rounded at low tide, and most of the way is simple sand and shingles, interrupted occasionally by short stretches of rough rock.

Sea stack near Hole in the Wall

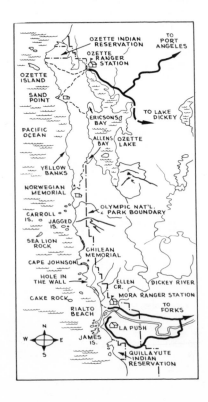

Near Norwegian Memorial

Be sure to obtain a tide chart beforehand and use it to plan each day's schedule. Much of the route can be traveled at high tide, but at the cost of scrambling over driftwood and slippery rocks, plodding wearily through steep, loose gravel, and climbing up and down points. Moreover, some headlands cannot be climbed over and the beach at low tide provides the only passage. Be prepared to hike early in the morning or late in the evening, with layovers during the day, if the tides so dictate.

Drive US 101 to 2 miles north of Forks. Turn west on the La Push road 8 miles, then turn right on the Mora Campground-Rialto Beach road 5 miles to the parking lot at the beach. (If the Dickey River bridge is closed to cars, as it was in 1978, be prepared to walk the final ½ mile to the beach.)

In ½ mile is Ellen Creek, the first possible campsite. Here and elsewhere the "brown water," colored by organic solutes, looks like tea, but is perfectly pure and delicious. At 1½ miles, just beyond the sea stack with the Hole in the Wall, are meager camps and the first headland, which has several small points, one requiring low tide to get around. At 2½ miles are camps near the Chilean Memorial, which commemorates one of the countless ships wrecked on this rugged coast, and at 3 miles begins the long, rough rounding of Cape Johnson, which has no trail over the top and can be passed at low tide only, as is true of another rough point immediately following. A point at 5 miles must be climbed over on a short trail and one at 6 miles rounded at low tide. At 6½ miles is Cedar Creek (campsites) and immediately beyond is a point that can be rounded at low tide or crossed on a steep, short path.

At the Norwegian Memorial (another shipwreck and more camps), 7½ miles, a trail leads inland 2¼ miles to Allen's Bay on Ozette Lake. (There is no trail along the lake, so unless a boat pickup by the resort has been arranged, this is not a shortcut to civilization.) Passing campsites every so often and at 10 miles a low-tide-only point, at 13½ miles the way comes to Yellow Banks, the point at the north end of which must be rounded at low tide.

At 15 miles a trail heads inland 2 miles to Ericsons Bay on Ozette Lake. At Sand Point, 15½ miles, are two more shelters, innumerable campsites in the woods, and a trail leading 3 miles to the Ozette Lake road.

Don't stop here. Continue on the wilderness beach 3 miles to Cape Alava, 18½ miles, where an archeological dig is uncovering a Makah village that was overwhelmed by a mudslide 500 years ago. The Washington State University student assistants give guided tours each year to some 60,000 visitors, most of whom have hiked the 3½-mile trail from Ozette Lake. To finish your trip, follow the crowds back to the lake, 22 miles.

PACIFIC OCEAN

102 Third Beach
To Hoh River

One-way trip 16 miles
Allow 3 days
High point 250 feet
Good all year
USGS Olympic National Park or La Push
   and Forks
Park Service backcountry use permit
   required

Wild forest and wild ocean, woods animals and sea birds, tidal pools and wave-carved stacks, the constant thunder of surf, and always the vast mysterious horizon of the Pacific. This south section of the Olympic National Park wilderness ocean strip is shorter but more complicated than the northern one described in Hike 101, requiring detours inland to cross headlands and creeks and demanding even closer attention to the tide chart.

Warning: Goodman, Falls, and Mosquito Creeks are high all winter, and after a period of heavy rain or melting snow are virtually unfordable.

Drive US 101 to 2 miles north of Forks. Turn west on the La Push road 12 miles to the parking lot at the Third Beach trail, elevation 240 feet.

Hike the forest trail, descending abruptly to the beach and campsites at ¾ mile. Head south along the sand and in ½ mile look for a prominent marker on a tree above the beach, the start of the trail over Taylor Point—which cannot be rounded at the base. The trail climbs into lovely woods, dropping to the beach at 3 miles and a small head which can be rounded at any time except high tide.

At 3½ miles is a point which can be rounded at low tide or climbed over by a short trail to reach Scott Creek, with campsites in the woods; another very small point immediately south can be rounded in medium tide or climbed over. At 4½ miles is Strawberry Point, low and forested and simple, and at 5½ miles, Toleak Point, ditto. Shortly beyond is Jackson Creek (camps).

At 6½ miles a trail ascends a steep bluff and proceeds inland through beautiful forest to crossings of Falls and Goodman Creeks (cliffs rule out a shore passage), returning to the surf at 7¾ miles. The beach is then easy to Mosquito Creek, 10 miles; ford the stream at low tide. (Camps here.) Climb small points at 10½ and 10.9 miles, and at 11.1 miles round another at low tide (the way over the top is strenuous). Two more points in the next mile can be crossed on rough paths but are better passed at low tide.

At 12 miles a trail climbs the large promontory of Hoh Head, which cannot be rounded in any tide, and regains the beach at 12¾ miles. Going by a campsite or two, at 13½ miles the way comes to the last point, a heap of big rocks which must be rounded at low tide. From here a narrow, low-tide-only strip of beach leads to the mouth of the Hoh River, 14¾ miles. A trail follows the river inland to the Oil City road-end, 15½ miles.

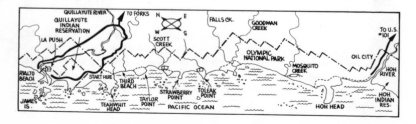

Toleak Point

The Oil City road reaches US 101 in 12 miles, at a point about ½ mile north of the Hoh River bridge.

Warning: Cars at the Third Beach parking area have been frequently broken into. Do not leave any belongings visible inside the car.

STILL MORE HIKES IN THE ALPINE LAKES, SOUTH CASCADES, AND OLYMPICS

The 102 hikes represent all provinces of the Cascades from Stevens Pass to the Columbia River, and of the Olympics. Heaviest emphasis has been placed on areas close to major population centers. There are other great hikes in the two ranges, and below is an additional list of over 150.

To take the following hikes, consult the books referred to, if any, or obtain the applicable maps and make your own way. The lack of detailed "recipes" or, in some cases, even a trail, may be compensated for by a greater degree of solitude.

Skykomish

Mt. Persis: Boot-made path from Proctor Creek road to the top of the 5464-foot mountain.

West Fork Miller River: An abandoned road, now a pleasant forest trail beside the stream. (See **Footsore 2**)

Hope Lake: 2 miles up North Fork Tunnel Creek to the Pacific Crest Trail and the lake.

Lake Josephine: Reached from Stevens Pass on the Pacific Crest Trail.

Nason Creek

Lanham Lake trail No. 1589: 1¾ miles to lake under cliffs of Jim Hill Mountain. (Closed to bikes and horses.)

Glacier Creek trail No. 1573: An access via Chiwaukum Creek to meadows on east side of Chiwaukum Mountains. A dead-end trail after 1½ miles—needs maintenance.

Lake Ethel trail No. 1585: Steep 4½ miles. Passes through a grove of lodgepole pine with contorted trunks.

Painter Creek trail No. 1575: Pleasant forest and meadows—long hike.

Hatchery Creek trail No. 1577: Access to Icicle Ridge trail.

McCue Ridge trail No. 1574: From trail No. 1584A to trail No. 1591.

White Pine Creek: From White Pine Creek road to Icicle trail No. 1551.

Icicle Creek

Icicle Ridge trail No. 1570: 25-mile ridge walk with lots of ups and downs and lots of views. 4-5 days hike.

Fourth of July Creek trail No. 1579: 5 miles to an old lookout site and Icicle Ridge trail.

Trout Lake trail No. 1555: 5 miles to shallow Trout Lake. Trail goes on to Windy Pass and Eight Mile Creek.

Icicle Creek trail No. 1551: 12-mile access to Crest Trail past Lake Josephine.

Jack Creek trail No. 1558: 11½ miles to meadows and Stuart Pass.

Solomon Creek trail No. 1593: Meadows. Long trail via Jack Creek or shorter from Cle Elum River.

Cradle Lake trail No. 1560: Long loop trip to meadows.

French Creek trail No. 1595: 12 miles to Paddy-Go-Easy Pass. Good trail in timber but boggy in meadows. Trail not maintained between Klonaqua Lakes junction and Meadows Creek trail junction.

French Ridge trail No. 1564: Open meadows on a steep loop trail.

Lake Leland trail No. 1566: Long hike in woods to lake on edge of meadow country.

Square Lake trail No. 1567: Interesting trail past a canyon, meadows, and views.

Chain Lakes trail No. 1569: Very steep trail from 10 miles up Icicle Creek trail to above timberline. View of spires on Bulls Tooth from hill north of lakes. Map shows loop via Doughgod Creek but trail is in very poor condition.

Klonaqua Lakes trail No. 1563: Steep trail (and long access) to two alpine lakes.

Mission Ridge Area

Devils Gulch trail No. 1220: Good trail 12 miles up Mission Creek to Beehive road and return on ridge via trail No. 1201. Good in May.

Red Hill trail No. 1223: Hike to top of 3800-foot hill in May.

Squilchuck trail No. 1200: 2-mile hike through alpine forest. Access to Clara and Marion Lakes.

Ingalls Creek

Hansel Creek Ridge and return to Ingalls Creek.

Negro Creek and Three Brothers Mountain.

Falls Creek trail and trail along ridge dividing the Teanaway River and Ingalls Creek.

North Bend Area

Bare Mountain from Lennox Creek: Stiff climb to lookout site on little-used trail.

Mt. Teneriffe: 7 miles up a jeep road from valley and then ¾-mile trail to summit. (See **Footsore 2**)

Granite Creek: Abandoned road and fishermen's path to Granite Lakes and Lake Thompson and connection with Defiance trail No. 1007.

Lake Thompson: From Granite Creek road and trail.

Pratt River: Possible for 7 miles but must first ford the Middle Fork Snoqualmie River.

Rainy Lake trail (not a trail) from Camp Brown: Route very difficult to find. 6 or 7 hours to lake.

Quartz Creek: Very difficult route to Rainy Lake or a ¾-mile fishermen's trail to Blethan Lake.

Nordrum Lake: Rough trail around logs and up creek beds from Taylor River to Nordrum Lake. Gateway to alpine country.

Middle Fork Snoqualmie valley trail: Unmaintained trail across river from road. Forest Service plans to rebuild this trail when money is available.

Rock Creek trail: Unusual approach from valley trail to Snow Lake (Hike 24). Trail not used much because of difficult river crossing.

Mt. Washington: Gated logging road through clearcuts to outpost summit (4400 feet) with grand views.

Mason Lake-Mt. Defiance: From Mason Creek on road No. 2218A. From Mason Lake, intersect Defiance trail (Hike 19). 5584-foot summit of Mt. Defiance easily reached.

Trail No. 1018 from Silver Peak to Hanson Creek: Presently closed through watershed and unmaintained for 15 years or more.

Snow Lake: 4-mile hike from the Alpental ski area.

Cle Elum Area

Roaring Ridge: Find abandoned road near Lost Lake. Follow it to road-end, then take a short trail to old lookout site.

Snowshoe Butte: Cross-country travel from road No. 204B or from Pacific Crest Trail between Tacoma Pass and Stampede Pass.

Lookout Mountain: Inquire at Ellensburg Ranger Station.

Cole Butte: Begins on the High Line Canal near Easton to Goat Peak and along jeep road to saddle between Log Creek and Big Creek.

Silver Creek: 16 miles to hanging valley, a beautiful meadow of berries and subalpine timber. Can also be reached from Cooper Pass.

Red Mountain trail No. 1330: 7 miles long, connecting with the Kachess Ridge trail a mile short of the Thorpe Mountain lookout.

Davis Peak trail No. 1324: Steep 5½ miles to an old lookout site and broad views. Possible roaming out along Goat Ridge.

Paris Creek trail No. 1393: A short 8 miles to open basin where trail is difficult to follow. One could spend a week here without retracing path, since the trail joins the Teanaway, Jolly Mountain, and Boulder-De Roux trails.

Boulder-De Roux trail No. 1392: 4-mile jeep trail connecting to the Paris Creek trail and others.

South Fortune Creek trail No. 1335: 4-mile jeep trail to mining claim and south to Boulder Creek, Paris Creek, Jolly Mountain, and Sasse Ridge.

Fortune Creek spur trail No. 2342: Jeep trail from Van Epps Pass.

Trail Creek trail No. 1322: From Waptus River to Fish Lake. Must ford the river.

Michael Lake trail No. 1336: Side-trip from Trail Creek trail. Best reached from the Fish Lake end.

Paddy-Go-Easy Pass: A 3-mile hike to a lovely lake from near the Fish Lake Guard Station.

Tuck and Robin Lakes: Spectacular alpine lakes reached by a boot-made route from near Deception Pass.

White River

Huckleberry Mountain: A once popular trail now nearly obliterated by logging.

Noble Knob trail No. 1184: From Corral Pass, 8½ miles in alpine trees and meadows with grand views of Mt. Rainier to road No. 196.

Dalles Ridge trail No. 1173: Starts from trail No. 1184. 3½ miles of scenic trail with views of Mt. Rainier. Ties to road No. 196.

Ranger Creek trail No. 1197: Being constructed by volunteers of the Boy Scouts of America. 8 miles to Dalles Ridge trail No. 1173. Good view overlooking White River in 2¼ miles.

Crystal Mountain trail No. 1163: 8½ miles from Silver Creek trail No. 1192 past Hen Skin Lake over top of Crystal Mountain (also reached by chairlift) down the ridge to Crystal Mountain highway.

White River trail No. 1199: 5-mile lowland trail in big timber paralleling US 410.

Deep Creek trail No. 1196: A steep 5 miles to Noble Knob trail No. 1184. Last ½ mile in open alpine country.

Greenwater trail No. 1176: Scenic trail following the Greenwater River 12½ miles. Passes 4 lakes.

Lost Lake trail No. 1185: Starts 3¼ miles up the Greenwater trail. Passes Quinn Lake, Lost Lake, and goes through alpine country to join the Noble Knob trail. Trail is 5½ miles long.

Maggie Creek trail No. 1186: Starts 5½ miles up the Greenwater trail. In 5¼ miles, all in timber, reaches Pacific Crest Trail.

Arch Rock trail No. 1187: Steep 3½-mile access to Pacific Crest Trail starting 7½ miles up the Greenwater trail. Last ½ mile in alpine country.

Carbon trail No. 1179: 9½-mile trail from Flip-O-Way road No. 1810 to a junction with the Summit Lake trail No. 1177. Scenic around Bearhead Mountain.

Cedar Lake: Steep, 1-mile fishermen's trail to lake, then ½ mile more to Celery Meadow.

American River

Bismark Peak trail No. 983: Reached from Bumping Lake or Indian Creek trails.

Fifes Peaks trail No. 954: Steep, dry trail to views of rugged cliffs. Map shows a nonexistent trail around the peak.

Richmond Mine trail No. 973: Long route from Bumping River to Rattlesnake Creek.

Bumping River trail No. 971: Long access to Crest Trail.

Mt. Aix trail No. 982: From Rattlesnake Creek road to Mt. Aix.

Rattlesnake trail No. 981: Long route to the headwaters of Hindoo Creek.

Randle Area

Langills Peak trail: Long scenic ridge walk. Water at Grasshopper Lake and Bear Creek.

Upper Green River trail No. 213: Woods walk to Norway Pass or Meta Lake.

Green River trail No. 213: O.K. to National Forest boundary, then contact Weyerhaeuser Company for conditions on its land.

Vanson Peak trail No. 217: Best reached from Ryan Lake over Goat Mountain. North end of trail is in private land (U.S. Plywood-Champion Papers).

Vanson Lake trail: A 1-mile side-trip from trail No. 217.

Blue Lake: A large lake surrounded by virgin forest reached by a 3-mile trail from road No. 123. Trail is heavily used by motorcycles.

Tongue Mountain trail 294: Early season hike from road 111 or 123.

Trail No. 119: 3½-mile ridgetop trail from Blue Lake to Mouse Lake.

Packwood Area

Lake Christine trail No. 249A (901A on old maps): Near southwest corner of Mount Rainier National Park.

Puyallup trail No. 248 (900 on old maps): On west side of Mount Rainier National Park.

Carlton Ridge trail No. 42: Old-growth Douglas fir, views of narrow valley, and access to Crest Trail at Fish Lake.

Cowlitz and Jug Lake trails, Nos. 44 and 43: Access to Crest Trail and shallow Jug and Fryingpan Lakes. Many marshy meadows.

Sand Lake trail No. 60: A way to Crest Trail.

Cartright Creek trail No. 57: Access to Crest Trail.

Bluff Lake trail No. 65: Long route to Coyote Ridge and Goat Rocks Wilderness.

Clear Fork trail No. 61: River access to Goat Rocks Wilderness.

5030 trail No. 83: On Snyder Mountain, joining trail No. 86 in 1 mile.

Angry Mountain trail No. 90: Ridge hike to Lily Basin.

Jordan Creek trail No. 94: Long access route to Goat Ridge (Hike 61).

South Point trail No. 123: A lookout and a long ridge hike on a dry access route to Klickitat trail (Hike 57).

Coleman Weed Patch trail No. 121: Access route to the Crest Trail. A timbered plateau with small lakes.

Teeley Creek trail No. 251: Can start on road No. 149 for longer hike to Granite Lake.

Tieton Area

Sand Ridge: Long, dry, flat, and wooded ridge hike from near Rimrock Reservoir to Blankenship Meadows.

Spiral Butte: A side-trail from Sand Ridge to a wooded hilltop going through the site of a recent forest fire. Excellent view of Mt. Rainier and Mt. Aix area.

Bear Creek Mountain: Exciting viewpoint of the Goat Rocks reached from Section 3 Lake (see **Trips and Trails, 2**) and North Fork Tieton River road.

Tenday Creek trail No. 1134: Starts from Conrad Meadows. A long creek and ridge route to Cirque Lake. Just above lake is a fine view of Goat Rocks.

Jump-off Lookout: Trail to lookout. Jeep road on other side of ridge.

Trout Lake Area

Snipes Mountain trail No. 11: From road No. N80, trail climbs along a lava flow 5 miles to alpine meadows and a junction with Adams Highline Trail.

Cold Springs trail No. 72: 15-mile loop hike is possible by starting on trail No. 11, going to the Adams Highline Trail, following it westward to timberline, then down the timberline road to trail No. 72, to trail No. 40, and walking road No. N80 ¾ mile back to car.

Bird Lake trail No. 100: Beautiful flower walk—see **Trips and Trails, 2.**

St. Helens Area

Miners Creek trail No. 212: Lower end in poor condition with some phenomenal mudholes. Upper end is fairly good.

Trade Dollar trail No. 246: Poor condition. Used mainly by tough hunters who want to be alone.

Butte Camp trail No. 238A: Widened for jeeps during a forest fire. Now closed to jeeps, but there are enforcement problems.

Trail No. 242: Lange's Mine trail from Boy Scout camp 2 miles to open meadows on side of Mt. Margaret.

Lewis River

Quartz Creek trail No. 5: Miles of forest and creek. The largest virgin forest in the area.

Snagtooth Creek trail No. 4: Climb from Quartz Creek to Boundary Trail.

Lava Caves: Interesting ¼-mile trail.

Wright Meadow trail No. 80: Through forest between roads N920.2 and 933.

Trail No. 17: Recently reopened from Lewis River road to Craggy Peak trail No. 3.

Wind River Area

Lost Lake trail No. 133: A small gem-like lake near Government Mineral Springs.

Falls Creek trail No. 152: 2-mile trail from road N73 to a falls in a secluded little valley.

Little Huckleberry Mountain trail No. 197: Starts from road No. 500. Camping near the top and views from the rounded 4202-foot mountain. Crossed by Crest Trail.

Silver Star Mountain: Impassable jeep road to a lookout in the Yacolt Burn. Generally closed during fire season.

Hamilton Mountain, in Beacon Rock State Park: 4-mile hike to a tremendous overlook of the Columbia River. See **Trips and Trails, 2.**

Table Mountain: 3-mile hike to views of the Oregon and Washington volcanoes.

Dog Mountain: 2½-mile hike along the Pacific Crest Trail from the Columbia River to the top of the mountain.

Thomas Lake trail: 3 miles from road No. 605 to Crest Trail and the heart of Indian Heaven.

Huffman Peak trail No. 129: 8 miles from road N66 starting in forest, climbing to a ridge top with panoramic views, and ending at road N617 on top of Siouxon Peak, an old lookout site.

Siouxon trail No. 130: 9 miles between road N66 and N63 following Siouxon Creek through forest and past a small waterfall in the Siouxon Roadless Area.

East Side Olympic Peninsula

Mt. Washington trail No. 800: Starts from Big Creek road No. 2419. An easy grade 1½ miles to ridge top. Does not go to summit of mountain.

Mt. Rose trail No. 814: Steep, strenuous climb 3 miles to within ¼ mile of the 4301-foot summit. For experienced hikers only.

Dry Creek trail No. 872: Starts from road No. 2357 near the Park boundary. The first 1½ miles are along the shores of Lake Cushman. Ideal for family hiking.

Wagon Wheel Lake way trail: Located near Staircase. Trail is a steep (12 to 15 percent) 3-mile climb to a small tarn. Good views of Mt. Lincoln and upper Slate Creek Basin.

Six Ridge trail: From North Fork Skokomish River trail. **Long, steep, dry** way trail to subalpine meadows, elk country.

Putvin trail No. 813: Starts at head of Hamma Hamma valley near Boulder Creek. A long-abandoned trapper's trail to alpine country. Very steep but offers access to Mt. Stone, Mt. Skokomish, and acres of flowers and wildlife.

Constance Pass: Scenic route between the Dosewallips and Dungeness valleys.

Graywolf trail: 20-mile hike to 6150-foot Graywolf Pass and descent to Dosewallips. Can be shortened by starting at Deer Park.

Cameron Creek trail: Reached from the Graywolf trail. A very long hike to 6400-foot Cameron Pass and on over Lost Pass to Dose Meadows.

North Side Olympic Peninsula

Grand Ridge trail: 8-mile ridge walk from Deer Park to Obstruction Point. Splendid alpine hike. Carry water.

Little River trail: Lovely and little-traveled 8-mile route to Hurricane Ridge.

Lake Creek: Begins at Heart O'the Hills Campground, Loop E. 2-mile woods walk, no lake.

Cox Valley way trail: Starts 1 mile along Obstruction Point road. Trailhead not marked. Goes into Cox Valley.

P.J. Lake: A way trail starting at base of Eagle Mountain on the Obstruction Point road. ½ mile down to lake. Way trail not marked.

Storm King way trail: 1½-mile steep trail to viewpoint of Lake Crescent on side of Mt. Storm King.

Barnes Creek trail: Indistinct way trail through forest to Aurora Ridge trail. Fades out as it reaches 5000-foot Lookout Dome.

Aurora Creek way trail: 3½-mile shortcut to Aurora Ridge trail. Very steep.

Aurora Ridge trail: 16-mile ridge walk, mostly in trees, then down to Olympic Hot Springs. Some good views of Mt. Olympus.

Long Ridge trail: From the Elwha trail to Dodger Point, a long, dry ridge with views. Ends in scenic meadows. Route to Bailey Range. Good trail.

Boulder Lake trail: 3½ miles from Olympic Hot Springs to Lake Crescent.

Happy Lake Ridge trail: Long hike with views and a lake, starting from Olympic Hot Springs road. Can be a loop with the Boulder Lake trail. 3½ miles between trailheads.

Martins Park way trail: 2-mile side-trip from the Elwha trail at Low Divide to glorious meadows and views.

North Fork Soleduck trail: Woods walk 9 miles to dead-end.

West Side Olympic Peninsula

Geodetic Hill trail: Very indistinct route, abandoned in 1945, from the Bogachiel to forested Spruce Mountain.

Hoh-Bogachiel trail: Follows the Park boundary from the Hoh over and down into the Bogachiel at Flapjack Shelter.

Indian Pass trail: Forested route from the Bogachiel River to Calawah River and on to Rugged Ridge and Forest Service road.

South Fork Hoh trail: Short trail to canyon. Very easy. Fades out in unspoiled rain forest. Trailhead difficult to find.

Mt. Tom Creek trail: A difficult ford of the Hoh River leads to seldom-visited forest.

Queets River trail: A difficult ford of the Queets River leads to 15-plus miles of primitive rain forest.

Kloochman Rock trail: From Queets trail past largest Douglas-fir tree to lookout site. Seldom maintained.

Tshletshy Creek trail: From the Queets to Quinault.

Higley Peak trail: 3-mile climb from Lake Quinault or a short walk from logging road. View of lake. See **Trips and Trails, 2.**

Elip Creek trail: Intersects the Skyline trail from North Fork Quinault. 4½ miles.

Skyline trail: Long, strenuous, scenic route to Low Divide. A late-summer trip, since snow obscures route at head of Promise Creek. Minimal way trail between Seattle Creek and Kimta Creek.

Three Lakes trail: Starts at North Fork Quinault Ranger Station. A 7-mile trail connects at divide above Three Lakes with Tshletshy Creek trail. 18 miles from Three Lakes to Queets River.

Graves Creek trail: 9-mile hike from the Quinault to Six Ridge Pass and Sundown Lake.

Second Beach (near LaPush): See **Trips and Trails, 2.**

INDEX

Adams, Highline Trail—160
Adams Glacier Meadows—148, 161
Adams Wilderness, Mount—148, 160
Aix, Mount—118
Alaska Lake—71
Alpine Lakes Wilderness—24, 28, 30,
    32, 34, 36, 38, 40, 42, 44, 46, 50, 52,
    58, 62, 68, 70, 74, 76, 80, 82, 86, 90,
    92, 94, 96, 98, 100
American Ridge—116, 120
Anderson Glacier—194
Anderson Lake—47
Anderson Pass—194
Angeles, Lake—202
Angeles, Mount—202
Annette Lake—65
Apple Lake—129
Appleton Pass—208
Avalanche Valley—161

Badger Lake—152
Bandera Mountain—56
Basin Lake—110
Bear Lake—24
Beverly Creek Trail—95, 97
Big Crow Basin—110
Blankenship Lakes—128
Blankenship Meadows—129
Blue Lake—172
Bogachiel Peak—213
Bogachiel River—214
Bolt Camp—174
Boundary Trail—151, 152, 173
Bridal Veil Falls—22

Cape Alava—226
Caroline, Lake—38
Chicago Camp—207
Chiwaukum Creek—35
Chiwaukum Lake—34
Cispus Point—135
Colchuck Lake—40
Colonel Bob Mountain—218
Commonwealth Basin—166
Constance Lake—192
Copper Lake—30
Cougar Lakes—117, 120
County Line Trail—94
Coyote Ridge Trail—137
Craggy Peak—172
Crow Lake Way—113
Crystal Ridge—108
Cultus Lake—159

Deception Creek—26, 154
Deception Lakes—33, 154
Deception Pass—33, 92, 154
Deep Lake—90
Deer Lake—213, 215
Devils Horns—131
Diamond Lake—81
Diamond Meadow—195
Dorothy Lake—24
Dose Meadows—196

Dutch Miller Gap—52, 87
Dumbbell Lake—124

East Fork Foss River Trail—29
Echo Lake—107
Eight Mile Lake—38
Ellinor, Mount—180
Elwha River—206
Enchanted Valley—194, 220, 222
Enchantment Lakes—36
Esmerelda Basin—95, 98

Falls Creek Camp—44
Fifes Peaks—113
Fish Eagle Pass—88
Flapjack Lakes—184
Fortune Creek Pass—95, 99
Foss Lakes—30
French Cabin Creek Trail—78

Gem Lake—69
Glacier Lake—32
Glacier Meadows—217
Gladys, Mount—184
Goat Lake—143
Goat Ridge—143
Goat Rocks Crest—146
Goat Rocks Wilderness—127, 130,
    136, 138, 142, 144, 146, 148
Gold Creek—71
Government Meadows—104
Grand Lake—205
Grand Valley—204
Granite Mountain—60
Gravel Lake—70
Greenwater Trail—107
Grizzly Lake—166

Happy Four Camp—217
Hart Lake—223
Hayden Pass—196
Heart Lake—138
Hester Lake—50
High Divide—212
Hogback Mountain—127
Hoh Head—228
Hoh Lake—212
Hoh River—216, 228
Home Sweet Home—186
Honeymoon Meadows—195
Humes Ranch—206

Ingalls Creek—44
Indian Heaven—158
Ingalls Lake—45, 100
Ivanhoe, Lake—53

Jade Lake—93
Joe Lake—71
Jolly Mountain—84
Josephine, Lake—156
Jumbo Peak—151
Juniper Mountain—150
Jupiter, Mount—191

Kachess Ridge—78

Kendall Peak—70
Killen Creek Trail—148, 161
Klickitat Trail—134

LaBohn Gap—52
LaCrosse, Lake—186, 221, 222
Ladies Pass—43
Larch Lake—34
Lena Lake, Upper and Lower—188
Lennox Creek—47
Lewis River—174
Lillian, Lake—72
Lily Basin—138
Little Heart Lake—31
Little Paradise—133
Long's Pass—95, 98
Low Divide—206

Malachite Lake—31
Margaret, Mount (Snoqualmie
  Pass)—72
Marmot Lake (Cascades)—92
Marmot Lake (Olympics)—223
Marmot Pass—198
Mary, Lake—42
McCall Basin—170
McClellan Butte—54
Melakwa Lake—59, 62
Mildred Lakes—183
Mineral Creek Park—76
Moose Lake—205
Myrtle Lake—50

Naches Wagon Trail—104
Nada Lake—37
Nannie Peak—144
Nannie Ridge—144
Navaho Peak—95
Necklace Valley—28
Nelson Ridge—118
Norse Peak—110
North Fork Quinault River—207

Obscurity Lake—167
Observation Peak—163
Olallie Lake—58
Olallie Meadow—66
Old Snowy—143, 147
Olympus Guard Station—217
O'Neil Pass—222

Pacific Crest Trail—32, 66, 70, 77, 82,
  86, 90, 110, 114, 124, 127, 143, 144,
  146, 158, 160, 176
Packwood Lake—136
Paddy Go Easy Pass—168
Park Lakes—77, 83
Pear Lake—129
Pete Lake—83
Pleasant, Camp—186
Point of the Arches—224
Polallie Ridge—80

Pratt Lake—58
Purcell Mountain—132
Pyramid Mountain—210

Rachel Lake—74
Rampart Ridge—74
Red Butte—161
Red Pass—166
Rialto Beach—226
Ridge Lake—70

Sand Lake—124
Sand Point—227
Sawyer, Mount—26
Scatter Creek Trail—89
Serene, Lake—22
Seven Lakes Basin—213
Shark Rock—172
Sheep Lake (Chinook Pass)—114
Sheep Lake (Goat Rocks)—145
Shoe Lake—127, 146
Si, Mount—48
Silver Peak—66
Snoqualmie Lake—24
Snow Lake (Snoqualmie Pass)—69
Snow Lakes (Icicle River)—37
Snowgrass Flat—142, 146
Snowgrass Mountain—43
Sourdough Gap—114
Spade Lake—86
Spectacle Lake—77, 82
Sprite Lake—168
Squaw Lake—90
St. Helens, Mt.—165
Stuart, Lake—40
Stuart Pass—45, 100
Summit Lake—102
Sunrise Peak—151
Surprise Lake (Stevens Pass)—32
Surprise Lake (White Pass)—130
Surprise Mountain—33
Susan Jane, Lake—156
Swamp Lake—120

Tatoosh Lake—141
Tatoosh Ridge—140
Third Beach—228
Thorp Mountain—79
Tired Creek Trail—80
Toleak Point—228
Tonga Ridge—26
Townsend, Mount—200
Trails End—132
Trout Lake—30
Tumac Mountain—122
Turnpike Trail—97
Twin Sister Lakes—123

Waptus Lake—86
Williams Lake—53
Windy Pass (Icicle River)—38
Windy Pass (Mount St. Helens)—169

OTHER BOOKS IN THE "HIKES" SERIES:

50 Hikes in Mount Rainier National Park
101 Hikes in the North Cascades
102 Hikes in the Alpine Lakes, South Cascades and Olympics
Companion volumes guide you to the best hiking in the mountains of Washington State
. . . valleys and ridges, forests, glacier views, subalpine meadows, ice caves and
snowfields. Easy-to-use sketch maps and complete trail directions. "101" covers from
Stevens Pass to the Canadian Border. "102" covers from Stevens Pass south to the
Columbia River. "50" includes the Wonderland Trail and Mount Rainier. Text by
Harvey Manning, photos by Bob and Ira Spring.

103 Hikes in Southwestern British Columbia
The most scenic trips from Vancouver Island to Manning Park, from the U.S. Border to
Lytton at the head of theFraser Canyon. (Includes Garibaldi Park.) Maps and photos for
each trip. Prepared by the B.C. Mountaineering Club, with text by David Macaree, maps
by Mary Macaree.

109 Walks in B.C.'s Lower Mainland
Delightful walks to see the best in Vancouver and vicinity. Complete directions and
maps for each trip; scenic photos of the highlights. Text by David Macaree, photos by
Mary Macaree.

**Trips and Trails, 1: Family Camps, Short Hikes and View Roads Around the North
Cascades**
**Trips and Trails, 2: Family Camps, Short Hikes and View Roads in the Olympics,
Mt. Rainier and South Cascades**
Companion volumes geared for beginner hikers and families, with maps, photos and
complete trail directions for short hikes (under two miles) starting from campgrounds.
Also describes facilities of each campground. "1" includes the San Juan, Whidbey and
Fidalgo Island areas. By E. M. Sterling, photos by Bob and Ira Spring, maps by Marge
Mueller.

Bicycling the Backroads Around Puget Sound
Bicycling the Backroads of Northwest Washington
Bicycling the Backroads of Southwest Washington
Full details, maps on cycle tours on quiet backroads, including scenery, mileages,
elevation change, estimated times. Companion volumes, no duplication of trips. By Erin
and Bill Woods.